The Promise of the Present and the Shadow of the Past

*For Keith
with
best wishes
Ben Dawn
12/11/11*

The Promise of the Present and the Shadow of the Past

The Journey of Barbara Frass Varon

Bension Varon

Copyright © 2011 by Bension Varon.
Cover by Carolyn Gambito.
Maps by Nicole Wynands.

Library of Congress Control Number: 2011906615
ISBN: Hardcover   978-1-4628-5829-3
             Softcover   978-1-4628-5828-6
             Ebook   978-1-4628-5830-9

All rights reserved. No part of this book may be reproduced or transmitted in any form or by any means, electronic or mechanical, including photocopying, recording, or by any information storage and retrieval system, without permission in writing from the copyright owner.

This book was printed in the United States of America.

To order additional copies of this book, contact:
Xlibris Corporation
1-888-795-4274
www.Xlibris.com
Orders@Xlibris.com
97812

CONTENTS

Acknowledgements..11

Introduction..15

PART ONE—FROM PRUSSIA TO AMERICA

I.   Roots..23

II.   The War and Its Aftermath...................................43

III. East to West 63

IV. The Last Years in Germany.................................85

V.   Becoming American 103

PART TWO—MY JOURNEY OF RECOVERY

VI.   The Polish Mystery Man 155

VII. The Ambiguous Exit of Werner Frass, Theater Director 167

VIII. A Life Lost and Remade: The Story of Ernst Jurkat........181

IX.   The Buchenwald Memoirist 223

X.   From Berlin to Elkins, West Virgnia................241

*To the memory of a special person
for whom everybody was special.*

Acknowledgements

This enterprise—it was not meant initially as "a book"—was suggested by my daughter Elizabeth soon after I completed my memoirs in 2009.[1] Having read about my Turkish and Sephardic upbringing, she expressed interest in learning more about her mother's German past. The last two years have been difficult for me. Yet the pleasure I derived from the work has greatly outweighed the pain. I therefore wish to thank Elizabeth before anybody else. Elizabeth deserves credit also for the title. Moreover, like her brother Jeremy, she provided me insights into her mother, my wife, not a simple person, as well as valuable criticism and suggestions. Not surprisingly, *Elehie Skoczylas*, Barbara's oldest and closest friend, was of equally valuable help—not surprisingly, because she was like a sister to her and like family to Elizabeth, Jeremy and me. She knew Barbara intimately and longer than I did. I asked her not only to read the entire manuscript, but to "approve" it, which she did. Whenever she offered me comments on the draft, I grabbed a pen and paper even before she opened her mouth. I am especially grateful to Elehie because I know that reading about her close friend and sister Barbara took an emotional toll on her.

Peter Jurkat, a semi-retired mathematician, is Barbara's first cousin. He lives currently in New Mexico and has the distinction of being her only German-born relative in the United States and the senior-most person bearing her mother's maiden name, Jurkat.

---

[1] *Cultures in Counterpoint: Memoirs of a Sephardic Turkish-American*, Xlibris, Bloomington, Indiana, 2009.

He graciously helped me fill in some holes about that side of the family and did a reality check of the text. I understand that, in the process, I injected him with the bug of genealogical interest, for which I have no regret.

Several other people have helped me to write about specific aspects or episodes of Barbara's life. I have thanked them individually in the relevant chapters or sections. In terms of providing me "raw information" about Barbara's German family, no one has played the rich role that *Tim Frass* has. Tim is Barbara's and my nephew who lives currently with his own small family in Krefeld, near Düsseldorf. He has served as my eyes, ears, feet and more—my alter ego—in Germany. He has dug out documents, initiated inquiries, and contacted relatives. Among those relatives was *Ernst Cecior*, a first-cousin of Barbara, who emerged as the resident historian of that branch of the family and elucidated a number of things for me with great precision of time and place. I extend him my thanks through Tim. Tim did all this with patience, humor, enthusiasm, and a strong sense of family, using his considerable charm when he had to.

With her intimate knowledge of government and other archives and the Internet, *Arden Alexander* identified relevant sources of information unknown to me, dealing particularly with, but not limited to, the rescue of German political refugees during the Second World War, and pointed me to new paths or tools of inquiry, such as ships' manifests and others. This made for more work but immeasurably enriched both me and the work. She also served as my "designated listener"—not an easy task because, like most researchers, I had my ups and downs.

It is more sad than ironic that I had to rely on the services of a German translator to write about a person who had an extraordinary command of the language and mastered the skill-and-art of translation. I blame myself for not learning the language. My only excuse has been that I did not need to—but, in retrospect, I feel that I did need to. Barbara left behind some forty family letters and postcards, in addition to meticulously preserved school and other records, all in German, and I acquired, through Tim Frass, some additional forty letters or documents. I was lucky to be assisted throughout my project by *Dr. Simone Seym* of the Goethe Institute in Washington, D.C. She did much more than translation for me; she provided context for what she translated; she supplemented and enriched my knowledge of German history, society, institutions, and customs whenever I needed it; and she undertook numerous inquiries on my behalf in Germany.

I shall conclude by acknowledging not another help but a vulnerability. It is more difficult to write a biography of another person than of oneself, and for more reasons than one. One of these, which I became keenly aware of, is that one keeps wondering what the subject of the biography would be thinking about what one is writing. This was driven home to me in one specific regard. I ventured into history a great deal in the following pages to provide necessary background and color. History was Barbara's favorite field, a first love that grew exponentially over the course of her life—a subject she never stopped studying, she excelled in, and she had a deep intellectual affinity for. Her knowledge of history was exceeded only by her understanding of it. Her eyes lit up and the sense of time and place disappeared whenever and wherever she talked about it. And talk she did. She asked piercing questions of herself and others. While reminiscing about this recently, our daughter Elizabeth remarked that no museum guide was safe. She was right. When the children and I visited a museum with Barbara, we often wondered how many minutes it would take her to question or enlarge upon what the guide was saying. Writing about history under her watchful eyes, I have felt nervous like a museum guide who has been warned in advance that she is in the audience and who must, therefore, summon his best performance.

Introduction

Fairfax County is a jurisdiction in Northern Virginia with a population of about 1.1 million. It is made up of nine administrative districts of roughly equal population size. The county is governed by a Board of Supervisors consisting of elected representatives of the nine districts, plus a chair person elected at large. The administrative seat is Government Center, an impressive modern building located on Government Center Parkway in the western part of the county. At the Government Center, a few feet past the main entrance, on the left wall, is a plaque which reads "Barbara Varon Volunteer Award, Enriching Fairfax County through Dedication and Community Service." The plaque contains an engraved picture of Barbara and the names of the seven awardees to date: Toa Do, Louise Pennington, Kimberli Costible, Nancy Portee, Hung Nguyen, Louise Rooney, and John Mayer. The award was established in March 2004 in recognition of Barbara's dedication to community service and especially her fight for the rights and privileges of all citizens to participate in the electoral process. It is given annually (in October) to a volunteer selected by a ten-member committee consisting of representatives of the nine districts, plus one nominated at large.

Barbara Frass Varon was born in Berlin, Germany, in 1940. She came to this country as an immigrant in 1959. She enrolled, on arrival, in the undergraduate program of the University of Pennsylvania, where we met, and she graduated with a B. A. degree in 1961. Barbara and I were married in 1962 and had our daughter, Elizabeth, in 1963. We moved to Northern Virginia in late 1964. Barbara became a United Stares citizen in January 1965. We had our second child, Jeremy, in 1967. As our children reached their teens, Barbara became actively engaged in local politics and community service and devoted two decades of her life enthusiastically to these passions. She served on the Fairfax County Electoral Board as Chairman and Vice Chairman between 2000 and 2003, when she passed away.

This book is about Barbara's dual and simultaneous life journeys: the physical one and the intellectual (or mental) one. The main markers of the physical journey were as follows. A Berliner by birth, Barbara spent the second half of World War II in Elbing, a small city in German-occupied northeast Poland where her maternal grandparents had a home. Her mother took her there to seek refuge from the heavy bombardment of Berlin. Her father, Herbert Frass, was then serving as an ordinary sailor in the German navy. At war's end, the Frass family, which had grown to four with the birth of a brother to Barbara in 1944, was reunited in East Germany and spent the next five years there, though not by choice. The family had moved—after advance planning—to Gotha, a city near Erfurt in central Germany on the path of the advancing American forces. However, soon after occupying the city, the Americans withdrew from it, ceding it to the Soviet forces. The family fled to West Germany in 1950, settling in Herne, a town in Germany's coal-mining region. Barbara lost her father to illness there within a year. This made the surviving family members dependent on refugee assistance and welfare support and bound them to the city they had first moved to. Barbara lost her mother in Herne in 1958 and came to the United States a year letter. She came directly to Philadelphia where she had an uncle. We met and were married there. Our next moves followed my career path as an economist and consisted of relocation to the Virginia suburbs of Washington, D.C. in 1965, where we lived the rest of the time, with the exception of a two-year work-related interlude in New York City. In all, Barbara spent the first 19 years of her life in Germany, divided among five cities, and the next 44 in the United States, 37 of them in Virginia.

Concerning the mental journey, what characterized Barbara's life first and most notably was the relatively happy childhood she had, despite life under bombs or the threat of them, the severe shortages during the closing years of the war and its immediate aftermath, the long absence of her father, and life under Soviet occupation. The credit for the happiness she nevertheless experienced as a child belongs fully to her mother. Barbara received her entire primary school education—four years under the German system—in East Germany. There is no evidence that the education she received at that level was inferior or lacking in any significant way. Moving—fleeing—to West Germany in 1950 did not represent for young Barbara the happy change it seemed to promise for her parents, because she lost her father within a year. Besides, with the loss of its main breadwinner, the family's standard of living did not improve and may have even deteriorated. Her mother tried to fill the shoes of her father as much as she possibly could, although the loss left a non-fillable void. She also used all the energy, imagination and skills she had to make up for the limited recreational, educational and cultural opportunities that tiny Herne offered.

Beginning in her middle teens, Barbara went through a series of transitions that shaped her: from dependence (on her mother) to independence in decision making; from dreamer (like most German children and even many adults had to be in the postwar period) to realist; and from self-identifying as a German to viewing herself as a Western European, like many Germans increasingly did. She started life in the United States in 1959 as a German immigrant; she quickly became in people's eyes a German-American; but she acted and lived the life of a non-hyphenated, fully integrated American. (More on this shortly.) The main thing she retained from her German upbringing and heritage was the German language. With time, she also grew from daughter to mother, and, as the children reached their teens, from political observer to political activist—from outsider to insider in the fights she cared about: civil rights, human rights, voting rights, women's rights, and others. She moved for good from the shadow of the past to the bright light and promise of the present.

The above sketch of Barbara's twin journeys can lead to two misunderstandings. The first one concerns the role of the war—the all-encompassing horrible war—in shaping her life and personality. The following pages are full of references to the war and examples of its impact. Yet it would be a mistake to view Barbara as a product of the war. Nothing, not even the war, had as big and as lasting an impact on her as did the loss of her parents at a young age due to natural causes. Hers was a story of human relationships, not of inter-country conflict . . . of a love affair between mother and daughter, of family loyalty, of dreams, and of unmet but undiminished ideals. Besides, Barbara did not fit into a mold, any mold; she was in many ways unique, self-made and unconventional, like her mother and father, her models in a German society that, at least then, valued conformity.

The second possible misunderstanding is about her "Americanization," a process which millions of immigrants have gone through and still do. She did not fit the classic model of an immigrant who becomes acquainted with America through school or work, learns English, falls in love with and adopts America's values, and is helped along in many cases by an American spouse. First of all, I was not an American. We became American together; if anything, rather than lead, I lagged behind. More important, like me, she came to this country fully bilingual, with considerable familiarity with its history and society, and a developed set of values. America "fit" those set of values; she did not have to discover them. Theirs—America's and Barbara's—was not love at first sight. This is why it endured despite ups and downs like in any relationship. My earlier reference to her being a non-hyphenated American was intended to indicate not that she was a pure or flawless American (whatever that may mean) but, rather, that her relationship to America was that of a family member—not of a passing admirer or friend of convenience. She would agree with that. The family concept was something she understood well and cared about a great deal.

Why this book? This book is in large part for those familiar with Barbara's community service and political work who wish they had known her longer or more closely. The knowledge vacuum exists because although Barbara loved history so much, she invested in and talked little about her own. This book is also for the many whom Barbara would have wished to know personally—those committed to community service who, like herself, believed strongly in voting rights, human rights, and women's rights, who shared her limitless curiosity, and who loved history as much. The book is at the same time about my own journey. When our daughter asked me to write about her mother, I embraced the idea enthusiastically because it offered me, despite the pain, the opportunity not simply of knowing her more fully but of living with her a second life, so-to-speak. I traveled not only wherever she went during this journey, but in her constellation. I met in the process her spiritual kin, people linked to her by history, alleys she had not gone into, and relationships she had not fully explored. As a result, the book grew in scope and is, therefore, in two parts. *Part One* is devoted to Barbara's life. It traces her mixed German-Polish-Lithuanian roots. It describes the tough decisions which her parents, who met and became parents in 1940, had to make during the rest of their short lives. It chronicles Barbara's childhood in East Germany, her coming of age in West Germany, the events that led to her coming to the United States, her initial adjustment to this country, and her public service which spanned more than two decades. *Part Two* presents the remarkable stories of five selected people from her constellation:

- a Polish ancestor—an artillery officer—who fought tyranny during the Napoleonic wars, was imprisoned by the Prussians, and is believed to have written a history of Poland while in captivity;
- an uncle, who was a theater director during the Nazi era, whose death in 1942 is still shrouded in mystery;
- another uncle, a social scientist, who faced a brilliant future but felt compelled to oppose the Nazi regime, had to flee the country and was separated from his wife and child for seven years before being reunited with them in the United States;
- another related person who fled the country, joined the French resistance against his native Germany, was caught and sent to Buchenwald, and somehow survived—an experience about which he wrote a memoir for an American school teacher and her high school students who had taken his story to heart;
- a medical doctor from Berlin who found himself in Elkins, West Virginia during the war where he raised a son who

returned with the U.S. team of prosecutors to Nuremberg to seek justice.

What do these people have in common? Why are they here? I'll reply anecdotally. Occasionally, I buy greeting cards—to express thank you, congratulations, friendship and the like—in advance, that is, for future use. Recently, while at the supermarket, I bought a card for such an undefined purpose that said in five lines, and in increasingly larger and bolder letters (as in a reverse eyesight chart), "Never never never never give up!" The above people never gave up in the face of adversity and would recognize themselves in Barbara.

Part One

From Prussia to America

Chapter One

Roots

Barbara Frass was born on July 22, 1940 at Humboldt University hospital in Berlin, Germany. She was the daughter of Elisabeth Emma Jurkat and Herbert Frass (no middle name), both of them Lutheran (*Evangelisch*). Elisabeth was born on April 9, 1903 in Graudenz, a small historic city on the lower bank of the Vistula River in north-central Poland. Herbert, Barbara's father, was born on July 2, 1902 in Berlin. Barbara's maternal ancestors were of mixed German (West Prussian), Polish and Lithuanian background; her father's ancestors were Berliners and East Prussians for at least several generations.

We know more about Barbara's mother's family than about her father's, partly because of her father's Berlin roots, that is, because of the effects that the war had on the survival of both his relatives and information about them. Moreover, Barbara's father had a smaller family and one with generally shorter longevity than her mother's. Her father had just one brother who never married and who, like her father, died before the age of fifty. Their father died at forty. On the whole, there have been far fewer Frasses (than Jurkats) to preserve the name and family knowledge. Barbara, for example, had no single Frass cousin, compared to four on the Jurkat side.

Background

Before going back in time beyond Barbara's parents, it is helpful to provide a minimum of geographical-historical background. The relevant background is considerable; I shall focus here merely on Prussia and the last two centuries. Historically, Prussia referred to a vast region of northern Europe extending from The Netherlands, Belgium and France in the west to Lithuania and Russia in the east. It encompassed parts of current-day Germany, Poland, northern Lithuania, and eastern Russia. Its population, which was highly diversified, included Germans, Poles, Lithuanian, Kashubians (a West Slavic ethnic group), other Slavs, Huguenots, and others, although the vast majority were Germans. The predominant majority were also Protestants, with important concentrations of Catholics, Mennonites, and others.

Most of Prussia was ruled by the independent Kingdom of Prussia, established under Frederick I (1657-1713) in 1701 out of the earlier Polish province of Royal Prussia. The Kingdom was made up of thirteen provinces, including West Prussia, East Prussia, Brandenburg (Berlin), Hanover, Rhine, Saxony, and others. The most important of these provinces from the perspective of Barbara's family were West Prussia and East Prussia in the Baltic region. The capital of West Prussia was the port city of Danzig, and the capital of East Prussia was the port of Königsberg. It is important to note that West and East Prussia were just two provinces of the Kingdom, that is, the two Prussias did not make up the whole of Prussia. And, despite their names, both provinces, which shared a border, albeit a shifting one, were on the *northeast* of Prussia.

With the unification of Germany by Bismarck in 1871, the Kingdom of Prussia became part of the German Empire, or a state within a state, albeit by far the most important part of the Empire. Berlin was the capital of both the Kingdom of Prussia and the German Empire. With the defeat of Germany in 1918 following the First World War, the situation changed dramatically, and the bisection, dissection and dissolution of the Kingdom of Prussia effectively began.

A major physical feature of the geographic area where the above took place is the Vistula river, modern Poland's main waterway and economic lifeline, which originates in the western Carpathian Mountains in the south and empties into the Vistula lagoon at the Bay of Danzig in the Baltic Sea. Without access to the port of Danzig, Poland would be a landlocked country. The Vistula crosses both Warsaw, Poland's capital, and Krakow, its second largest city, as well as many of the secondary cities Barbara's ancestor lived in or by, as I shall discuss later.

At the end of the First World War, Poland was declared an independent state in accordance with U.S. President Wilson's Fourteen Points, creating the Second Polish Republic.[2] To allow the new state access to the Baltic Sea, *per* Wilson's Point 13, the Allies gave Poland a part of West Prussia along the Vistula river, up to but excluding the port of Danzig. The sliver-like area became known as the Polish Corridor. Danzig was declared a Free City under the protection of the League of Nations. The city enjoyed political autonomy in domestic affairs and, after a period of transition, it acquired a number of the attributes of statehood, such as its own flag, currency and postage stamps.

The creation of the Polish Corridor resulted not only in the dissection of West Prussia but also in the separation of East Prussia from the rest of Germany, namely, from Weimar Germany between 1919 and 1933 and Nazi Germany thereafter. In 1939, all of West Prussia, including the Polish Corridor and Danzig, came under Germany's control. After the war, West Prussia reverted to Poland. The Soviet Union, which had occupied East Prussia during the war, retained the northern third of it. The rest went to Poland and Lithuania, which promptly began to rename the region and its cities. None of the formerly Prussian lands retained the name, either. As a result, with the exception of Berlin, none of the dozen or so towns and cities Barbara's ancestors came from are currently German territory. In 1947, the United States, Britain, France and the Soviet Union formally agreed to declare the end of a region or state named Prussia.

---

[2] The reference is to the points enunciated by President Woodrow Wilson in a speech to a joint session of Congress on January 8, 1918, which became the basis for the German surrender.

In the family history that follows, I shall describe briefly each of the localities mentioned for several reasons. Barbara's family history unfolded in a region, comprised of northern Germany, Poland and part of Lithuania, marked by high population density, national, ethnic, linguistic and religious diversity, and high political volatility. Many of the localities concerned were small towns little known outside the region, despite their long history going back in some cases to the thirteenth century. Geographically, they were situated on sea shores, river banks, railway/road junctions, etc., which shaped their histories as well as destinies, and gave them their character. Many of them changed hands, often more than once, especially between, but not limited to, Germany and Poland. And each change often led to mass emigration and/or ethnic-cultural cleansing. None of the places which survive under different names bear a resemblance to the places where Barbara's ancestors spent their lives.

Finally, a note on sources. The information that follows comes from: vital records (birth, death and marriage certificates) preserved by Barbara; knowledge transmitted by her in writing or orally; and church records dug up recently (May 2010) by Doris, her sister-in-law, in Germany. Her writings include annotations in photograph albums and a three-page "biographical sketch" of her family, prepared for a history class at the University of Pennsylvania, shortly after arriving from Germany. The church records I mentioned raise intriguing questions unrelated to their accuracy, which is not in doubt. They refer to a so-called *family book* which Doris located recently, and cover Barbara's parents, grandparents and great grandparents on both sides. They include copies of some original birth and marriage records, but they consist mostly of official *recordings* of the vital information on the people concerned, extracted from the original documents. The information given for each person consists of the name, date and place of birth, date and place of baptism, names of both parents, religion, parish, church, and recording office. The entry for each person is certified with the stamp, date and signature of the recording officer.

All of the above records were prepared and certified in Elbing, East Prussia, on May 27, 1940. Why Elbing, why all on the same date, and why that date? Clearly, the records were prepared on request—almost certainly at the initiative of Barbara's mother or her parents who lived in Elbing at the time. But why? Two possibilities come to mind. Barbara's mother and father were married in Elbing on March 23, 1940, that is, two months earlier. The happy event may have stimulated interest in the couple's family background. But could the request have been induced or imposed by the need to document one's Aryan, non-Jewish background? We do not know. Horrifying as the whole subject is, a by-product of the initiative was to indicate beyond doubt that Barbara was of pure Aryan (I hate using the term) background.

Maternal Ancestors

Barbara's maternal grandparents were Olga Hedwig Teske, born in 1880, and Martin Jurkat, born in 1876. (See Jurkat family tree.) They were both from West Prussia. Olga came from Graudenz, a historic city founded in 1260, mentioned earlier.[3] Originally a part of the Kingdom of Prussia, it passed on to Poland after the First World War as part of the Polish Corridor ceded to it by the Treaty of Versailles in 1920. It was re-occupied by Germany in 1939 and remained under its control until 1945. Martin Jurkat, Barbara's grandfather, was born in Elbing, a seaport on the mouth of the Vistula River originally in West Prussia.[4] Like Graudenz, Elbing became Polish after the Second World War and has been called Elblag since. Olga and Martin were married in Graudenz; they settled in West Prussia and brought up a family there. They had three children, in descending order of age: Elisabeth, Barbara's mother, born in Graudenz; a son, Ernst, born in 1905 in Ottlotschin, a town south of Graudenz on the Polish Corridor; and Gertrud, born in 1907 in a suburb of Danzig.

---

[3] Barbara remembered her grandmother's place of birth as Kulmsee, although church records show it as Graudenz. The discrepancy is not important, since Kulmsee, now the Polish town of Chelmza, is not far from Graudenz.

[4] When the Polish Corridor was carved out of West Prussia, Elbing, which was on its eastern border, was excluded from it. It was, as a result, incorporated into East Prussia.

Both of her maternal grandparents were alive when Barbara was born in 1940. Her grandfather Martin died of natural causes immediately after the Second World War, and Barbara had, therefore, little recollection of him. However, she got to know her grandmother Olga well—her grandmother was in fact the only grandparent from either side she truly knew—and she was very close to her, and vice versa. Her grandmother had a significant, lasting impact on Barbara, being instrumental in her coming to the United States. She also blessed our marriage and supported it with words and thoughtful deeds/gifts. I never met her; I shall refer to her nevertheless several times as if I did.

Barbara's grandmother, a housewife, was a source of wisdom and a pillar of strength. These qualities served her well, as they did the many family members who depended on her, especially since she was married to a seemingly quiet, introverted man. Martin Jurkat, her husband, came from a centuries-old line of Lithuanian farmers. As a younger son, he had no hope of ever taking over the family farm.[5] He became an officer in the Prussian army and, later, a customs director (*Oberzollsekretär*)—a position he held for most of his professional life. Martin was a very private person, a proud man in every way, a real Prussian, and a civil servant who took his work as "duty." He was probably formal in his relations, behaving at home as if at work, communicating mostly through aides or his wife, which was not uncommon in that era. In most of the pictures of him that survive, he seems to pose with authority and relish. He is in military regalia in some of them, even in those taken after leaving the army (see photograph). His pride in his Prussian identity is reflected in a photograph (also added) of his son Ernst, probably at age 9-10. It was customary or popular in many parts of Europe, indeed the world, then to photograph boys in military/court-style attire, including a sailor's uniform, as I was. In his photograph, young Ernst is featured, instead, in a Prussian hussar officer's uniform, complete with the tall, cylindrical headgear, the gold sash, and the ceremonial sword.

---

5   In most of Europe then, land was not subdivided among survivors upon the death of the owner; it passed on in its entirety to the eldest son.

Despite his seriousness, a few anecdotes do survive about Martin Jurkat. While they reveal a softer side of his, such as the love of tobacco, and even a penchant for humor, they throw no light on his substantive side. I would have loved to know, for example:

- what influence, if any, he may have had on his children's choice of career: bacteriology by daughter Elisabeth, and social sciences (sociology, statistics, economics) by son Ernst;
- his political activism, if any, and views, since Elbing, where he was born and spent his last years, was a Social Democratic Party stronghold before it turned pro-Nazi after 1933;
- whether Barbara may have inherited her love of history from him, considering that he lived all his life in a part of Europe that made history and was changed by it;
- and, on a personal note, the extent to which he may have inspired or encouraged the love of music of daughters Elisabeth and Gertrud who were accomplished violinist and pianist, respectively.

Following Barbara's maternal ancestors back in time leads to the discovery of not just geographic diversity (in terms of place of origin) but also cultural/ethnic diversity, Polish and Lithuanian in particular. One set of her great grandparents, namely, the parents of grandmother Olga (*née*) Teske, were Fredericke or Frederika Theofilie Kotowska, born in 1848, and Karl Ludwig Ernst Teske, born in 1851. Fredericke Kotowska was born in Graudenz like her daughter Olga, but she was of noble Polish lineage on her father's side. He was Anton or Antoni Kotowski, who belonged to one of Poland's foremost families. He was born in Poland's Poznan province, a Catholic, and a military man who fought on the side of Napoleon. He was married to Elisabeth Kroll, born in Königsberg, and a Lutheran. (See Chapter 6 on Anton Kotowski and his military career.) Karl (or Carl) Teske, Frederika Kotowska's husband, was born in Kamin or Kamien Pomorski, a small city still (current population less than 10,000) in the Pomerania province of the old Prussian Kingdom, situated west of West Prussia, and currently part of Poland. Very little is known about them, except that they had at least two more children besides Barbara's grandmother: a daughter, Anna, and a son, Paul.

Barbara's other set of great grandparents, the parents of her grandfather Martin Jurkat, were Wilhelmine Surkus, born in 1846 in Endrejen in East Prussia, and Dows Jurkatis, born in 1846 in Bendiglauken (or Bendigsfelde) near Tilsit on the border of East Prussia and Lithuania. Tilsit has been known by the Russian name Sovetsk since 1945. There is reason to believe that Dows Jurkatis had strong Lithuanian roots and may have been Lithuanian. The family name Jurkat means "house by the river Jur," Jur being a river *in Lithuania*. The addition of the suffix "*is*" seems to be the Lithuanian way of making the name toponymic, that is, derived from a place name. Note in the family tree that the Jurkatis version of the name goes back more than one generation. Some of Barbara's remote ancestors had old or classic Lithuanian names such as, for males, Friczus and Krihtups, and, for females, Annuhze Zamaitikke and Aguzza Adomatikke.

Tilsit and its surroundings, where some of Barbara's ancestors originated, while not Lithuanian, had a large Lithuanian population and a role in preserving and/or disseminating Lithuanian culture. In the nineteenth century, when Russia controlled Lithuania and banned the Lithuanian language, Tilsit served as an important center for printing Lithuanian books for smuggling into Lithuania. Incidentally, Barbara recalled being told by many people in her youth that she had Lithuanian features!

It is possible to go back one more generation, a fourth, in the case of Barbara's Teske great grandparents—to Susanna Stoike and Karl Teske, who was a school teacher like Barbara's (and my) Elizabeth and Jeremy five generations later.

To recapitulate, the main family names which occur on Barbara's maternal ancestry are Teske, Jurkat, Kotowski, Krall, Surkus, and Stroike. The places they came from are varied, including Graudenz, Kulmsee, Elbing, Endrejen, Ottlotschin, Kamin, Tilsit, and others. Most of these are strung like pearls on a string, along the old Polish Corridor. Nearly all of them had historically large, in many cases majority-German populations, and a Polish and Jewish presence, and they are *all* currently part of Poland. The most important among them in terms of the length and quality of the years Barbara's relatives spent in them and the nostalgia they generated are Graudenz and Elbing. These two cities, together, represented for Barbara and her family what Çanakkale (Turkey) has represented for me and mine for similar reasons and with similar effects. To elaborate, three of Barbara's female ancestors in a direct line—her mother, grandmother and great grandmother—were born in Graudenz. The history of the Kotowskis, who preceded them, weaves in and out of Graudenz, too. Barbara's Jurkat grandparents were married in the same city, and her mother Elisabeth spent her late teen years there. Elbing, too, is a city where Barbara's immediate family lived a long time, longer than at Graudenz, including during the critical World War II years. Her parents were married and her brother Knut was born there. Both cities were picturesque, owing to their location on or near the Vistula River and lagoon. One other factor that may explain the nostalgia about them is the fact that the family left both places when they did because they were forced to, as I shall explain later.

The attachment that Barbara's relatives had toward the above two cities is reflected in the souvenirs or reminders of them which they preserved from generation to generation. Among them is a series of unused postcards of Elbing dating from the turn of the century, in perfect condition, which Barbara inherited and preserved with the care of an old family bible, even though, and maybe because, she never knew Graudenz or Elbing.

To these two cities that have a special place in Barbara's family history one must add Danzig, now Gdansk. Although just one of Barbara's relatives (aunt Gertrud) was born in that city, a number of them lived and/or worked for many years there. Her grandfather's customs inspection office was probably attached to and/or reported to a central office in Danzig, the province's capital. More important, Danzig was the political as well as cultural center of West Prussia which, as such, influenced Barbara's relatives' Social Democratic political leanings as well as their cultural contacts and aspirations.[6]

---

[6] One of the prominent personalities from Danzig is Günter Grass, the winner of the Nobel Prize for literature, who was born there in 1927 and authored the *Danzig Trilogy*, among other works.

Nearly all of Barbara's maternal ancestors were Lutheran, with the exception of the Polish Anton Kotowski. There was no intermarriage across religion or region, except for the union of Kotowski-Teske. The clan and the culture were entirely northern. And the culture's guardian and transmitters were mainly the women, not merely because they generally outlived the men, which they did, but because of their strength and gender solidarity. I experienced the same in my own extended family where the women were similarly strong, outlived the men, and supported each other as if members of a sorority or decision making council. Over the years, I have told the story of how such a "council" endorsed my engagement outside my culture and religion before the men could take a position on it, which was in fact made redundant.

Paternal Ancestors

Barbara's paternal grandmother was Anna Schiemann who was born in 1874 in Berlin. Her full first name was Maria Anna Emma Ida. Schiemann can also be a Jewish name, but Anna came from a Lutheran family. She was married to Otto Paul Frass, known as Paul, born in 1869 in Königsberg, then capital of East Prussia. Königsberg was heavily damaged by Allied bombing during World War II and liberated by the Red Army. It was annexed by the Soviet Union and renamed Kaliningrad after the war. Anna and Paul were married in Berlin in 1899. She was a housewife and he a businessman *(Kaufmann)*, although the nature of his business is not known. She lived to see Barbara as a child, but he died young, at age 43, even before Barbara's father could reach maturity. His year of death was a mystery until recently. I became intrigued by it when I discovered that Barbara's father had volunteered for the navy at age 16, which made me wonder about any personal reasons, including a broken family, that may have led him to it. One of the wonderful aids for genealogical research on Berlin roots nowadays is the availability on line of the Berlin city directories (*Berliner Adressbücher*) for the years 1799 to 1943. The entry for Barbara's father's father in the volume for 1912 is replaced, in the volume for 1913, by an entry for his mother, with the abbreviation for "widow," in the same address, and similar entries for her appear annually in subsequent volumes. This leaves little doubt that he died in 1912 or 1913.

The question that arises is how Anna Frass was able to raise two young sons: Barbara's father Herbert, age 10, and his elder brother Werner, age 12. Incidentally, photographs of them survive, showing them in sailors' uniforms at a young age—in contrast to the hussar's uniform Barbara's Prussian uncle was photographed in at about the same time. What support network could the widowed Anna have had, since there is no evidence that either she or her departed husband had any siblings or live parents! The only certainty is that she was a strong, independent-minded and self-reliant woman. Incidentally, research into Frasses through the Berlin address books revealed that, as I suggested earlier, Frass households were rather rare: just a few most of the time and just one in 1900.

With the exception of her paternal grandmother Anna, who was a Berliner, all of Barbara's paternal ancestors were East Prussian, at least for 200-plus years, unlike her West Prussian maternal ancestors. They came from cities like Assaunen, Gumbinnen (now Gusev), and Gerdanen (now Zeleznodoroznyl) in the vicinity of Königsberg. And they carried family names like Kringer, Rogall, Girke, Rabiger, and Schmidt (see Frass family tree). We know very little about these outer ancestors, what they did and when or where they died, except that they were all Lutheran.

None of the cities Barbara's paternal ancestors came from or lived in—neither Berlin nor Königsberg or the surrounding towns—left a mark on the family or generated the Çanakkale-like nostalgia that Graudenz and Elbing did. Barbara showed some affinity to Königsberg, although she never visited it. Her affinity or interest was more intellectual than emotional, as she was fully familiar with the important role that the city had played throughout history. She showed this affinity by selecting some years ago as a birthday gift for herself an old map of Königsberg and the eastern Baltic region which hangs in our dining room.

Barbara's Frass ancestors were mostly merchants. The oldest one we know about is Christian Frass, grandfather of her grandfather Paul Frass, or nine generations removed from our grandchildren Benjamin, Emma and Arlo. One would have to go back to the thirteenth century to encounter another Frass. I refer to Hugo Frass,

Lord Mayor (*Stadtvogt*) of the city of Augsburg, who in 1284 was granted a Frass family coat of arms by the Holy Roman Emperor. This is somewhat ironic, with hindsight, because Augsburg is located in Bavaria, Germany's south, to which Barbara had no affinity—cultural or of any other kind. She may have had, rather, an antipathy for it. It is not clear when and why Hugo's descendants may have moved or turned northward physically or culturally. They may have run away from the plague that afflicted southern Germany in the middle of the fourteenth century. Coincidentally, Barbara's uncle and godfather, Werner Frass, the theater director, and a Berliner, spent some of his professional carrier in Augsburg. I describe his Augsburg years in Chapter 7 on him.

Barbara's Parents before Her Birth

Her Mother

Barbara's mother Elisabeth was thirty-seven years old when Barbara was born. She spent those years in at least five different places as a result of her father's occupation as customs director. He was reassigned frequently because the region where he served had, in addition to border crossings, several import-export ports and transshipment points along and across the Vistula River. Moreover, several of the cities, like Danzig and Elbing, were members of the Hanseatic League—a commercial alliance of cities along the North Sea and the Baltic Sea in northern Europe which offered its member significant trading advantages and generated a great deal of international and inter-city trade.

Elisabeth spent the first few years of her life in Graudenz, where she was born in 1903, and Ottlotschin, where her brother Ernst was born two years later. She and her family were living in Berent by the time she turned ten. Berent is a town in the north of modern-day Poland which is currently called Koscierzyna. The family then moved to Neufahrwasser, the outer harbor and a northern suburb of Danzig, and spent the next two years (1913-14) there. During the First World War years we find Elisabeth and her family mostly in Lautenburg (now Lidzbark), a town in southern West Prussia. About her mother during that period, Barbara wrote:

> "She spent the war years in a boarding school, grimly following each morning under the supervision of a stout Prussian teacher the movements of the battle lines, marking each change in position of the conflicting armies. From home she had learned that the Germans were to lose this war, and she said so, much to the dismay of her educators. Disrespect of majority opinions had always been one of her chief characteristics."[7]

From late 1918 through the establishment of the Polish Corridor, the family was back in its beloved Graudenz. And the next two decades were spent in Elbing, away from the ancestral West Prussia.

Some family documents (mostly correspondence) survive from each of these places and periods. They form the basis of the chronology I presented. An unusual source proved unusually helpful in this regard. I refer to an "autograph book" kept by Barbara's mother Elisabeth through her late teens. Autograph books, which were popular among the young in those years (my sisters had them, too), were fancy, attractively-bound notebooks where close friends, classmates and family members expressed their feelings and best wishes in writing, embellished with drawings and glossy stickers. They were sometimes called or sold as *Poésie* books, because the entries were often in verse and limerick or haiku-like. What the entries in Elisabeth's book say is difficult to decipher because most of them are in the now-archaic *Sütterlin* cursive script, but this did not matter since every entry indicated clearly the place and date of signature, which was more important for my purposes. It is interesting to note that since Elisabeth could not fill her book, she passed it on years later to Barbara, who used it for a similar purpose herself. I wonder if genealogists recognize the potential utility of this source and have "mined" it in the past . . . Autograph books can shed light not only on places and dates but also on changes in script, language, style, and social mores.

The Jurkat family's move from Graudenz to Elbing after the war must have been traumatic as it was induced/imposed by the creation

---

[7] From the biographical sketch she drafted at Penn.

of the Polish Corridor, that is, by the change in Graudenz' control from Germany to Poland. Such changes, which were historically common and characteristic of the region, were never easy or limited to one side. They were accompanied by forced relocation and imposition of language and culture—Germanization or Polonization—by either side. The Polonization measures imposed by Poland on the West Prussian territories it acquired after the war were particularly severe, however. Elisabeth's family, nevertheless, survived them relatively well, since her father must have moved to Elbing carrying his senior civil service job with him.

The war and the creation of the Polish Corridor out of West Prussia in its aftermath intersected Elisabeth's life at a critical time—her teen years and early adolescence. As a result, we do not know where, when and how she received her education. The considerable extent of it is suggested by a letter of recommendation which she obtained in 1940 from the city government of Elbing for which she worked as a bacteriologist for twelve years (1928-1940). According to the letter, she worked in the city-run laboratory serving the port and its slaughterhouse by checking for animal diseases, particularly parasitic *Trichinosis* in the live animals and raw meat imported and processed. She was in charge of a team engaged in this work and with maintaining the trade and other data on it. She was also responsible for the considerable technical correspondence the work generated. Other documents, such as her marriage record, give her occupation as *Laborantis,* which means laboratory technician, although she functioned as chief bacteriologist. We have no information on where she may have received the necessary technical education and/or training. Based on the knowledge which she passed on to Barbara, there is no doubt that Elisabeth had a well-rounded education and spoke Polish and probably other languages as well.[8]

The same letter described Elisabeth Jurkat as a competent, dedicated, well liked, discreet, and cooperative team member, and

---

[8] With the exception of Danzig and Elbing, which were nearly 100 percent German, most of the places where Elisabeth grew up and lived in West Prussia had large Polish populations even before the establishment of the Polish Corridor.

as a person with a quiet temperament, which she no doubt was, but probably mainly at work. Outside of work, she led a vigorous life, pursuing diverse interests, including reading, skiing, skating, swimming, walking—the German pastime—and music. She was an accomplished violinist and steeped in art, literature and history. She had numerous and assorted friends—as many males as females—with whom she pursued the above interests—which added up to an active social life. Although tradition loving, she was a liberated woman with liberated female friends with whom she often visited the big cities like Danzig, Berlin and Könisberg on holidays. She loved to party and to dress well. She was at the same time and inevitably, given the times, interested in politics and a Social Democrat, like much of Elbing, at least in the twenties. There is, however, no evidence that she was a political activist, overtly or secretly, like her brother Ernst. She was the oldest of three siblings but the last to marry.

Her Father

Herbert Frass, a Berliner by birth, was orphaned at age ten when his father died in 1912. This had no doubt dire consequences for his family and seriously disrupted his life. His brother, however, managed to plan and pursue a career as a theater director, as I describe in Chapter 7. One of the earliest and most important decisions young Herbert made was to enlist in the Imperial German Navy (*Kaiserlich Deutschen Marine*) on October 14, 1918, three months passed his 16th birthday, and to serve in it until 1922.[9] There is strong circumstantial evidence that he volunteered for service rather than being conscripted. He joined the navy less than a month before Germany signed the armistice agreement of

---

[9] The *Imperial* navy ceased to exist as such when the war ended. Shortly thereafter, Germany established a new navy called *Vorläufige Reichsmarine*, or Interim German Navy. Two years later, the word *Vorläufige* was dropped and the navy became simply *Reichsmarine*, or the German Navy. With hindsight, the German navy was "interim" in every way until 1935 when the *Kriegsmarine*, the war or Nazi navy, long under secret planning and preparation, came into being.

November 11, 1918 ending the First World War. Far from recruiting then, the German armed forces, including the navy, were about to embark on a massive, forced and controlled demobilization. This was especially true of the vaunted "Imperial" navy, with its fleet of dreaded submarines. The Versailles Treaty, signed on June 28, 1919, later put harsh restrictions on the size, equipment, role, movement, and expenditures of the German navy.[10] To say that in 1918 the German navy was no fun place to be would be a gross understatement.

Rather than being drawn to the navy at the time and under the conditions just described, Herbert may have been pushed to it by personal factors such as economic considerations and/or unhappiness at home. We do not know the latter for sure, nor the specific reasons for it, except that they must have been important, because the decision to join the navy when Herbert did meant quitting formal education at age sixteen. This was quite a different course from the one followed by his brother Werner who went on to become a successful theater director.

Herbert entered the navy as a ship's boy, cabin boy, or trainee, the lowest possible rank. Ship's boys, *Schiffsjungen,* were referred to informally as "Moses" then, alluding to baby Moses' discovery floating in a reed basket—an expression that has fallen out of use since. Upon enlisting, Herbert served for a few months in the *S.S. König Wilhelm*, an ironclad built in 1868 which served as a barrack hulk in the port of Kiel. In the following eighteen months Herbert was attached to a marine brigade and a coastguard unit in the naval base of Pillau, east of Kiel. Coincidentally, Pillau, which now serves as a Russian naval base named Baltiysk, is situated very near Danzig and Elbing, where Barbara's mother, was born and grew up, respectively. There is no evidence that Herbert and his future wife knew each other then. One wonders, nevertheless, if they later became aware of and talked about this coincidence.

Available military records place Herbert in Kiel, as attached to a U-boat flotilla and serving on the *SMS Hannover* during 1921-22.

---

[10] The navy's role was limited to defensive and perfunctory activities such as protection of coastal areas, performing courtesy visits, hydrographic surveys, and oceanographic work.

While a U-boat flotilla may have existed administratively, that is, on paper, Herbert almost certainly did not serve on a U-boat because, under the armistice agreement, Germany was not allowed to have any submarines. The *Hannover*, on the other hand, built in 1904, was one of the eight obsolete battleships that Germany *was* allowed to keep after the war. Once mighty and a key participant in the sea battle of Jutland in 1916, she was decommissioned in 1919, re-commissioned in 1921 and was serving as a guard ship in the Danish straits in the twenties.

There is scant information about Herbert's activities and personal life in the navy during 1918-22, except for two events—one of passing interest, the other significant. Medical records show that Herbert was incapacitated on June 12, 1921 due to a hernia on one side. He was moved to the naval hospital in Wilhelmshaven, where he was treated, probably surgically, and returned to duty on July 5, 1921. The hernia may have been caused by strenuous work, although Herbert may have had a predilection for it, since he was afflicted by it again after returning to the navy in 1941.

In May 1922, Herbert ran into more serious trouble. According to available records, he "disobeyed orders twice," this in a navy known for its strict discipline. He was jailed immediately, pending formal conviction. He was convicted on September 16, 1922 and sentenced to jail for eight months. The conviction did not describe the order or orders that he had disobeyed, except for stressing that he had done so twice, and had compounded his offense by talking back to his superior(s) and doing it in the presence of others. Since he had already served five months of his sentence, Herbert remained in jail for another three months until his release on December 15, 1922.

Herbert left the navy on the very day after his release from jail. Did he leave voluntarily or was he discharged? We do not know for certain; one can advance arguments on both sides. What is certain is that the navy and Herbert must have been disenchanted with each other, to say the least. It is possible and even probable that Herbert was discharged, and dishonorably, too, given his record of disobedience. He was nevertheless called back to service in 1941 and served until the end of that war.

Despite his mixed experience in it, Herbert left the navy with an enchantment for the sea and the possibilities it offered: adventure and discovery, including self-discovery. He was struck with a strong dose of "wanderlust," as Barbara aptly described it many years later. This led him before long to the merchant marine, which he joined without a specific goal or career objective, except the desire to explore the world.

Sadly, we have no concrete information about what Herbert did in the merchant marine, where he traveled, on which routes or ships, and what he achieved. What duties did he perform? At what level? What training did he receive? Having interrupted his formal education, how did he acquire the broad knowledge he seemed to possess? How did he live? How long did he persist on this physical and personal journey? His years of travel with the merchant navy must have shielded him from the ugly transformation taking place in Germany. Was this intentionall? No letter of his from the various places he visited survives, nor do any mementos from those places. In principle, it should be possible to learn more about his service in the merchant marine, since he must have belonged to a union, but one would need to know more about the specific year he served in and the names of one or more of the ships, as well as wait until the union records of that distant period are, if ever, scanned and computerized.

A few things about Herbert's twenties and thirties—which coincided with the 1920s and 1930s—are nevertheless known or can be surmised. At one point he became a businessman (*Kaufmann*)—his formal or official occupation for the rest of his life. We do not know with any certainty the nature of his business since Barbara was not specific about it. According to Barbara's first cousin Ernst Cecior, her father owned a tobacco shop on Elsastrasse No. 56 in Berlin, although this may not have been his only business or business interest. He was, by nature, a freewheeling entrepreneur not satisfied with a single, sedentary activity. Whatever his business was, it allowed him to lead a comfortable life, with leisure activities in the course of which he met Barbara's mother, Elisabeth.[11] Yet,

---

[11] In principle, as with his years in the merchant marine, it should be possible to learn more about Herbert's business, for example, through chamber of

he does not appear in the Berlin address directory until 1939. The above reflects who he was in essence: city-bred, well-traveled and well-read, a romantic, a dreamer, a person who lived from day to day, exhuberant, impulsive, infinitely imaginative, unconventional, and very unlike his brother. He was more Mediterranean than German, both emotionally and physically. He was short and dark—the German equivalent of the Black Irish.[12]

In the mid-thirties, Herbert fathered a child, Christa, as a single man. He could not marry her mother because, according to Barbara, her staunchly Catholic parents refused to allow it. I shall return to Christa in Chapter 4.

Her Parents' Marriage

Barbara's mother, Elisabeth Jurkat, and her father, Herbert Frass, met in 1939 at an entertainment locale—a casino, according to Barbara—in Berlin, where her father lived and which her mother was visiting with a friend. They were married on March 23, 1940, four months before Barbara was born. The marriage took place in Elbing, where Elisabeth lived, after which she accompanied her husband to Berlin.

Barbara's parents' decision to marry was rational and reasoned, rather than impulsive and emotional. An important thing (for those times) which they had in common was their anti-fascist political beliefs. I am not suggesting that love did not play the central role—Barbara was conceived five months before their marriage! What I am saying is simply that what drove Elisabeth's and Herbert's decision was to a large extent that they were *ready* to get married. She was 37 and he was 38. They were both mature and

---

commerce records of the time or the like, if and when they are computerized. I am not optimistic, however, because Herbert was not the type of person to be tied down to a given activity or place. Besides, the term businessman (*Kaufmann*) is one which, like the term housewife, is often used to describe what is too general or hard to describe.

[12] The above description of Herbert's personal traits, despite the lack of primary information on it, is based largely on and confirmed by what Barbara heard from her mother.

self-confident individuals who entered into their relationship with full awareness and openness. There is reason to believe, for example, that Elisabeth knew that Herbert had fathered a child previously. He had gotten over his wanderlust and was ready for a settled life. She wanted to have one or more children. I am simplifying but not a great deal.

What is more intriguing to me than the reasons for their decision to marry is what impact if any, the turbulent, ominous times had on it. Germany's new and ugly face was in full view, and the war with all its horrors was in full swing. *Kristallnacht* had occurred not too long before. Elisabeth's brother Ernst had had to flee Germany in 1939, pursued by the Gestapo. Germany had already occupied Czechoslovakia and Poland, and was about to invade Belgium, Holland and France. And Herbert's induction into the navy was inevitable. How did Elisabeth and Herbert see the future? What were their fears, dreams and expectations? Did they realize or imagine that the yet unborn Barbara would be five years old before the war ended? We'll never know. What their decision to marry nevertheless implies is that they did not lack courage, nor love for and an abiding commitment to each other.

Chapter Two

The War and Its Aftermath

As noted earlier, Barbara's mother, Elisabeth Jurkat, married Herbert Frass on March 23, 1940 in Elbing where she had been living with her family. After the event, she followed him to Berlin and they settled at *Elsa Strasse No. 36* there. Barbara was born on July 22, 1940 in Berlin and was baptized a week later. The first ten years of her life, which are the focus of this chapter, can be divided in equal segments between the war (1940-1945) and life under Soviet occupation (1946-1950).

The War Years

For the purpose of presentation, I shall relate Barbara's father's personal experience and his close family's experience separately and in that order.

Herbert at War

Herbert was called back to the navy, where he had served for four years after the First World War, in February 1941. The course of the war was favorable to Germany then, to put it mildly: Denmark, Norway, Belgium, and Holland had been occupied; German troops were already in Paris; Italy had joined the war on Germany's side; and the Unites States' entry into the war was ten months away. Herbert was thirty-seven years old in 1939, and he did not seem to possess—to have acquired during his prior service—skills especially in demand by the army. He must have been recalled as part of the ongoing, non-stop mobilization to achieve the Reich's expansionary goals and to perform mostly support services, thus liberating the younger, more able-bodied recruits to fight the war. Nor did Herbert make any mark in the navy. The highest rank he achieved, effective August 1, 1943, was that of *Matrosenobergefreiter,* equivalent to seaman corporal. This was deliberate on his part. Upon being recalled by the navy, his wife, who was staunchly anti-Nazi and against the war, is believed to have told him sternly, "If you return from the war with a rank higher than corporal, I'll divorce you." Herbert must have acted accordingly, lying low, avoiding being noticed and, above all, controlling the temper which had gotten him into trouble during his prior service.[13]

Back in the navy, Herbert received some indoctrination or re-training for about a month aboard the *SS Cap Arcona*, docked in Kiel. Once a luxury ocean liner, the *Cap Arcona* had been taken over by the German navy in 1940 and was being used as an accommodation ship in the Baltic Sea. The rest of Herbert's wartime service was ostensibly associated with the U-boat fleet. He served first at the headquarters of Germany's U-boat operations headed by Rear Admiral (*Konteradmiral*) Karl Dönitz. The headquarters were located near Lorient, or L'Orient, in Brittany in northwestern France. Lorient was one of several U-boat bases on the Atlantic coast and one of the largest. At its peak, it serviced and sheltered as many as thirty U-boats in fortified, special bunkers, called "pens." In March 1942, after the U-boat base at Saint-Nazaire suffered a deadly attack by the Allies, the headquarters near Lorient were considered too exposed and moved to Paris. Herbert was transferred to Paris along with the headquarters, and he served there until January 1943. That month Dönitz was promoted to Grand Admiral (*Grossadmiral*), became supreme commander of the entire German navy, and relocated to the German capital.

---

[13] See Chapter 1.

The Promise of the Present and the Shadow of the Past

Almost simultaneously, Herbert was moved to the command of Germany's "U-boote West" fleet. Between March 1943 and June 1945, he served sequentially at Waldbeutel, Pillau (where he had spent some time after the First World War), and the town of Neustadt/Holstein in Schleswig-Holstein. He was then assigned to Zeven, a naval port near Bremerhaven. He spent nearly eighteen months there, longer than at any other place, including Lorient, during the war. The only wartime photographs of him that survive are from Zeven. In February 1945, three months before the end of the war, he was reassigned to Cuxhaven, a port at the mouth of the Elbe River on the Baltic coast. He must have been captured there, since the information on him in German military records stops then. He was very likely captured by the Canadian forces which had been advancing through Holland.

What did Herbert do in the German navy? What tasks or duties did he perform? He was attached mostly to U-boat "training units," except for taking part in a special workshop in June 1944 in Plön, a small city which lies by the lake of that name in the state of Schleswig-Holstein. The workshop is noteworthy; it dealt with protection from gas attacks, as the course of the war had begun to turn against Germany. Yet, Herbert's U-boat training affiliation is misleading. It is highly unlikely that he ever served on a U-boat or trained those who did in any capacity. He was in his early forties through most of the war; he never received any technical training for any length of time; and, as previously noted, he never advanced beyond the rank of corporal. He probably served in an administrative or office support and service capacity. According to the information that has come down through the family, he worked in the mess, or food preparation and service facilities, at Dönitz' headquarters. However, his transfer to Paris when the headquarters were moved there in March 1943 suggests that his responsibilities as a non-combatant may have been broader than "mess duties."

What about Herbert's state of mind? In a letter which he sent to his mother from Zeven on March 21, 1945, a few weeks before the end of the war, he wrote "There is not much news to tell about me. . . . Things are still unchanged. . . . Everything seems to be bombed out. . . . We have to wait and see. I am curious to see how this is going to end." In a brooding mood as dark as the clouds above, he continued, "Who knows what life has in store for us? We should not make plans. Who knows what is going to be left for us? Who is going to survive?"[14]

Herbert became a civilian citizen again by September 1945, living temporarily in Upjeven, a small town near the Baltic coast in Eastern Friesland. He was issued an identity card confirming his new status on September 21, 1945 in Oestringen, a town in the southern region of Baden-Württemberg which must have had some Allied administrative office. Although the card indicated that he had no physical identifying mark (such as one resulting from an injury), the photograph attached to it showed a poorly-clad (jacket, probably borrowed, and no shirt), sad and exhausted man almost in a daze.

Herbert's overall *non-fighting* responsibilities and record may have contributed to his quick release after capture by the Canadian forces. His major achievement was surviving the war, and he had done that without bodily injury. With hindsight, his decision to volunteer for the Imperial Navy at age 16 in 1918 was not all that foolish, since it led to his induction into the navy, rather than the far more dangerous army, during the Second World War.

The Family Back Home

Herbert's wife, Elisabeth, and their newborn Barbara remained in Berlin very likely until the second half of 1943. Elisabeth's main focus was her baby daughter. She doted over her with utmost care, pride and love, arranging for photographs to be taken of her and often with herself every month and from every angle. This was a happy period for Elisabeth despite the gathering clouds and the separation from her husband. The couple maintained contact through the mail. While he was in France, Herbert sent his wife a beautiful handbag and Barbara a black bear. Both gifts are featured prominently in family photographs that survive. Elisabeth visited her parents in Elbing frequently with her child during 1941-1942,

---

[14] The letter was probably passed on by his mother (in Berlin) for information to his wife (in Elbing) who, in turn, passed it on to Barbara years later.

sometimes for extended periods. On occasion, her sister Gertrud and her children visited simultaneously. Her parents lived in a house with a yard in a quasi-rural setting, which allowed the four grandchildren to have a good time together.

During the same period, Herbert's mother was still living in Berlin, and his brother Werner was working in theater in Danzig. Elisabeth's brother Ernst had managed to reach the United States, although his wife, young son and mother-in-law were roaming as refugees in France. Elisabeth's main concern, however, was her daughter Barbara.

After the massive Allied bombardment of Berlin in the spring and summer of 1943, Elisabeth and Barbara moved permanently to Elbing. Berlin had been bombed before, especially during night raids in 1940-41, but those air raids were neither sustained nor very destructive. Those of 1943 were so serious in comparison that they caused the chief of staff of the German air force, Hans Jeschonneck, to commit suicide out of embarrassment.[15] On one night alone, more than 700 bombers participated in the air attack. According to survivors of such attacks, the sounds of the bombs and the planes overhead were as terrifying as the destruction they wrought.

The atmosphere in Elbing had some air of normalcy, compared to Berlin. Holidays were celebrated the traditional way, and children were shielded from the horrors of war by organizing special diversions for them, which little Barbara enjoyed. Herbert managed to come to Elbing on leave at least once during this period, and Elisabeth and Barbara visited him in Zeven as well.[16] As a result of one such occasion, Elisabeth produced a brother for Barbara, Knut, on May 15, 1944 in Elbing—a happy occasion no doubt but in an apocalyptic setting for Germany. The Allies had landed in Italy; the Allied armada was preparing to land in Normandy; and the Red Army was advancing westward. Internally, shortages

---

[15] Richard J. Evans, *The Third Reich at War*, Penguin Books, 2008, p. 459.

[16] During a brief reunion in Zeven, Herbert and Elisabeth wrote jointly a sweet letter to Herbert's mother expressing the "bliss of spending some time together as the bombs fell" and drawing a small flower on behalf of little Barbara, who was with them.

were acute, food rations were being steadily reduced, and travel was nearly impossible. And the persecution of Jews was in full swing and hard to overlook. Elisabeth's parents had Jewish next-door neighbors who disappeared practically overnight.[17]

Beginning in the war years, the life of Barbara's close family and that of her mother's sister Gertrud became intertwined. It is, therefore, appropriate to provide some background. Gertrud married at a young age, before her older siblings. Her husband was Wilhelm Cecior (1908-1983), known as Uncle Willi to Barbara and her brother. His parents were from Winsken (Wientzkowen)—a small town in today's northern Poland, situated east of Graudenz, origin of many of Barbara's ancestors. The area is part of the Masuria region, known for its numerous lakes, which was at one time part of East Prussia.[18] Willi could not shed his geographic/ethnic origins. He was often referred to by family and friends as a *Masur* to describe his earthy, coarse, peasant-like manner.

Willi at War

Willi Cecior's personality, profession and particularly his war experience were quite different from those of Barbara's father. Willi was a policeman for most of his adult life. He received his policeman's training in the mid-1920s in Sendsburg, then German, now Mragowo and Polish. He became an active policeman around 1928 in Elbing where he must have met his future wife. They had three children together: Ernst, born in 1933, Manfred (1938), and Ingrid (1941). The two sisters were close while growing up and remained so after Gertrud was married. Willi,

---

[17] Elisabeth's parents were close to their Jewish neighbors, as suggested by friendly joint photographs. Elbing had had one of the oldest Jewish communities in East Prussia, but by 1939 the community had dwindled to 53 member, including Barbara's grandparents' neighbors. We do not know what happened to them during the war. See Shmuel Spector, Ed., *The Encyclopedia of Jewish Life Before and During the Holocaust*, New York University Press, 2001.

[18] Masuria gave the name to the Polish national dance, *mazurka*, made famous by Chopin who composed many pieces of that title for the piano.

Tutta, as Gertrud was known within the family, their young children, and Elisabeth lived together for a while in Elbing. In the late 1930s, the Ceciors moved to Königsberg where Willi worked for the criminal investigation (*Kriminalinspector*) unit of the police department. In 1941, as the German army advanced into Russia, Willi moved with it to Bialystok—a city with a large Jewish population in northeastern Poland. After occupying it at the beginning of the war, Germany had ceded the city to the Soviet Union in accordance with the terms of the German-Soviet Pact of 1939, and it had re-occupied it in June1941. At first, Willi was there alone, but soon after he brought his wife and two children to Bialystok where they spent most of the war years. Ernst, the eldest son, who was of school age, was sent to live with his grandparents in Elbing.

What Willi did in Bialystok is not entirely clear, but what we know of Bialystok's history suggests ugly possibilities. The German occupiers dealt with Bialystok's Jewish population brutally. Soon after occupying the city, they placed its 50,000 Jews in a specially created ghetto. They employed the healthy among them in forced-labor projects. And, in August 1943, they started deporting them to extermination camps or murdering them *in situ*. These activities were carried out in part by mobile paramilitary "killing units," known as *Einsatzgruppe*, which followed the invading forces of the German army into Eastern Europe. According to Willi's son Ernst, who lives currently in Krefeld, while in Bialystok, Willi served as "an instructor for the army and a member of the *Sicherheitsdienst*." The last mentioned was the notorious Security Service, a sister of the Gestapo and the intelligence arm of the SS, whose activities included intelligence gathering, criminal investigation and, most importantly, finding and *eliminating* the enemies of both the Third Reich and the Nazi party (NASDAP), namely, the Jews, Communists, Gypsies, and other undesirable groups. We do not know exactly what Willi did as part of the *Sicherheitsdienst* or in any other capacity, but given the unit or units he was employed by, and regardless of his own beliefs, it would be very unlikely for him not to have be associated with criminal activities.

The Closing Months of the War

The Soviets re-took Bialystok in August 1944. Willi managed to escape to Danzig, which was still under German control, before then, and he worked for a few months for the police force there. His wife Gertrud and their two children went back to Elbing where the elder Jurkats still lived. The two sisters, Gertrud and Elisabeth, and their families were reunited around that time. The reunification took place in the region of Thuringia in central Germany. According to Barbara, her mother was absolutely terrified of being in Elbing when the Red Army arrived; she followed the army's advance daily by listening to the BBC. It is known that as the Soviet army approached Elbing, thousands of German citizens fled westward, as they did other cities on its path. Elisabeth and her children must have been among the first to do so. Elbing was occupied by the Red Army in February 1945 after a siege and bombardment which destroyed two-thirds of the city's infrastructure, including much of the historic city center. Elisabeth and the children missed this, moving to Erfurt in Thuringia in a hurry shortly before it was occupied by the American forces, General Patton's Third Army, on April 12, 1945.

The above account is confirmed by other family members, but it constitutes only the broad outline of what happened. According to Ernst Cecior, Elisabeth and her young children moved first to Gotha, a historic city 13 miles west of Erfurt, where Elisabeth had close relatives, namely, an uncle—her mother Olga's brother Paul Teske and his wife Grethe. This could have been a supporting reason, if not the main one, for moving to Thuringia. It may also explain why, in his last two "censored" letters to his mother, Herbert had been suggesting to her that she leave Berlin and move to Thuringia without giving any reason. Ernst reports that Elisabeth and her children moved in with her Teske relatives, while the Cecior family, as well as the Jurkat grandparents, who had left Elbing in the meantime, occupied the house next door.

The Frass, Cecior and Jurkat families' move to Gotha contributed to their survival unharmed. During the closing months of the was, Gotha was under the command of Colonel Josef Ritter von Gadolla, who was Austrian-born. When the American forces reached the outskirts of the city, he was summoned by his superiors in Weimar and ordered to defend the city to the last man, which he was forced to agree to. He knew, however, that the situation was hopeless since his forces were slim and ill equipped. A man of conscience, he wished to avoid the inevitable carnage at all cost. After discussing the options with the city representatives, he embarked on the unusual step of driving to the American front line to deliver the city's peaceful surrender in person. He was intercepted by a loyal anti-aircraft unit and driven to Weimar where he was tried on the spot and executed by firing squad the following day. Since Colonel von Gadolla had previously ordered his troops to withdraw, the American forces were able to enter city the same day, April 5, 1945, without firing a shot, avoiding military as well as civilian casualties, and leaving the city unscathed. Erfurt fell to the Americans eight days later.

The Postwar

Herbert and Willi, the two families' men under arms, joined their loved ones in Thuringia soon after the war ended. For Herbert this meant soon after he was released by the Canadian forces to which his unit had surrendered in the Baltic region. For Willi, the closing months of the war were more dramatic. He was caught—also in the Baltic—in the sinking of the German boat *MV Wilhelm Gustloff* with about 9,400 people on January 30, 1945. The ship was named after a Swiss Nazi leader who was assassinated by a Jewish man in 1936 and declared a martyr by the Nazis. Since its launching in 1937, the *Gustloff* had served successively as a passenger ship, a hospital ship, and floating barracks for naval personnel. In January 1945, it was participating in the evacuation of civilians, *Kriegsmarine* sailors and German soldiers who were surrounded by the Red Army in East Prussia. On this, its last voyage. the *Gustloff* sailed from the port of Gotenhafen (Gdynia) near Danzig, where Willi had sought refuge from the Soviets. Its final destination was the port of Kiel.

These were dangerous times and waters. The *Gustloff* was under the command of four captains—three civilians and one military—who could not agree on the best course of action to guard against submarine attacks. The ship was hit by three torpedoes fired by a Soviet submarine and sank in less than forty-five minutes. An estimated 1,200 people were rescued by various German vessels in the area and 9,400 perished. This remains the largest loss of life resulting from the sinking of single vessel in maritime history. It has been referred to for that reason as the Nazi Titanic and Hitler's supership. The record loss of life was caused by the excessive load of the ship: a total of 10,600 people, far exceeding its capacity, partly caused by the boarding of thousands of panicked civilians without authorization, the resulting mayhem, and the trampling of women and children when the ship was hit.

Willi Cecior was among those who survived. He was rescued by the free Danish navy and taken to a reception center in Denmark. He managed to escape his captors, making his way to his family in Gotha. Barbara never spoke of this event. The above account comes from Ernst, Willi's son, and conforms with the facts. The sinking of the *Gustloff* has been the subject of several books (both in German and in English), documentaries, movies, and television programs, including by the National Geographic and the Discovery Channels, and German film makers. The Nobel laureate Günther Grass wrote about the Gustloff in his 2002 novel titled *Im Krebsgang* (Crabwalk).

The Frass and Cecior families' first few weeks under Soviet occupation were not as horrible as those experienced by the residents of the other cities on the path of the advancing Red Army. Gotha did not experience the vengeful behavior by Soviet troops witnessed by cities like Berlin. Soviet troops left a mark, rather, by their naiveté since many of the recruits by the end of the war were young men from rural areas. Barbara's grandmother recalled observing Soviet orderlies washing potatoes in the standing water of toilets, not having seen such toilets before. And Barbara's mother, who was an accomplished violinist, liked telling of the evening when she heard an ominous knock on the door. She opened the door terrified, to find two Russian soldiers who said politely, "We heard you play the violin. We are wondering if we can bring our instruments and play with you tomorrow evening" . . . which they later did.

The above anecdote does not hide or minimize the horrendous reality that faced the citizens of defeated Germany right after the war, namely, the acute shortages of food and jobs, among others. Within weeks, the Frasses and the Ceciors moved from Gotha to Erfurt, the bigger city, where they anticipated employment opportunities to be better. While they suffered from the shortages as much as the rest of the population, they were pleased to be still under American occupation. However, on July 3, 1945, the American forces withdrew from Erfurt and ceded the city to the Soviets. This was not a last minute, post-occupation decision. In 1944 already, the Allies had determined the demarcation line for the areas of occupation. Erfurt and the rest of Thuringia were to belong to the Soviet occupation zone. The American forces (rather than the Red Army) had occupied Erfurt and its vicinity first, primarily because of the battlefield conditions which had led to unexpected and far-reaching territorial gains for them in central Germany. The Frass clan did not know that ahead of time and now found themselves in Soviet-occupied territory.[19]

Willi's Second Survival

What happened to Willi in the Soviet zone was ugly but uncomplicated. Given his professional background, he had no trouble joining the Erfurt police force. Within less than a year, however, he was arrested by the Soviets in Erfurt and sent to Buchenwald, site of the major concentration camp liberated by Americans, where he spent the next four years. There, the Soviets operated the *"Special Camp 2"* for their own prisoners: former Nazis, opponents of Stalinism, criminals, and others imprisoned due to identity confusion or arbitrary arrests. According to Ernst, his son, Willi was "probably" imprisoned for not fighting the black market operations vigorously enough as a law enforcement officer. Considering the prevailing economic situation and the severity of his punishment, Willi could have taken part in the black market activities himself. In the aftermath of the war, the black market was rampant throughout Germany. There were severe shortages of practically everything: food, construction materials, energy

---

[19] In addition to Thuringia, the Soviet zone included Saxony, Saxony-Anhalt, Brandenburg, and Mecklenburg-Verkommers.

(coal) for cooking and heating, etc. People traded family valuables for food. Illicit trade flourished. Under these circumstances, participation in the black market was considered both necessary and moral. Unavoidably, crime and corruption followed.[20]

Special Camp 2 was closed down by the Soviets and the facilities demolished in October 1950. During its five years of existence, according to Soviiet records, more than 7,000 people perished in the camp, most of them buried in mass graves in the woods surrounding the camp. Willi again survived. It is not clear whether he was released as a result of the closing down of the camp or the end of his sentence—probably the former. We have no information on Willi's experience at the camp. He never talked about it because, according to his son, he was made to sign a paper vowing not to divulge any information about life at the camp.

Herbert's Mysterious Work

Herbert's work in Erfurt is of particular interest because it had some enigmatic aspects; it sprang from some of the worst policies of the Nazi era; and it provided a glimpse of his character. I shall therefore discuss it in some detail. The broad facts are as follows.

On October 20, 1945, barely a few weeks after he joined his family in Erfurt, Herbert was appointed by the governor (*Präsident*) of the state of Thuringia as managing director (*Geschäftführer*) of a firm called MERKUR Handels-und Einkaufsgesellschaft Ahlburg & Co. (Trading and Purchasing Co.) located in Erfurt. The formal letter of appointment had a series of precise instructions covering both the do's and the dont's.[21] Herbert was to undertake an urgent assessment of the commercial status of the enterprise. He was to evaluate the actions and comportment of his "predecessors in his position" (the former managing directors) and review the report prepared by the state criminal police on the same. He was

---

[20] It is unlikely that the Soviets imprisoned Willi for atrocities he may have committed in Bialystok for the simple reason that the punishment for such acts would have been much harsher than four years in Buchenwald.

[21] The letter of appointment was discovered recently by Doris Frass, Barbara's sister-in-law, among the family papers preserved by her mother Elisabeth.

instructed, however, not to divulge information on the assets of the company or its financial situation, nor on the personnel and their Nazi party affiliation. He was expected to prepare a report on the appropriate course of action over the next three months. No other inquiry on this subject was to take place.

There is no evidence that Barbara's father applied for the job. His appointment raises a series of questions concerning why the Governor took this action regarding the company, its timing, and the selection of Herbert, all of which are linked to the nature of the company's activities.

After the Nazis came to power in 1933, it did not take them long to begin "cleansing" the civil service and all economic activities of people of the Jewish faith or of Jewish descent. The first measure was to approve the *Reichsgesetz zur Wiederherstellung des Berufsbeamtentum (*Civil Service Restoration Act) which had that principal objective. This was accompanied by an orchestrated attempt to transfer the ownership of businesses, big and small, to non-Jewish Germans. The process was tightly scripted and implemented. The tactical steps included boycott campaigns, refusal of bank loans, and other forms of harassment designed to force the owners to sell their businesses at drastically low prices equivalent to a fraction of their true value. The forced transaction was recorded in a contract between the parties to give it the appearance of being consensual, that is, voluntary on the part of the seller.

The process just described was known by the overtly racist term *Arigierung* (Aryanization). It amounted to a forced, calculated, step-by-step expropriation. Among the enterprises targeted first were the numerous department stores owned by Jews in the large urban centers because of their visibility or strong propaganda value. In November 1938, the Nazi government passed the Ordinance on the Elimination of Jews from German Economic Life[22] making Aryanization effectively mandatory. These actions resulted in what has been called "one of the most profound transfers of property in German history."[23] In Thuringia alone around 650 major

---

[22] *Verordnung zur Ausschaftung der Juden aus dem deutschen Wirtschaftleben.*
[23] Monika Gibas, Ed., *Fates of Jewish Families in Thuringia 1933-1945*, Landeszentrale für polische Bildung Thüringen, 2009, p. 7.

Jewish-owned family businesses fell victim to Aryanization. Many of them were in Erfurt.

Jews had been living in Erfurt since the twelfth century, although none were left there by 1945 as a result of "deportations and suicides."[24] One of the premier firms was the department store *Römischer Kaiser* (Roman King), which was the pride of the city. It was founded in 1908 by two brothers-in-law, Siegfried Pinthus and Arthur Ardtheim, who belonged to Erfurt's upper class. By the mid-1930s, the store employed as many as 450 people and was more than a store; it functioned, rather, or in addition, as a social center. It held band concerts and fashion shows. It had a lounge and a lending library of more than 5,000 volumes. And it boasted a sports club. By 1937, after an extended period of boycotts and other forms of harassment, the owners were forced to sell the store. The instant dismissal of all Jewish employees was stipulated in the contract. The new buyers were: Hans Quelh, en entrepreneur from the city of Leipzig; Dr. von Zabiensky, a bank director from Erfurt; and Dr. Walter Ahlburg, a lawyer from Berlin. The last mentioned specialized in acquiring Jewish-owned department stores and was very probably the person who put the buying partnership together. As he had done with some of his similar acquisitions, upon buying Römischer Kaiser he changed the name of the firm to MERKUR, with his own name in the long title. This is the enterprise to which Herbert Frass was appointed as managing director in December 1945.[25]

Merkur was taken over and put under trusteeship by the Thuringian government within six weeks following the war. The speed with which this was done, given the more pressing priorities after the end of combat (food and other shortages, for example) is striking. The quick action may have been prompted or imposed by the Americans soon after they liberated Erfurt. The American liberators relied on Dr. Hermann Brill, a Thurinigian politician, in setting up the governance framework for the state. Dr. Brill had government experience and a long history of resistance to the

---

[24] See *The Encyclopedia of Jewish Life Before and During the Holocaust*, op. cit.
[25] For an account of the firm's Aryanization, see Philipp Gliesing, *The Department Store "Römischer Kaiser" (KRK), Erfurt*, in Gibas, op. cit.

Nazis. He had served as a Social Democrat in both the Thuringian parliament and the *Reichstag* (the Federal Government) before 1933. He had made early on the decision to resist Hitler "at any time, everywhere and under all circumstances," and he had played a leading role in the creation of the secret resistance group known as *Deutsche Volksfront*. These actions led to his arrest for treason in 1938. He was imprisoned until the end of the war, the last two years of it in Buchenwald. As the war was ending, he began to draw up a plan for the administrative rebuilding of Thuringia. On the strength of this plan, in June 1945, the Americans appointed him *Regierungspräsident* (equivalent to governor) of Thuringia. He served in that position briefly—until Thuringia became part of the Soviet zone a few month later—following which he left the state and began working for the American administration in Berlin. Dr. Brill was a Thuringian to the core, born and educated in the state, familiar with its history, and concerned with both its future and its image. It is possible that the quick action on Merkur and other formerly-Jewish-owned firms was initiated by him.

The designation of Herbert Frass as managing director of Merkur, however, occurred after Brill left his post and the Soviets appointed Dr. Rudolf Paul as governor of Thuringia. Dr. Paul was a lawyer by profession who had been anti-Nazi, like Brill, and banned from practicing law after 1933. He did not get along with the Soviets, and in September 1947 he, like Brill, had to flee to the American occupation zone.

From the Frass family perspective the central question is why Barbara's father Herbert was appointed to such an important, politically-sensitive position which carried the heavy responsibilities itemized earlier. [26] He had survived the war as an ordinary sailor with no notable achievement. Although he had never joined the Nazi party, he had no history of sustained, known opposition to the

---

[26] It may be recalled that the aforementioned Dr. Brill's life had intersected with that of two of Barbara's relatives: Dr. Ernst Jurkat, her uncle, who had been a member of *Deutsche Volksfront,* and Hans Bergas, his brother-in-law, who had overlapped with Brill at Buchenwald. Both were Barbara's relatives on her mother's side. There is no evidence that Dr. Brill knew her father and recommended him for the Merkur position.

regime. He had been in business, but he had had no experience akin to running a large commercial establishment such as a department store. He had not made a mark in business or held an important position in the Chamber of Commerce, for example. While his lack of negative record may have been an advantage, even his main advantage, the fact remains that he had no positive record that recommended him for such a job. An exception, a key exception, may have been his *honesty*—an important quality for the job he was appointed to perform. He must have been selected for the job because of prior personal contacts with people—unknown to this day—familiar with at least this quality of his. A recently uncovered document in the Thuringian state archives hints at a possibility. It is a long letter written in 1947 by Dr. Ahlers, the key partner who acquired the Römischer Kaiser department store from its Jewish owners, to the State Interior Minister, arguing that the department store had been sold "voluntarily," ostensibly in order to build a case for its return to the new owners. In tracing the history of the firm, Dr. Ahlers stated that in 1945 the store was placed initially under the trusteeship of two "cigarette agents" (*Zigarettenvertreter*) called Heissner and Wermter. Herbert Frass had had a tobacco store in Berlin before the war and may have been known to these gentlemen through it. But this remains to be verified and leaves open the question concerning why the cigarette agents had been appointed trustees to begin with.

Herbert Frass worked at Merkur until the second half of 1947. The confiscation of the firm was lifted by the State on April 11, 1947, and the firm's return to its post-Aryanization owners was authorized on that date. The new (restored) owners asked Herbert to stay on as interim managing director for a short time until the firm was restructured and a permanent managing director appointed. The transfer of the firm's ownership appears to have been delayed until the end of the year for some reason. In all certainty, however, Herbert's affiliation with Merkur ended in mid-1947.

What precisely did Herbert Frass do at Merkur? We do not know with certainty or in any detail. None of the reports on the firm, which he may have written for the State in accordance with his letter of appointment, are available. What little we do know is more circumstantial than factual. On April 1, 1946, after barely six months on the job, Herbert received a letter from *Persische Teppich Gesellschaft A.G.*, an oriental carpet import firm in Berlin, thanking him for the "kind services" he had rendered the firm and offering him a carpet in appreciation—a carpet which Barbara inherited and brought, together with a second one, to the United States.[27] A possible explanation is that Herbert discovered a stock of such carpets in the department store's warehouse—carpets which may have been acquired illegally from their Jewish owners. And he may have sent them to the original importer for the purpose of identifying their owners. The department store itself was heavily damaged during the war and served as a warehouse and provisioning center following the war. Herbert's main preoccupation must have been regularizing the accounts and operations of the department store and creating the conditions for lifting its confiscation. This may have contributed to the eventual compensation of the survivors of the original owners. Siegfried Pinthus, the founding owner, died of natural causes a few months after the Aryanization of his beloved department store. His partner, Arthur Arndtheim, and his family immigrated to Palestine in 1939. The compensation of their survivors had to wait until after the reunification of the two Germanys. Herbert had long been deceased by then. He would have been pleased with the outcome no doubt, despite the long delay.

In the last few years especially, there has been a strong interest in the ugly experience with Aryanization in Thuringia, with a focus on Erfurt. After long research, which is ongoing, the Thurinigia State Archives, in cooperation with the Friedrich-Schiller-Universität of Jena, and under the direction of Dr. Monika Gibas, have prepared a traveling exhibition on it which was presented in Leipzig in German in 2007, and in Krakow, Poland, in English in 2009. The city of Erfurt is currently preparing an illustrated book on the Aryanized firms of Erfurt.

After leaving Merkur, Herbert worked for the Soviet Military Administration of Thuringia (SMATh). By then, the Soviets had moved the state capital from Weimar to Erfurt. SMATh must have

---

[27] The Persian carpet company concerned was an enterprise founded in 1911. It survives to this day and is located in Frankfurt am Main.

been the largest employer in Erfurt after the war. We know very little about exactly what Herbert did, except that he was in charge of the procurement and distribution of goods for SMATh. He had considerable authority and was given a to-whom-it-may-concern type document dated February 3, 1949 which stated his responsibility as well as authority and asked all parties to cooperate with him in his work. This was Herbert Frass' last job in East Germany. I shall return to this in the next chapter.

Life in Erfurt

As noted, the four Frasses spent five-plus years (1945-1950) in Erfurt. Those were important years for the family; and, despite the Soviet occupation, they may have been mostly happy years, too, compared to the five that followed. First of all, they were a period of welcome peace. The Frasses, together, had known only war up to that point: the parents had met and were married during the war, and both children were born in wartime, too. The family came together for the first time in Erfurt, enabling its members to truly get to know each other. Herbert had hardly spent any time with either of his two children. Despite having two children, he and his wife had lived together barely for eleven months, and needed to get acquainted—not just re-acquainted—with each other. As for Barbara, she went to school for the first time, completed four grades and made her first childhood friends in Erfurt.

Erfurt is a historic, medieval city of more than 200,000 people today. It is located practically at the geometric center of present-day Germany and very near notable cities such as: Eisenach, site of the Wartburg castle where Luther translated the New Testament into German; Weimar, an art center, where the Bahaus style was born; and Leipzig, a music capital, where Bach and other musicians too numerous to name either worked or were born. (See map of East Germany.) Erfurt was also very close to Buchenwald, the largest, most infamous concentration camp on German soil, which was liberated one day before Erfurt was. Generally, the Soviet Military Administration (SMA) left the administrative division of its occupied territories largely unchanged, but soon after taking over

Thuringia, it moved the latter's capital from Weimar to Erfurt, thus greatly enhancing its importance.

Erfurt is a beautiful city today, thanks partly to the Gera river which runs though it, carving Venice-like canals, and it was as beautiful when the Frasses arrived as it had been before the war, having suffered limited damage in 1945. Throughout their stay in Erfurt, the family lived at Milchensel Strasse, No. 3, a flat in a four-storey apartment building. In 1992, shortly after Germany's reunification, Barbara and I visited Erfurt, accompanied by our German relatives, and stopped by the building—an old, sturdy structure, dating probably from the 1920s, on a quiet residential neighborhood. Barbara recognized the building, even though she had left it when she was ten, but she did not wish to go in!

Life in Erfurt was not too bad, at least in the beginning. There were severe food and other shortages as elsewhere in Germany, but Herbert's occupation allowed him to go around them. Besides, the Soviet administration was at first less strict than one might imagine. The occupiers were preoccupied with shipping out of Thuringia the consumer and intermediary goods needed back home, thus exacerbating the shortages in Thuringia. Many of the senior officials were busy looting the art and other valuable goods they could find for the same purpose or in locating those looted by the Nazis before them. The border, or demarcation line, with the Western Zone was porous, with mail, some goods and people flowing in and out. The Frasses were able to visit neighboring towns in the Eastern Zone, like Weimar, on occasion.

More important for the Frass parents when they came to Erfurt was that the commitment to rigorous education was alive. Schools were open and functioning from day one after the war, although classes were larger than usual. Barbara was enrolled in the Theo Neubauer Einheit Schule.[28] Displaying her own disciplined temperament, Barbara kept her third grade (1948/49) and fourth grade (1949/50) grade books until her death. They show that she

---

[28]   The school was named after Thoedore Neubauer (1890-1945), German sociologist, educator and parliamentarian--as KPD (Communist Party) representative from Thuringia--who was honored by the GDR government by naming several schools and streets after him.

was an A/B student. She was described as "a good worker, consistent, attentive, and reliable."

Life was on the whole bearable. Herbert had a stable income which enabled the family to live decently by communist standards. He was issued a driver's license in 1946 although he did not have a car; he probably had access to one for official business. With hindsight, the Frasses probably had a higher standard of living—if not a better quality of life—in East Germany than they did later in West Germany. I am not suggesting that they were well off; I am merely saying that they probably did not lack necessities. And they had at least some close relatives in town: Elisabeth's sister Gertrud and her Cecior family. However, the situation did not last. The cost of the better standard of living they enjoyed—already quite high in terms of the lack of freedoms—became unsustainable.

Chapter Three

East to West

Leaving East Germany

The Ceciors, the family of Barbara's aunt, left first, and they did so in stages. Ernst, the eldest son, could not find work in Erfurt; he went to Cuxhaven in northern Germany to work on a farm. After his release from Buchenwald, his father Willi joined him there. He then moved to Bremen where he worked for a while as a salesman in the local branch of the Karstadt department store. His family followed him there. Willi eventually returned to his profession of a police officer, finding an opening in Krefeld, which became the Ceciors' permanent home.

For the Frasses, the impetus or urge to leave, at least when they did, came from Elisabeth, and the reason went beyond the desire to raise the children in a "free country." Nor was it related to the creation of the German Democratic Republic (GDR) in Germany' Soviet-occupied zone a year earlier. One evil had merely replaced another. In any case, the Soviets were still effectively in charge. Elisabeth shed light on the reason for leaving East Germany in a letter which she sent from Herne in West Germany, where they settled, to her brother Ernst Jurkat and her mother who was then living with him in the United States. She wrote the letter on May 21, 1951, shortly after the death of her husband, Herbert. (I'll cover his death shortly.) She was understandably bitter and reflective in more ways than one. She acknowledged that life had been better in East Germany but added that they had to leave because of what faced them. Herbert's co-workers had been arrested and sentenced to 10 to 15 years of hard labor. She continued saying, and I am paraphrasing, "Considering how much more Herbert knew, I wonder what punishment awaited him. The authorities must have been very upset to let him get away."

What could Herbert have known? This remains a mystery. We can only speculate about it. It could not have been a military secret. Herbert did not deal with anything of remotely military value. What he knew was probably related to corruption at various levels of government. The prevailing scarcity situation was conducive to the operation of a widespread black market and a system of illicit activities and bribes. Herbert's involvement with the procurement and distribution of goods for the Soviet administration must have given him access to information on both the illicit activities and the main actors. Given the severe sentences that his work associates received, the illicit activities must have involved goods of high value, perhaps even the smuggling of people, especially after the sealing of the border. There is no evidence, direct or circumstantial, that Herbert may have taken part in any of these activities himself. There is no evidence that he benefited from them materially. The Frasses left merely with a few personal belongings. They had savings neither in the East nor in the West. They were, in fact, dependent on welfare after moving to West Germany. Nor is there any evidence that Herbert may have spied for the West. As far as we know, he was never debriefed, on arrival, by the West German authorities nor did he receive any special treatment whatsoever.

The move out of East Germany must have taken place with little advance planning—it was executed carefully, nevertheless. Herbert left first, on July 1, 1950, arriving in Herne, a small coal-mining town in the Rhur area, which was to become the family's home for the next decade. Elisabeth and the children stayed behind until the end of Barbara's school year—the fourth and last year of primary school under the German system. The date of July 22, 1950 marked three events. Barbara turned 10 on that date. The same day, she received her last report card from school. About 300 miles away, her father registered at the public library in Herne. It is known that he was an avid reader; his early action to register with the library may be seen as an attempt to legitimize his residence in Herne—to drop one more anchor there, so-to-speak. His wife and children were very likely assisted by his friends and contacts in their move to the West three weeks later. Still, for Barbara's mother, crossing the border illegally with two children must have been a harrowing experience. Explaining to the ten and six year olds the reasons for the move and the way they executed it must have been even more difficult.

Three months after arriving in Herne, Herbert had to appear in person at the Transit Camp for Refugees in Siegen, a small town in south Westphalia, in order to establish his and his family's status—an important step which determined the assistance he and his dependents were entitled to receive. After a review of his record and a medical examination, on September 25, 1950, he was officially admitted as a "political refugee"—a standard designation for refugees from East Germany—and "able to work," with approved residence in Herne. As of that date, the Frasses were formally and legally in West Germany, but this was not an event to celebrate about, like crossing the Berlin Wall was for many East Germans years later. They were free of the threat of persecution, yes, but Herbert did not have a job. The West German economy had turned the corner but was overwhelmed by the flood of refugees. Refugees, moreover, including German refugees, were regarded with suspicion. And the Germany the Frasses found themselves in was quite different from the Berlin and peaceful East Prussia they had known before the war. The Federal Republic of Germany was almost as centralized and bureaucratic as the German Democratic Republic . . . as full of red tape and regulations which were little explained and had to be obeyed in the good German way. And the awful burden of the Nazi era weighed as heavily on the West Germans as it did on the East Germans.

Herne

Barbara lived in Herne from 1950 to 1959—the year she came to the United States—or longer than at any place in Germany. She spent her formative years through her late teens there. Herne compared poorly with either Erfurt, the East German city she had lived in before, or Krefeld, the city where her few German relatives lived and still call home. This is true in terms of size, history, economic base, education, culture, and physical environment.

Herne is located in the German state of North Rhine-Westphalia at the center of the industrial Ruhr area. (See map of Germany.) It was a tiny village until the middle of the nineteenth century. Like other villages in the Ruhr region, it became a town and later a city when the mining of coal and the production of steel began. The first coal mine was opened there in 1860, and the city was chartered in 1897. In contrast, the origins of Krefeld, which is also located in the Ruhr area, go back to Roman times. Krefeld was an important town already in the seventeenth century, and it remains a major commercial and manufacturing (textiles, chemicals) center today.

Erfurt was an important trading town as far back as the Middle Ages. It also boasted, among other assets, Erfurt University, founded in 1392, where Martin Luther matriculated. It had and still has a medieval city center dominated by two magnificent structures: the Erfurt Cathedral (*Mariendom*) and *Severikirche*, a fourteenth century gothic church, standing side by side. In contrast, Herne's skyline was dominated by the smokestacks of plants processing coal into coke for the region's blast furnaces. As a result, it had a highly polluted environment and none of the beauty contributed by the Gera river crossing Erfurt, with its magnificent canals and bridges, or of Krefeld's municipal botanical gardens.

Coal mining defined not only Herne, the city, but also its residents—a working class population with limited education and cultural interests who spoke, like much of the Ruhr area, a *sociolect,* or a dialect associated with that social group . . . The city had a public library but no university, museum, orchestra, concert hall or the like. To say Barbara, her mother and her young brother, especially, disliked Herne would be a gross understatement. They hated it. Their letters to each other, many of which survive, are peppered with remarks and jokes about Herne's endlessly boring, monotonous and depressing environment, gray skies, pollution, etc. It is telling that after leaving Herne permanently in 1959, neither Barbara nor her brother, Knut, ever revisited it. Since the

Frasses left and especially after the demise of coal mining, Herne has been trying to reinvent itself by building museums, parks, artist colonies, modernized shopping areas with pedestrian walkways, and an annual fair. Both Krefeld and Erfurt have experienced an expansion, if not rebirth, during the same period.

Why then did the Frasses settle in Herne after leaving East Germany? There seems to be no clear or single answer. They may not have had a choice. As refugees, they depended on the government for subsistence and subsidized public housing which Herne must have offered. Had they had a choice, Herbert Frass would have chosen a different place. He was a "big city" person and a born entrepreneur whose talents were better suited to a vibrant city environment. More important than why they settled in Herne is the question of why they remained there for so long. The latter is much easier to answer: namely, they did so because Barbara's father, the family's main bread earner, died within a year of their move to the West.

Death of Herbert Frass

Herbert, Barbara's father, died on May 5, 1951 at forty-nine years of age. Barbara, who was shy of her eleventh birthday then, had no direct recollection of the event. She no doubt learned the circumstances of the tragic loss from her mother later in life, but she did not like to talk about them. The circumstances are described in a letter which her mother, Elisabeth, wrote two weeks after her husband's death—a letter which crossed the Atlantic three times. The letter was addressed to her brother Ernst Jurkat, his wife Dora (Dorothy), and her own mother (Barbara's grandmother) who was living with them in Philadelphia at the time. The grandmother, with a sense of history or perhaps foreboding, kept the letter and brought it with her when she moved back to Germany five years later. And in 1959, when Barbara's mother died, she passed it on to her, as if she had kept it for her all those years. Barbara, in turn, brought the letter with her to the United States, where I discovered it among her family memorabilia two years ago.

Apparently, Herbert had not been feeling well for some time, although his state fluctuated. He was unable to work or to find employment, and he received unemployment compensation on which the family was dependent from the first day they arrived west.[29] Living from hand to mouth as they did must have been difficult, since Herbert, already sick, had to collect the payments weekly in person. Herbert's health deteriorated progressively. Elisabeth described graphically how his mental and motor functions, his vision and his ability to speak were affected. He was taken to St. Mary's Catholic Hospital (*Marienhospital*) in Herne. There, he was diagnosed preliminarily with a brain tumor, and he was moved to the University Hospital in Münster which had a clinic specializing in neurological disorders.[30] The specialists there confirmed the earlier diagnosis and performed surgery, with Elisabeth's prior approval. Herbert died a month later. Barbara and her young brother, Knut, had been aware of what was going on, since their father was hospitalized for nearly two months, during which their mother made several trips to Münster, leaving them with a neighbor.

Two sets of questions arise in connection with Herbert's death. As noted, according to his wife, he had not been well for some time, and this was reflected in his behavior. He was not his quick, active self; he was, rather, disinterested in his environment, pensive and moody, as if his spirits were broken. Could his ailment have started while they were in the East? If so, could this have been one reason why Elisabeth in particular precipitated their move? Could his broken spirits have reflected more his living and working experience in the East than his physical condition? We will never know. How accurate was the diagnosis, and how appropriate and good was the medical care he received? This we can answer. Today, the Münster University Hospital, where he was treated, is one of Germany's top medical institutions. It ranks first as a medical research center in the region and second in medical education countrywide. And it has a "Comprehensive Cancer Center" which treats all forms of cancer and focuses on neuromedicine. Although

---

[29] The booklet for the unemployed, which he was issued and which survives, did not specify the reason for his unemployed status.

[30] Münster is a city of about 300,000 people today, situated 35 miles north-east of Herne. (See map.)

Herbert was there sixty years ago, it is quite likely that the hospital was one of the best available then. Elisabeth was very comfortable with the care her husband received, noting that the doctors were "most qualified."

Concerning the diagnosis, while not doubting it, the medical and non-medical people I have talked to in this country have suggested the need for some caution if for no other reason that neuromedicine was not as advanced then, and that the doctors did not have at their disposal the modern diagnostic tools available today. Incidentally, the death certificate did not identify the cause of death; death certificates rarely, if ever, did in Germany. It is interesting that it gave Herbert's occupation as *Kaufmann*, or merchant, even though he had not worked as one since before the war.

Herbert Frass was buried in the large *Waldfriedhof* (woodland) cemetery in Münster—an 84-acre cemetery where some of the fallen soldiers of all nations of World War II lie. The decision to lay him to rest there rather than in Herne, where the family lived, was an inevitable and difficult one for Elisabeth, his wife. The government welfare agency on which the family depended would not pay for the transportation of the remains to Herne; it would cover the internment and associated expenses only if they took place where Herbert died. Elisabeth had no choice but to accept, although she had preferred Herne for the sake of the children and felt guilty about it. For those reasons, she went out of her way to praise the Münster cemetery in the letter she wrote her Philadelphia relatives, describing it as idyllic and peaceful. She explained that the cemetery was integrated into a forest, with only eighteen percent of it used as cemetery. The burial areas were carved out of the woods in plots accommodating just twenty graves, creating the impression of an archipelago of gardens. She was not exaggerating; the cemetery is indeed park-like today, with 260 benches, and acts as a refuge for endangered plants and animals.

In the same letter to her relatives in Philadelphia, Elisabeth made a poignant and telling observation. She said that she was not too unhappy with the outcome concerning the burial site because she was not sure that she wanted to live in Herne forever. She added in a *cri de coeur* (cry from the heart) way, "I would like to live with you [in America], but it's not easy." She could not have known that she would never leave Herne, let alone Germany.

Neither Barbara nor her brother ever visited their father's grave in Münster—and not because they did not care. Even in his darkest days, when he acted detached from the world, the father they called "Papi" spent time lovingly with them. They did not go to Münster as if they did not wish to disturb him or the memories they had of him. Financial constraints may also have been a reason.

Herbert's Last Year

During his difficult last ten months of life in Herne, Herbert's only pleasures, other than spending time with his young children, were reading and smoking an occasional cigarette. As noted earlier, one of the first things he did after arriving in Herne from East Germany was to register at the public library. He was issued a membership booklet for entering the abbreviated titles and author of the books checked out and the dates of check out and return. We are fortunate that Barbara preserved the booklet (see photograph), because it provides an insight into Herbert's tastes, interests, mood, as well as—and most importantly—the knowledge he was starved for after leaving East Germany!

Between July 28, 1950 and March 22, 1951, six weeks before his death, Herbert Frass checked out thirty-six books from the Herne public library. All of them were non-fiction. They dealt with (my grouping): the demise of Germany; world affairs, geography and history; and business, his field. Herbert must have left East Germany anxious to get an independent, uncensored account of what had happened during the war and its immediate aftermath, having spent the war years in the German navy and the following five years in Soviet-occupied East Germany.

One of the first books Herbert checked out was a memoir by André François-Poncet, France's ambassador to Germany from 1931 to 1938. François-Poncet was one of the first foreign diplomats to observe and warn of the Nazi regime's true intentions. He was arrested by the Gestapo during the wartime German occupation of France and imprisoned for three years. He returned to West Germany as ambassador again shortly after the war and wrote extensively about his experience. Herbert also checked out books with themes or titles such as the downfall of Germany, "illusion versus reality," how could it happen, and *The Leader and the Seduced* (by Hans Windisch).[31]

Herbert's interests extended to world history and politics, and books with a regional and country focus as well, such as the continent of Asia, the history of China, and the Incas of Peru. This must have mirrored partly the lingering wanderlust of his youth.

In 1951 especially, Herbert returned to his professional interests, covering subjects like accounting, bookkeeping, trade, employment, finance, and the experience of selected successful German entrepreneurs. The last two books he borrowed were a biography of the German industrialist, engineer and inventor Robert Bosch (1861-1942) by Theodore Heuss, and a description by Bernhardt Huldermann of the life of Albet Ballin (1857-1918), a Hamburg Jew of Danish origin who became the executive director of the renowned Hamburg-America Shipping Line and masterminded its expansion and rise to that status.

Could the return to his field have signaled Herbert's interest in returning to work? Not really, because his health had been deteriorating steadily. His reading list indicates that he was an avid reader—36 non-fiction books in less than eight month by a sick man—a businessman at heart, and a man of diverse interests who sought solace in books, much as his daughter did fifty years later in her difficult last months.

Coping Physically Without Herbert

Elisabeth's predicament cannot be exaggerated. She was widowed at forty-eight years of age and had to bring up two young children by herself—Barbara was eleven and Knut seven at the time. She must have been physically and mentally worn out after five years in the East, the escape and relocation, and nearly a year of caring for her unwell husband. She was, moreover, in a city she

---

[31] I am not providing the proper citation for the various books, because I am not sure of their exact German titles, due to the yellowing of the pages of the booklet and the illegible handwriting.

had had barely time to become familiar with and make friends in. And she had no family support. The whereabouts of Herbert's few close relatives were not known. Her own brother, sister-in-law and mother were in America. Although she had a sister, Gertrud Cecior, living not too far away, that sister had three children of her own and a difficult husband.

Above all, Elisabeth faced a dire financial situation. She had no widow's benefits accruing to her through her husband. Herbert had been mostly self-employed before the war and, according to prevailing regulations, she would have been entitled to "veteran's widow" benefits only if her husband had died at war. The family was, therefore, entirely dependent on welfare support. The amount was DM122 per month—an amount which, as Elisabeth put it in her letter to her brother in America, "is not much, but we do not starve." She was right, because it seemed to have been just enough for the family of three to feed itself. I am not sure whether Elisabeth had to pay rent from it, although education and health care were definitely free.

At the then rate of exchange, DM122 was equivalent to about $30 and would be worth less than $500 today. The amount has to be seen in the historical and national (German) context. The Federal Republic of Germany (FRG) was barely two years old in 1951. Its economy was doing well, but the "German miracle" (of economic recovery) was not yet in full fruition. And the Cold War was a bitter new reality. The Berlin airlift (1948-49), the formation of the communist-run German Democratic Republic and other factors had created a flood of refugees from the East, straining the FRG's resources. The country was awash with war widows and orphans. The network of social programs and safety net for which the country became known later was not fully in place.

Elisabeth's ". . . but we do not starve" assertion in her letter to her close relatives in the United States notwithstanding, her predicament did not go unnoticed by them. Her brother Ernst and his wife Dorothy responded to Elisabeth's letter promptly, lovingly and positively. They described their own tight financial situation, which had forced Dorothy to hold two jobs to help support the family, namely, working as a bookkeeper for a radio station, and teaching (bookkeeping?), which required hard, advance preparation.

They nevertheless offered to send Elisabeth DM 60-70 monthly, which would raise her income by about half. And they offered to consider Elisabeth's interest in moving to the United States in a few months. Shortly thereafter, they proposed bringing over Knut and raising him as their own.

It is not clear whether the financial aid offered materialized and, if so, how long it continued. The outcome concerning Knut was clearer. Initially, there was some follow up. The Jurkats made some inquiries both in the United States and Germany about the process for bringing Knut over. The process was not simple; it went beyond mere sponsorship of a prospective immigrant, since a minor with a living mother (not an orphan) was involved. They solicited the help of *Arbeiterwohlfahrt* (Workers' Welfare Association)—a decentralized German charity—which contacted Elisabeth on February 20, 1952, in turn, although there was no follow up by any of the three parties. Fourteen months later (on April 4, 1953), Ernst Jurkat wrote his sister a tightly-typed three page letter taking pains to explain why bringing Knut over was no longer feasible. The gist of the argument was that his work situation had changed drastically. He was between jobs, had no "stable" income, and Dorothy had to continue to work to help support the family. Without a demonstrable stable income, he would not qualify as sponsor vis-a-vis the Immigration authorities. A related, central argument was that since Dorothy worked, and worked hard, she would have little time to help raise Knut "as an American," which both Jurkats desired. The responsibility for raising him would fall on Ernst's mother, who lived with them and who would unavoidably raise Knut "as a German." Besides, Dorothy's health was not good, and the grandmother was becoming increasingly difficult. So, the offer was withdrawn.

It is noteworthy that Barbara never spoke of this episode, and that referring to the outcome, Elisabeth told her children that she had "refused the offer" because she did not want to lose Knut physically and legally. This is the only version that has survived within Knut's close family, at least. Although without result then, the episode is of interest because eight years later, following her mother's death, Barbara did come to live with Ernst and Dorothy Jurkat who welcomed her with great speed and open arms. It is not certain whether the financial help initially offered Elisabeth took place in the interim. It is doubtful it did, given the Jurkats' financial reasons for withdrawing the offer concerning Knut. Thus, the financial challenge faced by Elisabeth remained unalleviated.

The logical answer to the financial challenge she faced would have been for Elisabeth to try to supplement her income by working, at least part-time, as a bacteriologist, as she had done for twelve years in Elbing. She still had the strong letter of recommendation she had received from the Elbing city government, her last employer, before she quit her job upon marriage. Elisabeth chose instead a path combining severe economizing with doing some "seamstressing" at home. We can only speculate about the reasons. Her experience as a bacteriologist was quite specialized, focusing on the identification of the parasitic disease trichinosis in live animals at the slaughterhouse level. Herne may not have had a slaughterhouse or a need for such testing. The need in Elbing was related to its being a port which received livestock for slaughter, among other goods.

Elisabeth's tight budget necessitated limiting cash purchases. She must have been a gifted seamstress or became one quickly out of necessity. She made nearly all of Barbara's outer garments through her teen years competently, tastefully and fashionably.[32] Barbara was proud of her cloths. Her mother could duplicate practically any design she saw. Soon, Elisabeth began doing some sewing for her friends, neighbors and acquaintances as a favor, for barter or for some cash. This helped. The family nevertheless lived from welfare payment to welfare payment, modestly, with no money left for extras beyond the strict necessities, except for occasional movies (more on this later). Yet they managed to preserve a few possessions—the previously mentioned two carpets and some jewelry mostly of sentimental value. And the children, as they grew up, never worked to contribute to the family budget. Rather, in

---

[32] Although Barbara came to the United States a year after her mother died, the vast majority of the dresses she came with were made by her mother. I do not know if Elisabeth also made her son's clothing. She must have made at least some of it, at least when he was young.

their spare time, their mother enrolled them in any free recreational activity available for the sake of their health and entertainment.

Coping Emotionally

When a husband and father is lost, one worries first and most about the plight of the children. Yet the biggest hardship is faced by the wife and mother. This was especially the case with Elisabeth Frass who had been separated from the place where she grew up, her family, friends, profession—indeed her past—and now had lost her husband. She had to perform at her peak as a mother and fill in for her husband vis-a-vis the children materially and emotionally, ignoring her own needs for love, affirmation, sustenance, and the reason for being. She had to project to her children a sense of normalcy, family identity, and forward motion, if not optimism. And she had to do all of the above without showing her pain.

Elisabeth succeeded in this Sisyphean task through open communication with her children to get their understanding and cooperation. They knew, for example, when the money was not there, and they had to wait until the next welfare payment to get or do something which had been promised them. At the same time, Elisabeth adapted to Herne's community environment, taking advantage of whatever free or subsidized services the city offered. She made friends and encouraged her children to do the same, and she instituted mutual visits with her sister's family in Krefeld. She managed to replicate the rhythm of a normal family, with punctual birthday and holiday celebrations the traditional German way. As the Lutheran faith prescribed, Barbara was confirmed at church on March 29, 1953.[33]

As a mother, Elisabeth faced two persisting challenges among many. The first was that money was perennially tight. Most everything had to be home-made. This included clothes, toys and games. She instilled the idea, and demonstrated through her sewing, that something "new" could be made from something old. The idea stayed with Barbara for many years. She believed that a "new room" could be created by moving the furniture around,

---

[33] The original confirmation certificate survives.

which no doubt the family did in their modest Herne apartment. Years later, when Barbara lived with the Jurkats in Philadelphia, she occupied a Spartanly decorated room in their attic. Dorothy Jurkat remembered often hearing noises coming from the attic late at night when Barbara would be shuffling furniture between school assignments. Barbara's furniture rearrangement drive or passion was not limited to her residence. In the mid-1970s, we were crossing the Atlantic on the *SS France*. Upon entering the luxurious cabin, she rearranged the furniture in the generous sitting area—an initiative for which she received the compliments of the head steward.

Elisabeth's second challenge was that her children had no hero or model, especially male role model, to aspire to. The only males in their lives were their uncle Wilhelm Cecior and his two sons, none of whom had the charisma or record of achievement to constitute a model.

In difficult times, children, especially, are capable of making up or emulating fictional heroes—from fairy tales, for example. This is where movies come in. Movies played a very important part in the lives not only of Barbara and her young brother Knut, but also of their mother. In fact, their experience constitutes a case study of the positive, therapeutic effect of movies.[34] The Frasses, together, left a rich record demonstrating their near-obsession with movies. As I shall show later, the small family loved to write and to preserve letters as well as postcards. Rare is the letter that does not mention the movie the writer saw or expected to see, or that did not inquire about what movie the addressee had seen or planned to see. This was done even in the limited space of a postcard written from out of town when Barbara was old enough to travel.

Movies were not just the cheapest but also the only form of entertainment available in Herne for children and adults alike. There were no theaters, concerts, American-style amusement parks, circus, public swimming pools, river front, lake front, nor—for the Frasses—the money to travel to places that did. Movies were anticipated, planned, discussed, the event and impressions noted in diaries, etc. Young teens formed movie clubs and went to the movies in groups. The outing was a weekly activity. Barbara was

---

[34] Movies can also have, of course, negative effects and influences.

the president of her group—a position she cherished because it entitled her to select the movie the group would see, as well as to a free ticket, compliments of the theater owner.

Movie ticket buyers received at no additional cost an elaborate, often multi-colored program of 4-6 pages listing the cast and film credits, offering insights into the movie, and reproducing some of the scenes.[35] The programs were produced by the movie distribution companies or private publishers for all movie houses. They were cherished by all, young and old, and collected like baseball cards and comic books are in the United States. They are sought after still today, and old issues are traded or sold on the Web. Barbara cared enough about these programs to accumulate unfailingly 225 of them, bring them to the United States with her, and preserve them meticulously in a drawer for the rest of her life. To put the activity in perspective, the 225 programs would translate into five years of steady movie going.[36]

I shall not comment on the movies Barbara saw even though the vast number and coverage of the programs could lead to some interesting conclusions. I shall not do so largely because they would not mean much to the reader, given the fifty-plus years that have elapsed. It is not surprising that about ninety percent of the movies were Hollywood productions dubbed in German, and less than ten percent were German-made. Comedies, musicals and even mysteries were few; the vast majority were dramas—many of them historical dramas.

Barbara must have preserved the programs not—or not just—to remember the movies but, subconsciously at least, as a souvenir of her youth. She was a happy, cheerful child, even in the Erfurt days, smiling in all photographs. I am not attributing this to the movies, although they must have helped the children and the parents alike in those difficult post-war years. Focusing on the fictional or on the past brought the promise of a future. If it happened so far away in time and place, it could happen now and here as well. Everybody

---

[35] There were two series of programs: *Illüstrierte Film-Bühne,* produced until 1969, and *Das Neue Film-Programm*, produced until 1960.

[36] Based on weekly movie going, except during summer vacation when, in her late teens, Barbara was in camp or abroad.

dreamed—even Barbara, the hard-core realist of later years. To use movie terms, the chief producer and director of Barbara's childhood happiness was unmistakably her mother.

Overall, Elisabeth made life in Herne, life without a father, life with very modest means livable and even enjoyable for her children. She was a source of love, knowledge and hope, the sun which made up for the cloudy days, and the magician who added color to their black and white existence. She kept their father's memory alive, despite the pain she felt. She confronted them with the stark realities of their lives without robbing them of the right and the ability to dream. But it was not all one-sided. Elisabeth could do all this because of the strength and joy she drew from her children. She needed them just as much as they needed her.

Formal and Informal Education

Barbara was educated "at home" and in schools in East Germany, West Germany, and the United States. I shall cover here mostly the first three. One advantage she had was that she completed elementary school—all four years of it under the German system—in East Germany, all nine years of high school in Herne, and the last two years of college (she had received credit for the first two) in the United States. Although she changed cities three times, she did not have to change schools mid-stream.

I talked about elementary school in the preceding chapter. By home schooling above, I was referring to education outside or in addition to, not instead of, school, mostly through the parents. One of Barbara's earliest and fondest memories—even though she was just ten then—was of being taken by her father to register at the local public library, of returning to take out books jointly with him, and of talking to him about what she read. On March 22, 1951, the last time he took out books for himself before his death, she was with him. As I noted earlier, Herne did not have a museum or anything like it. Barbara remembered fondly how her mother would take out art books from the library to walk her through the pictures of art works to expose her to art history and "beauty," as if visiting a virtual museum. And when years later her mother made it possible for Barbara to go on vacation abroad, her motivation

The Promise of the Present and the Shadow of the Past

was to provide her just as much an extra educational opportunity as recreation.

From 1951 to 1959 Barbara attended the *Neusprachliches Mädechengymnasium,* a girls' high school in Herne. She took the same twelve courses for seven consecutive years, with evolving focus or at advanced level of complexity—namely: religion, German, history, geography, Latin, English, French, mathematics, physics, music, art/drawing, and physical education. The curriculum also included biology and chemistry in selected years. Like all students, in addition to the above subjects, Barbara was graded regularly on her conduct, leadership, participation, orderliness, and handwriting. As in elementary school, Barbara was a good student, but her performance varied from semester to semester and from subject to subject, depending on her level of interest in them. Understandably, she consistently scored higher in English than in Latin, as her relative proficiency in them later in life demonstrated. Young Barbara did not lack intellectual ambition, self-esteem or self-confidence. Her report card at age fourteen noted that ". . . she has to learn to think in a more humble way."

How about the quality of the education Barbara received? We can judge only by the results. Her stock of knowledge was remarkable. She had a broader, more diversified and deeper knowledge base than her years of schooling would lead one to expect. This was recognized by nearly all people who knew her, including those who knew her for a far shorter period than I did. She loved school and learning a great deal, but this is by no means unique. What distinguished her, I believe, was her knowledge absorption, retention and integration capacity. She got more out of what she read than most people I know . . . Perhaps she had innate gifts; perhaps she came to the United States with a hunger to learn and a determination to compete, to succeed. Regardless, I believe that some of the credit for her extensive knowledge base belongs to the formal education she received at high school in Germany. A notable aspect of that education was the focus on basic subjects such as history, geography and languages, including Latin, which were taught year after year. Her German education was also characterized by the application of rigorous, coordinated standards with remarkable degree of uniformity—long resisted in the United

States—regardless of region, background of the student body or the local tax base.[37] Underdeveloped Herne's high schools did not have different curricula or lower standards than, say, Frankfurt's high schools. Last but not least, German education placed a high value on getting the facts right, especially in a subject like history, Barbara's favorite—an approach with which she identified very closely. She was, by nature, a critical thinker who started by questioning what was presented as facts.

The specific high school which Barbara attended in Herne was unusual in several respects and better than one would expect to find in a place like Herne. It had been established in 1893 and was the pride of the small city. It enjoyed strong parental support as well as the active support of the municipal government and other local institutions. Its activities were routinely covered by the local press. It had better physical facilities—building, laboratory, training aids—than the city's limited financial base would suggest. It enjoyed strong alumni loyalty and support. And it tried to adopt new approaches to teaching and student management such as student government and a program of ambitious field trips. Barbara reported that some of her high school instructors had Ph.D.'s in their fields.

Learning About the War

The comments I offered above on the what, the why and the how in teaching inevitably bring up the question of how German schools, Barbara's in particular, dealt with World War II in the 1950s. It is important to specify the period because the openness about the horrible war no doubt increased greatly as time went by.

---

[37] Education in Germany is the responsibility of the states (Lander). Education policy is coordinated at the national level by a standing conference of the state ministers of education and cultural affairs which issues guidelines for teaching. What is actually taught is determined by "syllabus directives" issued by state governments in accordance with the national guidelines. The directives do not establish lesson plans. Rather, they determine the topics to be covered for every grade and subject and the "teaching objectives" to be achieved.

In the mid-1950s, when Barbara was in the middle of her high school years, the war was a mere ten years behind. Some of the Nazis or Nazi-sympathizers were still around, and their daughters were among Barbara's classmates. Her classmates included also the daughters of current and former communists.

Luckily, Barbara brought from Germany most of her high school textbooks—especially those on history, religion, literature, and art—less as a souvenir and more to consult, as needed. Broadly speaking and not surprisingly, the history textbooks dealt with the challenge of covering World War II by devoting much more space and attention to ancient history than to recent history. No doubt, the allocation of class time reflected this, too. Ancient history—not just European but also Egyptian, Greek, Roman, and Chinese history—took up four hefty textbooks. In contrast, the rise of National Socialism, the war and its immediate aftermath (the period 1933-1950) were covered in a slim volume and took up just forty pages, or less than the space devoted to ancient Greek history.[38] It is important to note that the book was drafted in 1955; it was intended for the *Mittelklassen*, the years overlapping junior high school and high school; and it was not the only source on the war. The textbooks on other subjects, such as literature and art, may have also dealt with aspects of the war. The history book mentioned is nevertheless of special interest, with the above *caveats*.

The treatment of the war in the Pinnow and Textor textbook of 1955 was mixed. The rise of Hitler, the evolution of the war, and Germany's central role as its instigator and prime belligerent were covered fairly, if too shortly. The gruesome acts and sheer atrocities committed by Germany were recognized quite explicitly, including the creation and operation of the concentration camps such as Auschwitz and others, mentioned by name, the "incredible mass (industrial) exterminations" in the camps and elsewhere, and the murder of "millions" of Jews and others "in a devilish way."

---

[38] Hermann Pinnow and Frtiz Textor, *Geschichte der neuter Zeit von 1850 bis zur Gegenwart* (History of Modern Times from 1850 to the Present), Stuttgart, 1955. I am grateful to Dr. Simone Seym of the Goethe Institute in Washington, D.C., for guiding me through the book and sharing her insights.

Yet the coverage was flawed and incomplete, if not biased, and gives one pause. For example, the treatment of the worst acts and atrocities in the frank language quoted above was squeezed into just three paragraphs—paragraphs which were remarkable but which either the instructor or the student could skip or overlook intentionally or by accident. The Nuremberg trial (1948-49) and judgments were given scant attention even though six years had elapsed. This is the textbook's biggest omission which, no doubt, was intentional. Referring to the trials would have brought out the criminal character of what the leaders and their collaborators were responsible for and the gruesome detail of the crimes. This and the young age of the student population for which the textbook was written may have been on the authors' minds. Finally, while the treatment of Hitler and the other German leaders was objective and deservedly harsh, the authors attempted to absolve the German population in subtle ways.

The above shortcomings notwithstanding, the book's treatment of the war surprised me since most Germans were probably still in denial about much of the war then. The authors, Pinnow and Texter, seemed to have made a sincere effort to draft a reasonably balanced account of Germany and the war. It is not surprising that the textbook is out of print, and that rare copies of it are still in demand.

What Barbara and her classmates or peers learned about the war was supplemented by what they heard from their parents, who had lived through the war. Barbara was privileged, in a way, in this regard. The war's scars were, in a manner of speaking, clearly visible on the faces of the family. They had been living as welfare-dependent refugees within their country. She had lived in five cities since her birth at the onset of the war. She lived without a father during her first five years. She had an uncle who worked against the Nazi regime, had to flee, and was now in the United States, and another uncle, a theater director, who had not been heard from for years. She also had a mother who had opposed the regime from the beginning and told her more than once, almost as bed-time story, how she had been harassed for having listened to foreign broadcasts on radio, for spreading anti-Nazi propaganda at her place of work, and for "evading her duties as citizen;" how her father had tried unsuccessfully to evade the draft; how the last thing she wanted was for him to become a war hero; and how, once drafted, she threatened him with divorce if he got promoted higher than corporal. As to the notion of collective guilt, her mother told her unequivocally that the German people "knew" about the deportations and the outcomes awaiting the deportees. Many Germans felt, nevertheless, that there was little they could do about what they saw or heard.

Chapter Four

The Last Years in Germany

This chapter deals with Barbara's late teens—the crucial years when the Barbara we knew began to emerge, revealing her personality, temperament, tastes, and passions. These years are of particular interest also because they were the last years she spent in Germany. The person Barbara evolved into during her late teens and beyond had no doubt roots in her childhood. But I shall not deal with those here. I shall focus, rather, on three sets of external factors that helped to shape her late teens: the return of her maternal grandmother from the United States, where she had been living with her son, Ernst Jurkat, and his family; the limitations of life in Herne; and, as a direct consequence, the extended time she spent away from home—both within and outside Germany—with her mother's encouragement. I shall conclude with the death of her mother Elisabeth and its immediate aftermath.

Despite the severe constraints she faced, Elisabeth Frass had brought up in Barbara a healthy, bright child with an insatiable appetite for knowledge, an active imagination, and limitless curiosity. She realized that she had to go beyond the experiences, stories, models, and whatever else she could provide herself in an environment like Herne. She, therefore, made it possible for Barbara to spend the summers of her late teens away from home, specifically and in chronological order, at a youth hostel in the Black Forest, on a multi-city tour organized by her high school, on a visit to a friend in London, and as an "au pair" girl in France. She did the above at considerable cost, material and emotional, to her. While the vacations (travel and room and board) were paid for by city or state agencies, the recreational activities had to be approved in advance and paid for by the parents. This, plus the associated non-negligible expenses (for suitable clothing, for example), strained Elisabeth's tight budget. The bigger cost or sacrifice, however, was the pain of being alone and lonely without her daughter and of dealing with a young Knut who suffered equally from his sister's absence.

An important by-product of those absences was the voluminous correspondence it generated among Barbara, her mother, her grandmother, and young Knut. Some forty letters and postcards from that period have survived and form the basis of a great deal of what follows. Barbara wrote almost daily. Some of her letters were 6-7 pages long. The extent of the correspondence reflects partly the family's financial situation. Communicating by phone was not an option largely for financial reasons. (The Frasses did not have a telephone to begin with for that reason.) Luckily for us and future generations, Frass/Jurkat family members were both writers and keepers/preservers of letters. But the survival of the rich correspondence in loving hands reflects more than that. It reflects the correspondents' strong bonds and, in particular, the close relationship between Barbara and her mother, which is a theme of this chapter.

The Grandmother Factor

Oma (grandmother) Olga, as she was known, returned from the United States in August 1956 after an absence of more than six years. She had gone there as a widower to live with her son, and had done so enthusiastically. Why did she come back when she did? For a combination of reasons. The first would not be a mystery to those who knew her daughter-in-law, Dorothy Jurkat—a talented and capable woman, but strong, assertive, opinionated, and difficult to get along with. The other reason was nostalgia, both toward her family in Germany—including two daughters and five grandchildren—and toward her culture. Referring to her, Elisabeth reported in a letter. "[Since her return] she enjoys that everybody understands her, and that she understands what everybody is saying." The entire family was happy to welcome her back. In fact, her return produced a holiday-like celebration.

Oma Olga settled in the house of her daughter Gertrud (Tutta) Cecior in Krefeld, where she would live for the rest of her life. Her return brought about a number of changes for the Frasses with both immediate and lasting effects. At the simplest level, the nuclear family, which stood at three after Herbert's death, immediately grew to four. The prime beneficiary of this was Barbara's mother, who acquired a source of comfort, advice, criticism, companionship, and help. The event also brought welcome diversion. As Elisabeth reported, "Oma talks a lot about America." There were also little but welcome benefits. Oma received a pension which, though modest, given her limited expenses, enabled her to spoil Elisabeth and the children alike with little luxuries or pocket money. Most important, however, Oma was both a source and an object of love. Her resourcefulness and availability added an element of flexibility to everyone's management of the present, as she could be nurse, teacher, babysitter, friend, and companion.

For Barbara, her grandmother's return left a lasting mark. Elisabeth had been very close to her mother. She was the oldest of three children and the last one to marry and to leave home. Oma's return provided Barbara an opportunity to observe at close range the special relationship between her mother and her grandmother and to be inspired by it. Oma's greater impact on Barbara's life, however, was to come after her mother's death in late 1958. As I shall discuss later, the grandmother was instrumental in Barbara's coming to the United States—both in the decision made and in its execution. It is not surprising, therefore, that grandmother was the only person—family member or friend—with whom Barbara retained contact after moving permanently to the United States. The reason for this went beyond love or gratitude. For Barbara, her maternal grandmother, Olga Jurkat, represented the link to her ancestral past—indeed, to her German identity and roots.

What about Barbara's other, paternal grandmother *Anna Frass*? We know very little about her, but enough to conclude that, although being a loving person and close to her son, she played a negligible role in Barbara's life. The main reason was physical separation. Oma Anna lived in Berlin, like Barbara and her parents, during the first few years of the war and felt close to her daughter-in-law and her family, the Jurkats. When conditions in Berlin deteriorated—especially after the massive bombardment of the city beginning in 1943—she moved to Elbing in East Prussia where Elisabeth and her baby daughter had sought refuge at her parents' home. This is confirmed by her entitlement to receive food rations in that city. In April 1944, her Elbing-specific entitlement was annulled, following her return to Berlin, where she had lived most of her life and had long-time friends. Apparently, her departure from Elbing was unpleasant. It ended with a disagreement or feud with Elisabeth's parents. The disagreement must have been serious or unpleasant enough to cause her son Herbert to complain to her—almost scold her—in a rare letter he wrote her from the field. In it, he left no doubt that he blamed her for the incident, which we know little about.

During the rest of the war, Anna Frass served as liaison between her son and not only his wife Elisabeth but also his out-of-wedlock daughter *Christa* (more on her later) and possibly her mother, too. For whatever reason, soldiers' mail must have reached Berlin more assuredly or quicker than it did Elbing in those days. All soldiers' mail was nevertheless censored. To cope with it, mother and son, knowing each other well, seemed to have developed a code to exchange messages concerning certain people, documents and sums which I have not been able to decipher to this day.

What happened to Anna Frass after the war is murky. What is certain is that Barbara never saw her or heard from her directly again. In his last two letters to his mother, Herbert had urged her to move out of Berlin, suggesting discreetly that she go to Thuringia. But she never appeared there, even after Herbert and his small family were reunited in that region where they spent five years. Anna reappears next in the early 1950s in a letter from Elisabeth to Barbara where she mentions that she had helped her mother-in-law submit (to an insurance company?) a claim for damages incurred in her residence, although it is not clear where she was living at the time. Oma Anna's last mention is in an inter-bank document dated March 13, 1954 transferring the balance of her bank account in Berlin to Elisabeth's bank account in Herne, presumably upon her death. We do not know how or where she died and where she may be interred. The above document makes it clear that she had no other survivors.

By all indications, Anna Frass was a strong woman. She had to be to bring up two young children on her own, after losing her husband at a young age. While we can speculate confidently about her coping skills, we know little about her softer side . . . which she must have had, having brought up a son who made a career in the arts and another who was a dreamer.

Life in Herne

In the preceding chapter I described physical Herne. Here I shall describe what living in Herne was like *for the Frasses*, in the late 1950s (Barbara's late teens), and in their condition. Herne was a small, ugly, economically-handicapped town with no redeeming features. The town was unattractive everywhere, with no central square or park like most other German towns or cities had. The weather was bad nearly always. There was no "good season." And there were no noteworthy entertainment venues or opportunities, except for cinemas which, for most residents, constituted the only consolation. Nor was there an active political or civic life. We know all this because the rich intra-Frass correspondence I alluded to was full of remarks about it, as if people felt a need to talk—to vent—about what I described, which the Frasses certainly did. Some of the remarks were ironic, as whan Elisabeth wrote to Barbara in camp suggesting that she return early, as ". . . one always has to get used again to the air in Herne." Elisabeth summed up her view of Herne by writing on another occasion, ". . . nothing ever happens here, days just go buy." And she was right. This, incidentally, was the decade that saw the start of Germany's rearmament after joining NATO in 1955, the Hungarian Revolution and the Suez Crisis in 1956, the launching of the earth-circling Soviet satellite Sputnik in 1957, and the "miracle" of Germany's economic recovery under Chancellor Konrad Adenauer and his Economic Minister Ludwig Erhard. Yet none of this seemed to matter or to have made a difference to those living in Herne.

One consequence of the reality I described was to make Barbara's absences from home during summer vacations particularly painful for both her mother and Knut. She, with her vivacious being, was the cure to their chronic boredom and made life in Herne tolerable for them. The main affordable and easy-to-experience diversion was to visit the relatives in Krefeld, although this was not a better alternative for Knut who hated Krefeld just as much. Krefeld was not as developed and diversified a metropolis then as it is now.

And then there was the financial constraint, which imposed a tight budget with little or no flexibility on the Frass family. Often the money was not there even for movies, and Barbara and Knut had to wait for the next welfare payment to indulge in this central entertainment in their lives. Barbara's mother worked as a seamstress at home to complement her welfare check. Once at least, Barbara asked her to give up sewing. Her mother replied in a letter firmly, "I have to work," avoiding the explanation that she had to do so in order to provide her and her brother the little extras they enjoyed. We do not know how Barbara reacted. It may nevertheless be of interest to note that, although Barbara developed basic sewing skills and did some sewing as a mother, she never expressed the desire to acquire a sewing machine, for Freudian reasons perhaps. Rather than giving up sewing, Elisabeth worked harder at it as time went by. In fact, she continued to sew until two months before her death. One factor seems to have been the changing needs of Barbara as she transited from girlhood to womanhood. The process was accelerated by Barbara's eagerness to reach adulthood and gain independence, prompted no doubt by the limitations of life in Herne. Elisabeth recognized that the transition necessitated expanding and upgrading her daughter's wardrobe. She had to take on more work to enable her to pay for the clothing and related items (shoes, make-up articles) she could not supply herself. The circumstances that necessitated it notwithstanding, Elisabeth enjoyed sewing and was good at it. Although she did not like the burden, she enjoyed the creative part of the work and was often proud of what she produced. She also enjoyed the social part, as sewing provided her opportunities to meet and interact with people, to get feedback and to be in demand.

The Promise of the Present and the Shadow of the Past

Soon after moving to Herne, especially following her husband's death, Elisabeth made a deliberate effort to establish a social circle—or, rather, a mutual support group—in the town. The nucleus of the group was constituted by her neighbors, and most of the members were widows like herself, of whom Herne, indeed Germany, had an abundance after the war. As often happens with small families, Elisabeth's friends became like family to her children. Her correspondence with Barbara had more references to her friends and neighbors—Frau Kampf, Frau Magdalene, Frau Lefke, Frau Lubbens, Frau Ransiek, Frauline Sefte and others—than to blood relatives. These provided welcome friendship, companionship, entertainment, as well as help, although their role fluctuated; it diminished when there were other demands on their time.

During most of her Herne years, Barbara's main interactions with peers were with her cousin Ingrid in Krefeld, with whom they exchanged visits and letters, and Gerda, the daughter of her mother's closest friend—the acquaintance she saw most often. The two young women were very different. Ingrid, daughter of Willi and Gertrud Cecior, was a year younger than Barbara and quite reserved. Gerda, on the other hand, though Barbara's age, was more mature and adventurous. She dated a married man, when Barbara hardly interacted with any boys. Neither Ingrid nor Gerda, by the way, were intellectually oriented. Barbara also had friends in her high school but their interaction was limited to life in school or to school-sponsored activities.

In her late teens in particular, for Barbara as well as her mother the prime friends were each other. The friendship was enhanced and sustained through free communication, uninhibited in time or content (subject). What this meant for her mother especially is reflected in how she felt when Barbara was away. "Life is not fun when you're not around," she wrote. "I feel very lonely. . . . The house is empty if you are not here. . . . I miss the intellectual mutual stimulation and understanding."

In Herne, Barbara had two other relationships, both unusual, which I shall discuss for that reason below—one with her half-sister Christa, whom she never met before, then or after, and the other with an English soldier her mother referred to as *Deine Englander* (your Englishman), as I shall, too.

Christa

Although we know little about Christa, her kinship to Barbara is not in doubt. Herbert Frass fathered her probably five years before he did Barbara. If we know little about Christa it is because of the paucity of contacts and documentation rather than secrecy. As I noted in Chapter I, Barbara's mother knew about Christa when she married Herbert. According to Barbara, her father had not married Christa's mother because her staunchly Catholic parents had objected to her marrying a non-Catholic. Far from denying her, Herbert maintained contact with young Christa, including during the war, through his mother, and he even sent her a gift or gifts on her birthday. (Both his mother Anna Frass and Christa lived in Berlin then.) Apparently, Christa's mother married and Christa assumed the surname of her stepfather (Belz?), who presumably adopted her.

After Herbert's death, Elisabeth kept in touch with Christa who felt close to her half-sister and half-brother whom she had never met. Elisabeth played this role willingly, as it helped to give her children as well as Christa an added sense of feeling connected after the loss of their father. Barbara and Christa exchanged letters in the mid and late-1950s, when they lived in Herne and East Berlin, respectively, and Christa, the elder of the two, occasionally sent Barbara gift packages. However, Barbara felt increasingly conflicted about her relation to Christa and did not keep up the correspondence. Christa may have reminded her too much of her father. Christa, nevertheless, continued to write to both Barbara and Knut into the 1970s—past Barbara's emigration to the United States, her marriage, and her motherhood. In her communications, Christa explained that in the meantime she had lost her mother, had gotten married (to a musician), taking the surname Brezina, and had had two sons: Roland, born in 1955, and Brend in 1960. Unfortunately, her husband had left her when her children were young and, therefore, Christa had to work in a hotel as a cook to bring them up.

In 1977-79, however, Barbara had a change of heart which led her to reply to Christa's annual Christmas greetings, as well as to call her. I learned this from Christa's side (from her next communication), because Barbara spoke rarely about her in any length. To my knowledge, no further contact between the two took place. My guess is that her relation to Christa must have pained Barbara, but not because of any ill feelings toward her but because of the empathy she felt. Christa referred to one of Barbara's letters as "affectionate." If Barbara seemed to shut her off during the last years of her life, she probably did so as part of the broader past she wished she could rewrite.

I tried to locate Christa and her sons for the purpose of this account, but I found no trace of either.

The "Englander"

In one of the visits to her relatives in Krefeld, Barbara met an English soldier. His name was Alan Armer. He was a sergeant in the Coldstream Guards who were stationed in the city. The barracks they occupied were built in 1936-38. They were then known as the Adolf-von-Nassau Kaserne. The initial occupiers were the 800-strong troops of Germany's Sixth Armored Reconnaissance Regiment. The barracks were taken over by British units after the war: the Coldstream Guards until 1955, the Royal Artillery until 1965, and the Royal Signals until 2002.

Barbara and Alan became close friends and saw each other frequently. Alan was, in a way, adopted by the family. In addition to being Barbara's friend, he represented novelty and a source of fascination. Elisabeth's mother in particular had been very drawn to the British all her life. Alan met most of the family members, both in Krefeld and in Herne. He called Knut Teddy Boy. Barbara's cousin Ernst Cecior, who is in his seventies and lives in Krefeld, remembers Alan to this day—after more than fifty years—by name.

After Alan was transferred to London, Barbara and he remained in touch by correspondence. Alan sent her magazines frequently, And in April 1958, Barbara traveled to England to see him. She was nearing seventeen then. This was not only her first trip outside Germany but also her first "solo" (unaccompanied) trip, and the occasion for which she acquired her first passport. She reached London via Brussels and Dover by a combination of train and boat, and stayed with his family in Croydon, Surrey for about ten days. More on her trip later.

Despite the culmination of their friendship with the trip, the relationship between Barbara and Alan did not last long. His letters became less frequent. Barbara's mother, who noticed that, attributed it to their growing intellectual difference. She wrote Barbara while she was on vacation, "The more you advance in your studies, the more Alan feels left behind." Clearly, the two young people had less in common than either of them would have liked.

The Summers Away from Home

Barbara spent her summer vacations from 1956 to 1958 away from home at the initiative and with the support of her mother. Her mother's objectives in this regard were: to get her daughter away from boring Herne; to contribute to her physical wellbeing through outdoor activities; to expose her to new places and people; and to benefit from her experience, that is, from what she saw. (The Frasses never vacationed outside Herne/Krefeld together for financial reasons.) The choices Elisabeth made helped her to achieve all of the above objectives.

Barbara spent the summer of 1956 at a youth hostel in Menzenschwand, a village in the southern part of the Black Forest. The location was suitable for youth activities like hiking and trekking and, therefore, popular for youth hostels. A main attraction was its proximity to Freiburg, a historic city, known for, among other things, its university; St. Blasien, a picturesque town; Rhine Falls, the largest waterfalls in Europe; and Lake Constance (Konstanz), or Bodense, which is shared by Germany, Switzerland and Austria and offers rich opportunities for tourism, recreation and sports. Barbara visited each of these places and took advantage of all the opportunities they offered.

In the summer of 1957, after her junior year in high school, Barbara toured some of the cities along the Rhine River with a group of her classmates. The tour was organized and directed by her high school. Because of this, we have the benefit not only of multiple photographs of the tour but also of write-ups about it in the local (Herne) press. The cities visited included:

the historic city of Köln (Cologne) on both sides of the Rhine; Koblenz, also on the Rhine, at the confluence with the Moselle River, and called Germany's most beautiful "corner city;" and the cities of Limburg and Marburg, both of them on the river Lahn, a tributary of the Rhine. The participants in the tour, including Barbara, were very different from the young girls at the hostel in the Black Forest a year earlier. They were "young women"—all of them seventeen—who, in the photographs, seemed proud of their physique and growing independence. They showed both of these in their appearance—fanciful cloths and high heels—and their happy, confident and made-up faces. The tour had the aura of a "coming out" celebration, with the participants more eager to show themselves off than to see the world. They exuded optimism, seeming to rejoice in escaping the gravitational pull of their collective ugly past.

In addition to visiting England in April, in 1958 Barbara spent her entire summer vacation as an "au pair" girl in France. This constituted her longest absence from home until then; it posed the challenge of physical work; and it offered the opportunity to learn about France and practice her French. The family she lived with—Mr. and Mrs. François Bataille and their six children she cared for—resided in Paris but split their summer vacations between Blonville-sur-Mer, a family-oriented seaside resort in the Calvados department in the lower Normandy region of northwestern France, and a farmhouse in a neighboring region. Blonville was known as a "children's paradise." It was situated about 120 miles west of Paris and less than three miles from the better known, fashionable resort called Deauville, famous for its beaches, casinos, and annual film festival. The farmhouse the Batailles owned was in Thienloy-St. Antoine, a locale too small to have a post office, near the town of Grandvilliers in the Oise department. Barbara benefited from the welcome and diversified experiences she had in both of these places as well as in Paris. She related her experience dutifully and enthusiastically in voluminous letters to her mother.

As noted earlier, Barbara's correspondence during the above absences permit a glimpse into her evolving interests and personality. From the Black Forest, after visiting Koblenz (Constance), she wrote the following, displaying—at age sixteen—her enduring love of history, her discerning eyes, and her articulation gift:

> . . . In Konstanz, I visited the Cathedral of Konstanz [*Konstanzer Münster*]. It is a conglomeration of different styles. The result is not particularly felicitous but unique. In contrast, the baroque chapel on the island of Mainau is charming. Konstanz has a most beautiful old town, full of twisted alleys with old gothic houses and renaissance buildings. There is a romanesque city hall as well as towers left over from the city wall dating from 1200. I would have loved to walk through the entire old town. You know how much I love everything that has to do with history. Konstanz is a good example of how the old and the new converge, and it is most beautifully located. I would love to live in such a town one day or at least to spend my holidays there. After that, we continued to Switzerland until Schaffhausen, where we visited the Rhine falls. The water drops 124 meters straight down from the rocks with restless thundering.

From England, the next year, she wrote her impressions of the historic places she visited, including Windsor Castle, Westminster Palace, Kensington Museum, the Tower of London, and the House of Commons. It is a safe bet that she drew up the program and chose the places to visit herself, as she was prone to do on European travel the the rest of her life.

While with the Bataille family in France, Barbara must have impressed them with her knowledge as well as her appearance about which she cared increasingly. This prompted her mother to remark in a return letter, "I am so happy that you made such a good impression. After all, not all Germans are stupid and without culture. Better be a little elegant than too primitive. But most likely it is not the clothes that make one elegant but the person in it." From France, Barbara also wrote how she had a lengthy discussion about politics with Mrs. Bataille's visiting brother-in-law, a lawyer, and that he had been impressed by it.

But the most interesting aspect of the correspondence is what it reveals about the close relationship between mother and daughter. Barbara addressed her mother lovingly as *Liebe* (dear) Mutti, Mum, Mammi, *Meine liebe süsse* (My dear sweet) Mutti, or *Meine liebe goldige* (My dear golden) Mutti. And she signed off sending *tousend küsse* (thousand kisses). Once she closed with, "Your Barbara who is very far away but very close to you." Her mother addressed her affectionately as Babs, Babschen or Babi.

The two women—Elisabeth and Barbara, mother-daughter, friends—gave each other comfort and pleasure, and they missed both when separated during Barbara's last three summers. One can argue that the separation, though painful, especially for Elisabeth, brought them closer together by driving home how much they meant to each other. One can also argue, however, that by the summer of 1958, her mother may have felt that she was beginning to lose her daughter. In her last letter to Barbara, dated August 18, 1958, two months before she died, she wrote, ". . . you could really come home a few days earlier," knowing full well that Barbara could not and would not since she had a fixed commitment to the French family she was living with. She had encouraged Barbara to be selfish—to enjoy her time away from home—for her benefit, and so had her grandmother. And Barbara did; she enjoyed focusing on the outside world, both literally and figuratively. She was already embarked on an orbit that would carry her away from Herne. The same thing happened to me several years earlier and more than a thousand miles away. As with Barbara, the present that my family built for me had the seeds of a future that carried me away from them.

Her Mother's Death

Barbara's mother died on October 26, 1958, at 6:20 pm, at her home in Herne. She was fifty-five years of age. We know relatively little about the circumstances of her death because Barbara did not speak about it in any detail. She was in Herne at the time, but we do not know where she was at the precise time of her mother's death. Whatever we can put together about the event comes from the letters her mother wrote her two months before dying, while Barbara was in France.

The event was unexpected. Elisabeth had not been feeling well but only for a few months, and her ailment did not seem to be life threatening. It concerned one of her legs (it is not clear which one), which was swollen. In early August 1958, she wrote that she had had eight days of rest, which "helped a little." She added, nevertheless, "My leg is still in bad shape . . . . I canot walk to the post office [which she wished to do, to mail Barbara a package]. I have to go to the doctor tomorrow." She then wrote that the doctor had diagnosed the problem as "inflammation of the nerve" and ordered bed rest. Apparently, that helped, enabling her to get up. She reported, "the leg is no longer swollen." A few days later, however, she complained of a migraine and the malfunction (non-function, to be exact) of her bladder. The doctor prescribed some medication which brought some relief. She died a few weeks later and was laid to rest in Herne. Ernst Cecior, her nephew who survives in Germany and whom I have quoted earlier, believes that—I am translating verbatim—she died "because she had some water in her body which rose to her heart." According to a medical doctor I consulted in the Washington area, based on these limited indicators, the most likely cause of Elisabeth Frass' death was a blood cloth that traveled to lung.

To set her mother's death in perspective, Barbara's upbeat letters from France notwithstanding, these were not happy times for the Frasses; none of their eight years in Herne truly were. In her last letter, Barbara's mother seemed in an uncharacteristically bad mood. She wrote: "How is your weather? Here it is always gray and humid. Herne is a terrible place. Your many children [the French children Barbara was caring for] will give you a hard time. It will be a practice for the future. Why are so many kids in so many countries badly behaved? Write again very soon since your letters are the only entertainment in my sad life." She gave the impression of being physically and mentally exhausted, which she almost certainly was. She had been largely self-sufficient despite the many difficulties she faced, rarely asking for help. She had never asked Barbara, for example, to help her with her sewing . . . which she could have. And she had to raise Knut, a challenge about which I have said little. As a boy and four years younger, Knut had needs that were quite different from Barbara's. He was, moreover, a somewhat difficult child, with a stern temperament and a fluctuating performance in and out of school. He was not a dependable, steady student. In 1958, when his mother died, he was attending the *Kaufmannische Privatschule Institut Kaiser*, a business-oriented trade school, in Bochum, a few miles southwest of Herne. He did so with the approval of and financing by the welfare administration. The institute was a boarding school to which he was sent probably for partly behavioral reasons.

Elisabeth's death came as a shock to her children. Barbara was eighteen and Knut forteen at the time. Barbara had finished high school but not obtained her Abitur diploma yet. A question that arises concerning Barbara's reaction is how she felt about the limited time she spent with her mother during the six months preceding her death. During that period, she had been to England to see her English friend, made a side visit to Berlin with her graduating class, and spent almost her entire summer vacation in France. She had spent just six weeks with her mother after her last trip. She may have regretted the separation with hindsight, but her mother was not the kind of person who would make her feel guilty for it. Barbara's love for and admiration of her mother must have been been at its highest level when she lost her. There is no better indication of this than her naming her first child, a daughter, Elisabeth and her doing so not sadly but in celebration. What is sad in retrospect is that Elisabeth I would have met Elisabeth II had she lived a mere five years longer. Elisabeth I's middle name, Emma, survives as the first name of Elisabeth II's daughter.

The mourning did not last long because there were important things to attend to. Barbara had to be declared "adult" by the Court to enable her to act as temporary guardian of her brother, as well as to receive and spend the support payments they were entitled to as orphans. Before her death, their mother received a total payment of DM 204 for the family as a whole, consisting of DM 120 for herself and DM 84 for the two children together. After her death, the payment was reduced to DM 65 for Barbara and DM 65 for Knut. There was much more to do, however.

The Big Decision

The decision to send Barbara to the United States was made most clearly by her grandmother, Olga, and soon after her daughter's death. Olga had been deeply affected by the loss. It is said that the loss of a child is much more painful than the death of a parent. (I have heard that myself from my maternal grandmother who lost two children in their forties.) Yet Olga displayed the strength, wisdom and cool-headedness of Teske women before her. The decision she had to make was particularly difficult and complicated because it involved separating the two siblings and arriving at a parallel plan for Knut. She was both empowered and the most qualified to make the decision, being the *doyenne* of the family and having lived with the Jurkats in the United States. She felt that even though Dorothy Jurkat was a difficult person, she, her husband and Barbara would be good for each other. The Jurkats' son Peter had recently gotten married and left home. His parents genuinely loved the company of young adults and would welcome Barbara. As for Knut, he had been neglecting school and associating with undesirable friends. He needed a strong man more than a loving sister at this stage in his life. The decision was made, therefore, to bring him into his uncle Willi Cecior's family with whom Olga herself lived.

The implications of the big decision were particularly painful for three people. Oma Olga herself would be separated from her beloved Barbara, probably for life. (She was seventy-nine then; she would die six years later.) In addition, she was assuming responsibility for the decision's implications for Knut and his uncertain future. Knut would not only be left behind without a Frass relative for the first time in his life, but he would be raised by his uncle, a police chief, with the toughness that that implies. And Barbara would be abandoning her young brother whom she often called lovingly my *Igel* (hedgehog) or *Igelus* (hedgehog man).

The decision was implemented quickly and methodically, with the grandmother's firm, guiding hand. The Jurkats, the Ceciors and Barbara agreed with the plan. None of them needed much persuading since they understood that there were no other or better alternatives. On February 15, 1959, less than three months after her mother's death, Barbara applied for a U.S. visa as an "immigrant." The application was approved quickly, as the German quota was far from filled. Barbara obtained her Abitur diploma a few week later. The Jurkats secured passage for Barbara on the ocean liner Queen Elisabeth. And the preparations for the trip started in earnest. The grandmother played a central role in it. The task was not easy because it involved, as a preliminary step, dissolving the Frass household in Herne—a household which contained some of the family heirlooms which she had passed on to her daughter when she left for the United States. While some of the family members concerned—Barbara, the Jurkats, Knut—may have viewed Barbara's move to the United States as not necessarily permanent, Oma left no doubt about what she wished, expected or predicted—Barbara was going for good! She packed Barbara a full wardrobe, spending some of her own modest resources, the two oriental carpets which had been in the family since Erfurt, and the lion's share of the Frasses' transportable items, including some silver, tablecloths, other linens, and family documents. Whatever she may have thought about the future, Barbara followed her grandmother's course by taking along her schoolbooks, school records, movie programs, and family photographs—in short, everything dear to her. This included her mother's German translation of *Gone With the Wind*, worn out from reading, and her skating boots, dating from her youth in Elbing or possibly Graudenz.

Barbara boarded the liner Queen Elisabeth on April 23, 1959 and arrived in the United States, her new world, on April 28, 1959.

Chapter Five

Becoming American

Barbara arrived in Philadelphia from Germany in April 1959. I arrived in the same city from my native Turkey eight months later, but I did not get to know her until the beginning of 1961. I described how we met in my memoirs, *Cultures in Counterpoint*. I shall return later to that event and how it transformed our respective lives. Barbara's first twenty months in this country, which I was not privileged to witness, were crucial in several respects. She faced the challenges of healing from the loss of her mother; adjusting to a new family and a new country; placing the past in perspective; forging a new identity; setting herself a new direction; and getting herself going. A tall order! She met all of these challenges, thanks mostly to the Jurkats who opened their home and their hearts to her. They played a crucial role, intentionally or not, in shaping or influencing how Barbara saw the past, the present, and the future, as well as the weight that each deserved. I shall, therefore, start this chapter with them.

Life at the Jurkats

Ernst Jurkat, Barbara's uncle, was fifty-four when Barbara arrived. His wife, Dorothy, was fifty-five. I describe the odyssey that brought them to the United States in Chapter 8. By 1959, Dr. Jurkat was an established marketing and urban planning consultant working mostly at home. The Jurkats lived in a historic neighborhood of Philadelphia, called Germantown, situated 7-8 miles northwest of the city. The neighborhood was founded in 1681 by German settlers from Krefeld, the very city where the Jurkats' remaining German relatives lived—where, in fact, Barbara had left her brother in the care of their Oma and the Ceciors. (This was merely a coincidence and had had no influence on the Jurkats' decision to move to Germantown.) The neighborhood was neither German nor, for that matter, American in character. It was, rather, Quaker and "Philadelphian," at least architecturally.[39] It had three private Quaker schools, including one on the street where the Jurkats lived. And its ethnic composition was representative of Philadelphia's population.

Germantown was accessible by public transportation, including a suburban railway—advantages which probably drew the Jurkats to it. It was a quiet, almost dull, neighborhood with an aging population. Although close to Philadelphia, it was more like Herne than Berlin. The Jurkats occupied a typical Philadelphia semi-detached row house on 6337 Greene Street, one with a covered porch at the entrance, two stories and an attic, and a small yard in the back. The porch opened onto a parlor, which doubled as a study for Dr. Jurkat; it led to a dining room and a kitchen in the rear. The main living room was on the second floor, which also had the main bedroom. Barbara was allotted the attic, which was comfortable and had the added advantage of privacy.

Ernst and Dorothy Jurkat lived a quiet life. Their lives revolved around Ernst's work, in which Dorothy often participated. They were serious people who, nevertheless, had a soft side. They enjoyed watching television—comedies, mysteries, and entertainment shows, in addition to the news. From the first day Barbara arrived, they made a concerted effort to lighten her spirits by talking about anything but her past, joking with her, and even teasing her. They tried to create, in short, a jovial atmosphere, despite the fact that Ernst's work fortunes had started to deteriorate. Barbara responded in kind, enjoying the atmosphere, and being vivacious by nature.

---

[39] I refer to the characteristic Philadelphia row houses.

There were also serious family discussions, which benefited Barbara and began shaping her interests. They involved American politics, national and local, among other topics. This was the year Kennedy was running for president. The Jurkats followed the campaign closely, being staunch Democrats who had supported Adlai Stevenson earlier. They were also concerned with state and city politics, partly because Ernst's work dealt with state and city planning. Thus, Barbara was exposed to how local government works early on—an interest which grew exponentially with time.

What Barbara may have found the most notable about the Jurkats is the extent to which they had adopted America and played down their German identity, at least outwardly. They were strong defenders of American democracy, American foreign policy, the American legal and economic systems, and American core values—but not American food! In short, they adopted America earnestly in every way they thought mattered. Dorothy Jurkat liked to recall the occasion when, shortly after coming to the United States, she met one of the self-identified "daughters of the American Revolution" who, sneering at her foreign accent, introduced herself with the words, "I am a true American." Dorothy promptly shook her hand, saying, "I'm glad to meet my first American Indian."

A more than symbolic manifestation of the Jurkats' strong identification with America was their adoption of the English language. They spoke English most of the time, even in private, and they read only American newspapers and literature. You could hardly come across a German magazine or book in their home. And they rarely, if ever, talked about the past, Germany's Nazi past, and how it had altered their lives. The impression they gave is not that they ignored the past, but simply that what mattered was the present and the future, anticipating the attitude that later generations of Germans, including Barbara, were to adopt. Even if Barbara's attitude toward the past was not modeled on or inspired by the Jurkats', the fact that they felt this way must have made Barbara comfortable about hers.

Barbara's readiness to break with the past and accept the new reality was reflected in a decision she made on her own soon after arriving at the Jurkats: she began calling them mother and father. There was no legal basis for this; she was over eighteen when she came; and there had been no talk of adoption, unlike concerning Knut nine years earlier. The Jurkats accepted this virtual parenting, although their relation with Barbara was and remained somewhat formal. The Jurkats commanded respect above and beyond love. There was something admirable about their inner strength and dignity. In both appearance and behavior, Dr. Ernst was the quintessential German professor: portly, imposing, brilliant, demanding, judgmental, intimidating, and exuding authority. He and Barbara had a special bond through her mother. Elisabeth and he had been each other's favorite sibling and intellectual kin. He must have tested Barbara's intellect in his own way early on, and she must have met his approval. Both Jurkats treated Barbara with respect, guiding her but never preaching or dictating to her. They set high behavioral and intellectual standards, which served her well. Incidentally, although the Jurkats were proud Quakers—as quietly proud as Quakers can be—to my knowledge, they never took Barbara to a Quaker meeting.

In short, while Barbara's relations with the Jurkats had ups and downs in later years, her quick and smooth adjustment to her new life and country owes, undeniably, a great deal to them.

Resuming Education

The first major action the Jurkats took on behalf of Barbara was to enroll her in school. School was the University of Pennsylvania—Ivy League, expensive. For years after the event, Dorothy Jurkat loved to say that they succeeded in this task because she knew the wife of the university's president, Gaylord Harnwell, a Quaker like them. If intervention was needed, it was probably because of the late application to enroll. Barbara's high school record was quite good in terms of both course content and grades. On the strength of it, she was given credit for the freshman and sophomore years and was admitted as a junior, starting in September 1959. The cost was manageable, being limited to tuition, since she did not live on campus; it was probably covered through a combination of a small grant and a student loan.

Attending university in her new country was an important step for Barbara. It exposed her to broader America; it also enabled her to make friends of her own age, to find an outlet for her grief, and to return to the activity that she loved above all others—learning. She seemed to have been attracted to peers of mixed background like herself. Her close friends were a second generation Armenian-American, a commuter like Barbara, and a first generation Ukrainian-American. The latter, Elehie Skoczylas, was to become a friend for life. She lived at the center of Philadelphia and was, therefore, easier to visit. Elehie's mother had three daughters, Elehie being the middle one—an advantage over Dorothy Jurkat who had just one son. Barbara opened up to her regarding the pain she felt about the loss of her mother. She got back understanding, empathy and sympathy at a time when she needed all three a great deal, which complemented the less emotional but no less valuable attention she received at the Jurkats.

Although new to America and to American education, Barbara had no difficulty with her classes. Her knowledge of English was as good as her classmates'. She did very well through her junior and senior years—this, despite her selection of subjects which were either inherently difficult or new to her. She liked to be challenged and was eager to get to know her new country—its governance, culture and history—as quickly as possible. She therefore took courses on the U.S. Constitution, American literature, political science, and U.S. and other history—lots of them on history. She graduated four semesters later with a B.A. degree with honors in history. She was twenty-one. I received my M.A. in economics at the same university on the same day.

Barbara accomplished the above despite working part-time, which she had to do in order to contribute to the family finances. Like many young people in those days, she sold Encyclopedia Britannica sets door to door. And she worked as a sales person in a department store on weekends and some evenings. Beginning in January 1961, she started a still part-time but steadier job: she was hired as a statistical assistant by the university's Population Studies Center, where I had been working part-time, too. I had met her once or twice before but hardly knew her. I merely informed her of the unadvertised vacancy at the Center; she got the job on her own merit. She worked initially, like me, on the development of internal migration data for the United States, which was the Center's focus at the time. She later had the more challenging task of creating a reference library for the young center.

The Population Studies Center was headed by the eminent sociologist-demographer Dorothy Swaine Thomas who was responsible for its informal, home-like atmosphere. The staff was multi-disciplinary, multi-ethnic, and multi-national. It included, in addition to a German and a Turk in the persons of Barbara and myself, a Chinese, an Indian, a Latvian-American, an African-American, and two Americans from the deep south. One thing the group had in common was fascination with the recently elected President Kennedy. The only subject that competed with him during the communal coffee breaks was what Jack Paar of the "Tonight Show" had said the night before.

Three Key Steps

These were: getting married, leaving Philadelphia for the Washington, D.C. metropolitan area, and becoming U.S. citizen.

Barbara and I started dating soon after she joined the Center. We were engaged after a year and got married six months later. In my memoirs, I described the event as follows:

> "We were married in a brief ceremony at the elegant suburban residence of Judge Adrian Bonnelly of the County Court of Philadelphia. This was arranged by Everett Lee, a professor of ours at the University of Pennsylvania who, knowing our limited means, asked the Judge, his neighbor, to marry us for no pay. The Judge did so on the ninth day of June 1962, solemnly, seriously and graciously, after putting on his black judicial robe and calling the court to order. The 'court,' other than his wife and Professor Lee and his wife Anne, consisted of eight adults and an infant: Ernest and Dorothy Jurkat, my wife's German uncle and aunt, long-time residents of Philadelphia; their son Peter Jurkat, his wife Mayme and their infant Alex; David Gabay, a Turkish friend and the only link present to my

past, and Pat, his American wife; and my future wife and me.

We exchanged rings, of course, but no personalized vows. There were no flowers, except the bouquet Barbara carried. There was no music of any sort either. Nor was there a commercial photographer.

After the event, we—the same eight people plus infant—went to the elder Jurkat's house in Germantown (Philadelphia) to celebrate the occasion over coffee, coffeecake, and cookies."[40]

That was the biggest day of our lives but it did not change much in the short term for us. We continued to study and work much the same way, with no significant change in our routine or lifestyle. We lived in most respects like other married graduate students. I resumed studying toward a Ph.D., and Barbara started on a master's degree program in demography, after the Center offered her an attractive fellowship she could not refuse. And we both continued our part-time work at the Center to support ourselves. What changed right away was our residence. We moved into a small apartment across the street from the Jurkats, which brought the benefit of a free meal at their home at least once a week.

Subsequently, things changed, although more for Barbara than for me. Barbara left the Pop Center, as we called it, to become chief demographer for a project carried out by Jefferson Medical College of Philadelphia. The project involved the evaluation of hospital services in the State of Pennsylvania as a whole. Her new job allowed Barbara to diversify her work and to make new friends. During this period, Dr. Jurkat was hired by the United Nations as an urban planning adviser for Turkey, and the Jurkats left the country almost right away. This represented a big change for the Jurkats as well as for Barbara. The Jurkats would be out of the country for some seven years thereafter, serving subsequently and in the same capacity in Ethiopia and Tanzania. And Barbara would be without her closest relatives and unofficial patrons in her new

---

[40] *Cultures in Counterpoint*, op. cit., pp. 116-117.

country. She was, moreover, left in charge of caring for and renting the Jurkats' house.

The first renters of 6337 Greene Street, directly across from us, were a couple consisting of a young woman from Germany and a medical doctor from Iran fulfilling his residency requirement in cardiology at Hahnemann Hospital in Philadelphia. We became friends almost right away. Barbara and Diana, the couple's German half, developed a special bond due to their similar age, marital status and common background. They were both from northern Germany (Diana was from Lübeck on the Baltic coast)—an important consideration for Germans from that part of the country. Diana identified much more with Germany than Barbara did. She liked to surround herself with all kinds of German objects—food products, clothes, cosmetics, music, magazines and books, and accessories and decorations of all sorts. And she took pain to celebrate special occasions, such as birthdays and holidays, the traditional German way. Barbara went along and enjoyed Diana's ways—especially, talking and joking in their native tongue—although without showing an interest in imitating or replicating them. For Barbara, Germany was already far away!

The closing weeks of 1963 were marked by two events about three weeks apart—one sad, the other happy—which affected us equally: the death of President Kennedy on November 22 and the birth of our daughter Elizabeth on December 16. Kennedy spoke for almost everyone of our generation, especially in the academic community we were a part of. He was so different from the other Western leaders of the time—Eisenhower, Adenauer, de Gaulle, Macmillan (Britain)—and in more regards than age—although his youthfulness was a part of his appeal and promise. We firmly believed that Kennedy was good not just for the United States but for the world as a whole. Barbara stopped outside work after becoming a mother, but she continued working at home on a paper, inspired by Dr. Thomas, which she had started drafting as part of her graduate program in demography. Barbara had not been happy with her choice of demography as a field of specialization. She was nevertheless attracted to the subject of her paper in progress. It dealt with the successful assimilation of Japanese-Americans in the 1950s, and it continued the pioneering work carried out by

Dr. Thomas on this subject after the war.[41] Barbara finished the paper, which was published with some delay in 1967.[42] In 1964, concurrently, I began drafting my doctoral dissertation and turning my attention to life after graduate school.

In the fall of 1964 I received an employment offer from the World Bank in Washington, D.C., and we relocated there in late December of the same year. We moved into an apartment in a complex of garden-type buildings in Shirlington, Virginia, five miles from Washington along highway I-395 in neighboring Arlington county. Barbara hated everything about the apartment: its size and construction, small with thin walls; its location, since Barbara did not drive then and Shirlington was not yet the "urban village" it became later; and the neighbors—mostly noisy single men. In retrospect, the apartment's only saving grace—other than the low rent—was the opportunity it gave us to meet a couple (Patti and Ron Kornell) who became friends for life. On balance, we were happy to leave Philadelphia—to cut the umbilical cord connecting us to the university and its Population Studies Center—and to step into a different America. Philadelphia was the only city Barbara and I had known since coming to the United States. The most precious thing we brought along from Philadelphia was our one-year old daughter.

I reported to work at the World Bank on January 4, 1965. Two days later, Barbara returned to Philadelphia for the day to be sworn in as a U.S. citizen. No elaborate application was necessary, since she had been admitted to the country as an "immigrant" in 1959, which qualified her for citizenship in five years. Her first act as citizen was to vote the following November in the gubernatorial election of the State of Virginia. This was the first time she had

---

[41] Dr. Thomas' two seminal works on the subject were *The Spoilage*, 1946, and *The Salvage*, 1952, both published originally by the University of California Press.

[42] "The Japanese-Americans: Comparative Occupational Status, 1960 and 1950," *Demography*, Vol. 4, No. 2, 1967.

cast a vote anywhere. The winner was Mills E. Godwin Jr., a Democrat.[43]

The Late Sixties and the Seventies

Our lives over the next fifteen years (1966-1980) were shaped by a series of decisions we made, both individually and as a team, along the way. We moved several times within and outside Virginia—from Arlington, where we had settled initially, to Alexandria and then Annandale, Virginia; then to New York City; and finally to Fairfax County, back in Virginia. Our first moves were prompted by the birth of our son Jeremy in 1967 and the need to provide our children larger play areas, both inside and outside our residence. The move to New York was entirely work-related; it followed my taking a leave-of-absence from the World Bank to work for two years (1975-1977) at the United Nations headquarters in Manhattan. I have written about my experience there in my memoir, *Cultures in Counterpoint.* Barbara's top priority during our children's formative years and beyond was to be as good a mother as she could. Her becoming a working mother was not an option either of us considered; nor was it realistic. The absence of high-quality day care facilities in those days made working unthinkable for most young mothers. Barbara's determination to become a full-time mother to her children was very likely influenced by how much she and her brother had benefited from the full-time attention they had received from their own mother. The decision was, in a way, unavoidable. I was much like an absentee father, being gone for long stretches of time because of my work. I traveled overseas 4-5 times a year; I worked long hours, including weekends, when not traveling; and I was preoccupied with work much of the time. I was more in need of

---

[43] I do not know for sure if Barbara voted for him. Goodwin was a Democrat but part of the conservative Byrd Organization that dominated Virginia politics for over three decades. He became a Republican in 1974 and was reelected for a second, non-consecutive term as one. He is the only governor in the history of the United States to be elected both as a Democrat and as a Republican.

caring myself than I was able to care for others, including my close family. Thus, Barbara had to be a full-time wife in addition to a full-time mother.

We were lucky to have two healthy children. Raising them physically was, therefore, not a problem. Attending to their intellectual and cultural development was a greater challenge, largely because we—a German and a Turk—wished to raise them fully as Americans. The challenge, or burden, fell almost entirely on Barbara. She had to become an American before the children did or simultaneously with them in order to guide them, supplement what they learned in school, public school, and answer their questions. This meant not only absorbing American history, language, traditions, sports, games, and popular music, but also keeping up with changes in them. She did all this successfully and enthusiastically while managing to retain her individuality. Typical of her achievement was her embrace of, and identification with, American football and baseball in record time. To serve as the mother I briefly described was not an easy task for Barbara, partly because of the limited help I offered her. Furthermore, neither she nor I had any relatives we could call upon in the country, let alone where we lived. Also, Barbara valued her independence and did not avail herself of services, except for the occasional babysitter. She did not engage the service of a housecleaner for thirty-five years—a decision unrelated to cost—as she took pride in and meticulous care of her inviting, orderly household.

To compensate for the time that child rearing took, and to steal a few hours for intellectual pursuit and quiet reflection, Barbara became the night owl she would be known as for the rest of her life. Her friends and political associates knew that they could call Barbara past midnight, often as late as 2:00 a.m. What she did during those late hours was mostly read, both fiction and non-fiction, ferociously. Many of the authors whose work she read were women, among them: the novelists Jane Austen, Ellen Glasgow and Edith Wharton, the biologist and environmental scientist Rachel Carlson, the feminist author and critic Rebecca West, the historian Barbara Tuchman, the biographer and novelist Antonia Fraser, and the novelist and essayist, Joan Didion. Barbara was attracted to them not because of their gender but because of the subjects they addressed and the sensitivity and language with which they covered them. The subject of history was an early love of Barbara which intensified with time.[44] Although her love bordered on addiction, it was based on a rationale which she explained in an assignment titled "Why I Study History" which she prepared during her first year at the University of Pennsylvania. The rationale was, in part, that the study of history helped her "to understand what is and what will be in the light of what has been," since she subscribed, as she put it, "to the spiral approach to history, whereby human existence is a continuum, civilizations rise and fall, one always being the heir of the achievements of the previous ones." Yet by far her favorite historical subject was the life and achievements of Queen Elizabeth I of England. Barbara read and left behind more books on her than on any other subject. I believe that she was more interested in the person than in the period. But I leave it to my children, both of them historians, to explain how their mother's favorite topic related to her rationale for studying history.

Barbara's only connection to her native country's "shadowed past" was through the German language. It is said that when the renowned German poet Heinrich Heine (1797-1856) was asked what his nationality was, he replied, "the German language!" This is consistent with how Barbara felt about her native tongue. She kept her knowledge of it alive and up to date by using it. For more than a quarter century, she worked as a freelance translator from German into English in various fields such as the physical sciences (medicine, engineering, nuclear energy), politics, law, sociology, religion, business, and current affairs. Her employers included the United States Joint Publications Research Service (JPRS) which—she was later informed—was, at the time, affiliated with the Central Intelligence Agency. She also worked for think tanks, the Konrad Adenauer Institute (a political foundation supported partly by the German government), and the private sector. The clients ranged from government agencies, both U.S. and German, and both civilian and military, to the academic community and

---

[44] She articulated and displayed that love in her description of the historic center of the city of Konstanz at age 16, which I quoted earlier.

the Lutheran church. The work required in-depth knowledge of German, which she possessed, and was very demanding. To illustrate, the demand for her skills jumped soon after the reunification of Germany in 1990. The reunification created a need to raise capital internationally for the many privatized East German enterprises. The stakes were high, as the Initial Public Offerings (IPOs) which she translated involved sums running into millions, sometimes hundreds of millions, of dollars.

Barbara proved very good at using her language skills, and she enjoyed doing so. What attracted her to the work and made her excel in it was not her love of the German language; it was, rather, her loyalty to it. She never flaunted her knowledge of German or seemed eager to use it. She rarely spoke German to the first German she met. But when she worked at translation, she gave the work all she had. Her effectiveness owed immeasurably to her insistence on precision—precision in the use of any language—a fact which leads me to her command of English. She impressed all those who knew her with her mastery of the English language. She used it with a flare, almost gusto, and justified self-confidence. I firmly believe that her command of the two languages sprang from one and the same root, namely, a love of clarity.

I have related above mostly what we *did* in the late sixties and the seventies. We experienced concurrently also a series of events which influenced what we *thought*, at least politically—events that shaped our politics for life. The year 1968 was an important one for us. We visited Germany and Turkey for the first time since leaving our respective countries 8-9 years earlier, and we did so with a spouse and children. This was a momentous, happy event for Barbara and me. But it was sandwiched between two horrendous acts: the assassination of Martin Luther King, Jr. in April 1968, a few weeks before we left, and the assassination of Robert Kennedy while we stopped in Athens (Greece) for a week on our way back in June of the same year. The late sixties were marked, in addition, by the expansion of the Vietnam War under President Johnson, the massive demonstrations against it, the election of President Nixon, and the escalation of the conflict during his early presidency through incursions into neighboring countries. This was followed by the leaking of the Pentagon Papers[45] and the Watergate Scandal—an event too well known to require an explanatory sentence or footnote. The Watergate Scandal in particular commanded our attention; we were captivated by it. I remember buying a portable, battery-operated television set in June or July of 1971, taking it with us on a rare family vacation, and planting it on the sand at Rehoboth Beach, Delaware, to watch the Senate Watergate Committee Hearings. Then came the impeachment-related actions, the Nixon resignation, and his pardon by the succeeding President Ford. I wonder, with hindsight, how we found time to care for our children the way we did in those days. The effect of the above experience was to solidify our center-left political identity, to radicalize us, and, at the very least, to hook us on politics.

Although we cared deeply about the outcome of the political processes, participating in them was not an option for me, not being a United States citizen at the time, and not feasible or realistic for Barbara. This would change for her around 1980 as both children reached their teens.

Public Service: The Early Years

Soon after we came back from New York, Barbara became involved in community work partly out of sheer disappointment with the lifestyle that suburbia offered, which contrasted so sharply with life in Manhattan. She was attracted to local politics in particular and became active in the Fairfax County and Providence District Democratic Committees on which some of our neighbors served. The crucial step came in 1984, when she joined the Fairfax County General Registrar's Office. Since 1983, the registrar had been Lilyan Spero, a person with a long history of public service, an activist/organizer, a "Roosevelt Democrat" at heart, a supporter of New Deal causes, and a veteran of past partisan struggles. The causes Lilyan pursued with energy and determination throughout her life ranged from voting rights to human rights and from child

---

[45] A top-secret United States Defense Department history of the United States' political-military involvement in Vietnam from 1945 to 1967, which was leaked to the press in 1971.

care to elderly care. She was particularly concerned with education and women's issues. She became later a co-founder and president (1993-94) of the Learning in Retirement Institute at George Mason University in Fairfax County. These and other activities earned her many awards, including the 1987 National Association of Cities and Counties National Award and the Fairfax County Citizen of the Year Award in 1997.

When Barbara came on board, the General Registrar's Office was engaged in an aggressive drive, led by Lilyan Spero, to sign up new voters. Virginia's record in voter registration and enfranchisement had been dismal, among the worse in the country. Despite the abolition of Virginia's notorious poll tax in March 1966, serious impediments to voting persisted and resulted from both the numerous, often overtly discriminatory regulations and their arbitrary or wrongful application. In the past, and at different times, both parties had pursued a policy of deliberately restricting the number of voters and done so selectively, aiming to disenfranchise racial minorities in particular, as well as voters from the opposition party. In addition to correcting these longstanding problems, the increasing proportion of Asian and other immigrants in Fairfax County's population constituted new challenges beginning in the early 1980s.

Against this backdrop, the strategy followed by Registrar Spero was to expand the accessibility of registration facilities for all—voters of all ethnic and other background and age groups. Shortly after she joined the Registrar's Office, Barbara was put in charge of conceptualizing and implementing a high school voter registration program as part of the social studies curriculum of high school seniors. She enjoyed doing that greatly, particularly the opportunity it gave her to make presentations at various high schools. She was very good at this task, having raised two teenagers, the second being about to reach voting age. She had been all her life very effective in communicating with young people. At the Registrar's, Barbara also designed a survey for measuring the effectiveness of student voter education programs and evaluated the results. She prepared, in addition, a training manual for field registrars. The Registrar's overall voter outreach efforts received enthusiastic support from

Virginia Governor Charles Robb and First Lady Linda Robb, as well as bipartisan praise.

Her association with Lilyan had multiple rewards for Barbara. It exposed her to the workings of county government; it convinced her that community service was the path she wanted to stay on; and it strengthened her self-identification as a Democrat, for although Lilyan was scrupulously bipartisan as registrar, she was an influential and model Democrat in the county. In Lilyan, Barbara acquired a supporter and friend for life. Although Barbara is gone, Lilyan still watches over her legacy: she has served for several years as the at-large member of the selection committee for the award named after her.

After leaving the Registrar's Office, Barbara devoted her energies to activist political work, which she was to continue for the rest of her life, regardless of other demands on her time, such as family priorities and her on-and-off translation work. She helped people running or contemplating to run for a variety of district, county, state and national offices such as sheriff, school board member, district supervisor, and U.S. congressman. Her help or involvement took a variety of forms: providing political advice, framing issues, assisting with campaign literature (design, content and mailing), fund raising, public relations, and voter mobilization. She often enlisted our children and me in the work. And she did all this with characteristic enthusiasm. Although many of the above tasks approximated those of a campaign manager, she never seriously considered serving in that capacity. She preferred to keep her independence and being available to help more than one person at the same time, with all the pressure that that often created in which she thrived.

Throughout, what motivated and drove Barbara was her determination to encourage and help people to register to vote . . . and to actually vote. She was not alone in this endeavor; she felt a kinship toward the many who shared the same objective or passion in Fairfax County, and she opened her heart and home to them, regardless of ideology or political affiliation. They became for her a "community" she was proud to be a part of. People like her at the grassroots level practically ran the show; they were responsible for identifying and running candidates, running campaigns, and designing actual public policy. This coincided with a period when the involvement of young people in political activities was scandalously low, being long before the internet, the blogosphere, the "netroots," and the like. Much of the work fell to political operatives or professionals, but also to people like Barbara and a preponderance of women who were civic minded and had, in relative terms, discretionary time because they did not have conventional careers and their children were grown up.

Happily, Barbara's interest in voting coincided with the evolving career focus of her oldest and best friend, the previously mentioned Elehie Skoczylas. Both were foreign-born and multicultural, and both belonged to families which had seriously suffered from the effects of the war. After a successful career at the United States Information Agency (USIA), Elehie devoted herself to surveying public opinion scientifically and to organizing and monitoring elections. She did this as a consultant to foundations, international organizations, individual governments, and private organizations here and abroad. The two soul mates supported each other's work by exchanging experiences, using each other as sounding boards, and critiquing each other, often over a glass of wine. They collaborated in at least one endeavor concerning Kazakhstan, thousands of miles away.[46]

Barbara's entourage of like-minded political friends was markedly different from my World Bank community. The majority of my colleagues, many of whom she met, were concerned at times with national politics, but more often with international politics, geopolitics, and change or management (macro-management) from the top. Hers vied for change from the bottom up. While we at the Bank worried about the deeds and misdeeds of former Zaire's Mobutu and other assorted dictators, Barbara and her friends worried about electing local officials ranging from members of the Board of Supervisors to the members of the school board. Barbara's involvement in local issues and politics pulled my interest away

---

[46] Elehie Natalie Skoczylas, Steven Wagner and Barbara Frass Varon, *Kazakhstan 1995: The Public Speaks—An Analysis of Public National Opinion*, International Foundation for Election Systems, Washington, D.C., September 1995.

from my World Bankese bias. I became a willing adjunct member of her community. I remember being happy when I appeared in a photograph in one of the early campaign mailings of the current Congressman Connolly, then running for Providence District Supervisor in Fairfax Country. The photograph showed me as a supportive neighbor of the candidate, raking leaves.

The Fighting Years

In early 1990, Barbara started working for Virginia State Senator Emilie Miller, a Democrat, as legislative assistant. The senator's term ran from 1988 though 1991. Although the Virginia legislature is in session only two months out of the year, the work involved is not limited to that period, as the various committees meet year around. The next two years were hectic, super challenging and super enjoyable for Barbara. This was entirely due to the senator's work responsibilities, multiplied several fold by her activism, the areas she focused on, the resistance she met, and her work style. Like Lilyan Spero, Emilie Miller defined activism. The senator was the only freshman to receive four standing committee assignments: Education and Health, General Laws, Local Government, and Rehabilitation and Social Services. She was also active in the National Conference of State Legislators and was appointed to their Labor Committee. She had been politically active before, at both the country and state levels, and knew many of the issues. She therefore joined the Senate running. She focused on a wide range of areas concerning, among others: *child care*, which she viewed not as a woman's issue but as a family issue; *mental health, mental retardation, and substance abuse,* areas in which she had been closely involved for a long time; and *women's rights*. As the first woman to represent the Fairfax area in the state senate, she felt a special responsibility to fight for gender equality in education and other areas. Barbara identified fully with these concerns.

Senator Miller was results-oriented and had a legislative agenda in each of the areas she got involved in. The agenda met stiff resistance by the conservative, male-dominated legislature. She was often the only female in the committees she served on. The resistance was sometimes stiffened by what some saw as her combative style. This was prompted by her aggressive questioning of the status quo on issues like gender discrimination or established ways of doing the people's business. She produced a culture shock in the legislature, and she undeniably rocked the boat. (The boat kept rocking even after she left the senate in 1992.) This atmosphere and configuration forced Barbara to give the work all she had in terms of long hours, analytical skills, communication skills, skills of persuasion and diplomacy, and even knowledge of history and the law.

The senator and her legislative aid had, nevertheless, a number of successes, including assuring the adequate and uninterrupted funding of programs to combat mental retardation, mental illnesses and substance abuse, prevention of the execution of the mentally retarded, and the symbolically important acts of declaring March as Virginia Women's History Month and April 22, 1990 as Earth Day in Virginia. But none of these deeds took as much energy, drew as much attention and had as important an outcome as did their efforts to integrate the Virginia Military Institute (VMI).

VMI is a state-supported military college founded in 1839 and located in Lexington, Virginia. Since its creation, it practiced a males-only admission policy. When Senator Miller joined the state legislature, the school had fifty full scholarships exclusively reserved for men. The Senator thought that this was discriminatory and against state law, which forbade such discrimination in state-funded institutions. Some past politicians had recognized this and had even been concerned about it, without however, attempting to change VMI's practice, being intimidated by the latter's vast political clout. The Senator began the fight by proposing that the State fund fifty scholarships reserved for women who wished to attend college in Virginia institutions in order to equalize the rights of the genders. She also introduced legislation providing that "all public institutions of higher education shall admit qualified students without regard to race, sex, religion, national origin, or political affiliation." Both attempts failed, although the issues that drove them began to attract national attention, culminating in a whirlwind of publicity.

The U.S. Department of Justice had filed a discrimination suit against VMI. At first, Virginia's newly elected Attorney General decided to defend VMI against the Justice Department, but she reversed course under unrelenting pressure from the Senator who was on the daily television show circuit. The steps the Senator took included threatening, with the governor's support, to impound state funds intended for VMI's defense. VMI continued the litigation on its own. The process, which went through several Appeals Courts, took many years. Finally, on June 26, 1996 the U.S. Supreme Court, by a vote of 7 to 1, ruled in favor of the Justice Department. VMI enrolled its first female cadet in August 1997. This sweet victory for the Senator and her legislative aid came five years after the Senator lost re-election in large part because of her stand on VMI, a decision she has not regretted to this day. Incidentally, like Lilyan Spero, the senator has been serving on the Barbara Varon Volunteer Award selection committee.

Barbara emerged from her experience with VMI on Senator Miller's side with a renewed dedication to the cause of women. Soon thereafter, she joined the local chapter of the Virginia Business and Professional Women's (BPW) Foundation. This was an arm of a nationwide organization of the same name, founded in 1921 and headquartered in Washington, D.C. The organization works at many levels to support the economic interests and advancement of women, including lobbying for women's issues, supporting women candidates (through dedicated Political Action Committees), promoting female entrepreneurship, and granting scholarships to qualified women. At the local chapter, Barbara took an active part in the establishment of a "Women of Virginia Historic Trail," honoring women who made an outstanding contribution to Virginia history. She enlisted our daughter Elizabeth, who was then enrolled in Yale University's Ph.D. program in history, to research the background of, and draft biographical notes on, the thirty women being honored. The project was co-sponsored by the Virginia BPW Foundation and the Virginia Foundation for the Humanities and Public Policy.

Barbara then resumed her political work at the local level. In 1994, she was elected chair person of the Providence District Democratic Committee and served in that capacity for two years. This was a period of intense activity and challenges for the district Democrats, as it coincided with the election of governor, the state legislature, the county government, the school board, sheriff, etc.

Many of the candidates were from the district, and at least two of them had to run twice: in mid-term special elections and for full terms. March 1995, when the now Congressman Gerry Connolly (Democrat) won his first election as Providence District Supervisor, marked the beginning of a strong and enduring professional relationship and friendship between Barbara and him.

Ideologically, particularly where *national* politics are concerned, Barbara belonged squarely on the left wing of the Democratic Party, and she defended, articulated and voted her beliefs. She fought against the encroachment of social conservatism, embodied in restrictions on abortion rights and curricular battles in public schools, and for an enlightened, common-sense liberalism that was about "smart growth," the protection of organized labor, the expansion of rights (for gays and lesbians), the preservation of the environment, and the pursuit of real integration, gender equality, and citizen empowerment through voting and education. Barbara saw her work in these areas as contributing to social justice. Yet she was not an ideological purist. She appreciated the inevitability of ideological and even moral compromise, especially at the local level, where issues tend to be crisper and political decisions can touch citizens quickly and directly. She also learned from experience, particularly with the Virginia legislature, that the party label did not necessarily define the positions of politicians on given issues—that one could learn a great deal from thoughtful opponents. She was a loyal Democrat but she fought for ideas rather than the party.

Non-Partisan Service

In early 2000, Barbara was nominated by Emilie Miller, who was then chair of the Fairfax Country Democratic Committee, for the position of chair person of the Fairfax County Electoral Board. She was appointed to the Board formally (by the Court) on February 21, 2000. This was the last county position Barbara would hold, and, in retrospect, it proved important for her in several respects. The appointment returned her to the world of voting—an area through which she had entered public service and one she had never stopped being concerned about. Since her work at the Registrar's Office fifteen years earlier, the population of the county had grown markedly and become more diversified. By the year 2000, nearly a fifth of the population was Asian and 16 percent Hispanic, which posed special challenges for election officials. Finally, Barbara's new appointment would test her impartiality, which she demonstrated by alienating elements of both major parties on two major occasions, as I shall explain.

The main responsibility of country electoral boards in the State of Virginia is to apply the state electoral laws and to supervise the elections, including primaries. Each county board also appoints the country registrar. The makeup of the boards is governed by strict rules. Each board consists of three people, two of whom are from the Virginia governor's party (whatever it may be), and the third from the opposition party. Although in the minority, the member of the opposition party serves as chair. When the governor changes, the composition of the electoral board changes according to the above rules. Board members are nominated by the two major parties. Each party submits three candidates for a vacant post. The selection and appointment are made by the County Circuit Court Judge. When Barbara was appointed, the governor was James Gilmore, a Republican. Barbara, being a Democrat, joined the electoral board as chair person.

Barbara took her work seriously. For example, to make sure that things were running smoothly, she visited as many voting places as she could on election day, which her predecessors never or rarely did. One of the challenges she faced the first year was the appointment of a new Registrar when the office holder had to resign before his term was up. She encouraged one of the two Republican board members, whom she thought was well qualified for the job, to apply for the post, and she voted for her. About a year later, she voted to reappoint the same person as Registrar, this time casting the deciding vote for the Republican incumbent. This drew the ire of some of her fellow-Democrats in the county. Barbara herself was reappointed to the Electoral Board for three years beginning in February 2001.

The next year on the Board was very problematic and unpleasant for Barbara. Shortly after the general election of November 2001, the State Board of Elections sued Barbara and a fellow-member of the Electoral Board, a Republican, petitioning the Fairfax Circuit

Court to remove them from the Board for "neglect of duty"—an unprecedented change. The facts of the case were as follows. On November 6, 2001, election day, 18 people showed up to vote in the wrong precinct (a precinct other than the one they were entitled to vote in). The Electoral Board allowed them to cast "conditional" ballots, subject to a review the following day—a common practice. At the meeting the next day, Barbara and one of the two Republican members of the Board voted to admit the said ballots; the other member abstained. The State Board of Elections took the position that this violated the state law and ran against the specific instructions it had issued earlier. The Circuit Court dismissed the case, saying that incompetence and negligence were not involved. The State Board pressed the case, nevertheless, arguing that its authority "to obtain uniformity in the practices and procedures of local electoral boards" was at stake, and it threatened to appeal to the State Supreme Court.

In the numerous litigation moves and countermoves that followed, the defenders had the assistance of the county lawyers but the county government did not get involved. The defenders consistently acknowledged that the 18 votes should not have been approved but that they did so in good faith. (It is worth noting that the general election was decided by 270,000 votes.) The case was finally resolved on February 26, 2002 through a *Consent Order of Compromise and Dismissal* under which the two sides agreed that "there must be uniformity in the Commonwealth of all election practices and proceedings to insure [*sic*] the legality and purity of all elections concluded in the Commonwealth," and Barbara stated publicly that she did not intend to violate the provisions of the applicable law. She retained her seat on the Board, although since the recently elected governor, Mark Warner, was a Democrat, a newly appointed Republican became chair and Barbara became Vice Chair.

Barbara Varon continued to serve on the Fairfax Country Electoral Board without any bitterness. She remained concerned with voting and other civil rights until her fatal illness put a stop to it in 2003. She was Vice Chair of the Electoral Board at the time of her death. The last board meeting she attended was in May 2003. She died in the county on October 12, 2003. A memorial for her, attended by the members of her public service "community," was held two weeks later at the home of Gerry Connolly, then Providence District Supervisor. Gerry Connolly was elected Chairman of the Board of Supervisors ten days later—an occasion Barbara would have liked to witness.

Eight days after Barbara's death and even before her memorial meeting was held, a motion was introduced at the Fairfax Country Board of Supervisors to request the County Board of Elections, in conjunction with the Office of the General Registrar and the Office of Equity Programs, to establish "an annual volunteer recognition award to honor Barbara Varon in our memories and to celebrate the spirit of her commitment." The award was approved formally in March 2004. Of the seven recipients to date, four have been women and three men. The seven included two Asian-Americans. The awardees were honored in part for their efforts to enable residents to participate in the political process, beginning with their registration to vote, and encouraging them to perform their civic duties.

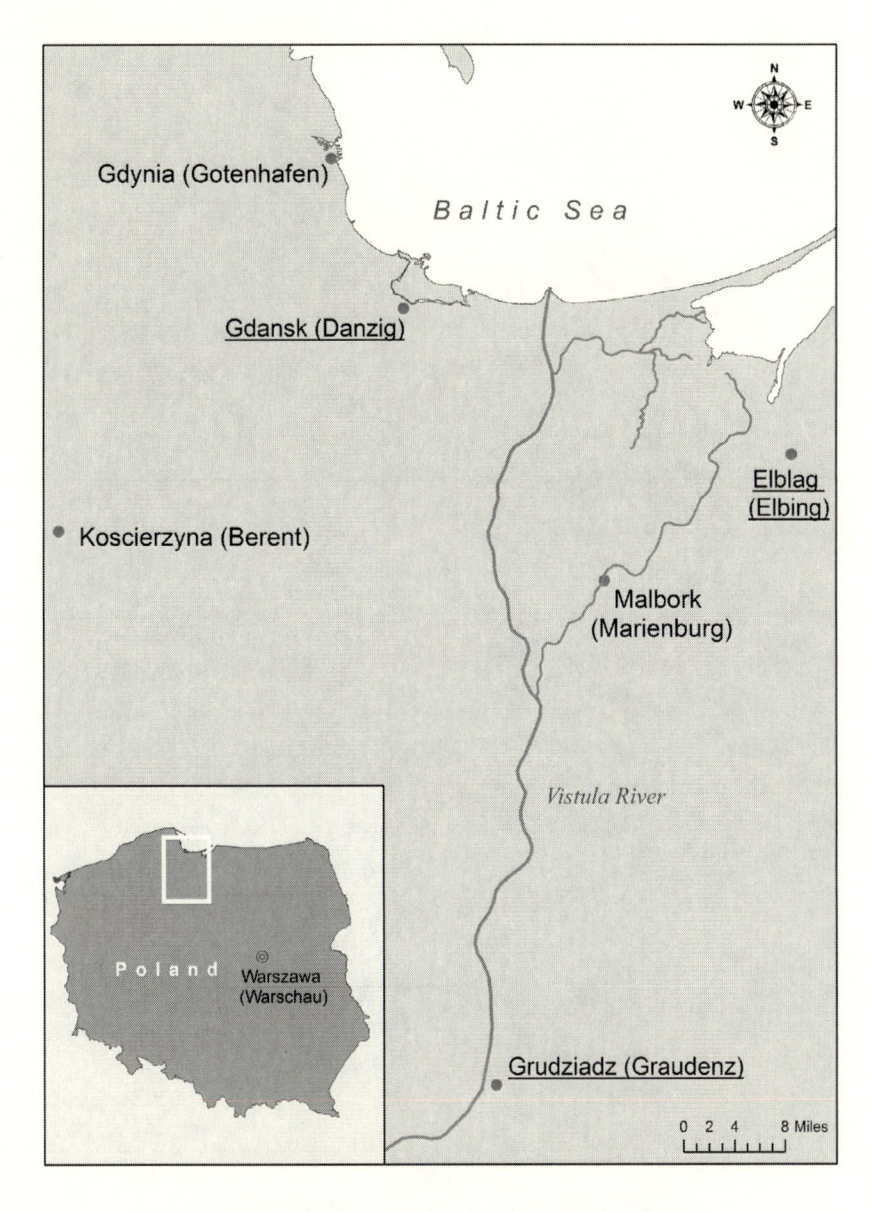

Prussian areas, now in Poland, where Barbara's Jurkat
ancestors came from. Key cities underlined.
Old German names in parentheses.

Cities (underlined) in East and West Germany where Barbara and her close relatives lived after the Second World War.

Barbara's FRASS Side

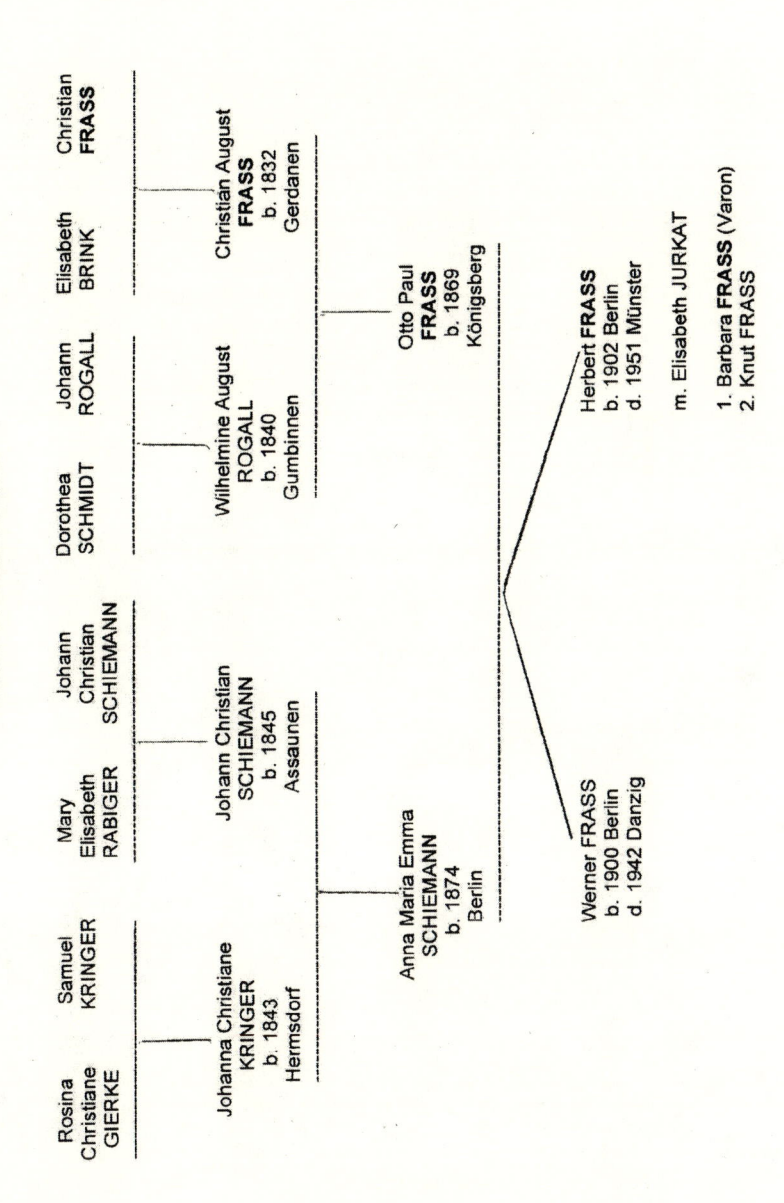

| Rosina Christiane GIERKE | Samuel KRINGER | Mary Elisabeth RABIGER | Johann Christian SCHIEMANN | Dorothea SCHMIDT | Johann ROGALL | Elisabeth BRINK | Christian August FRASS | Christian FRASS |

Johanna Christiane KRINGER
b. 1843 Hermsdorf

Johann Christian SCHIEMANN
b. 1845 Assaunen

Wilhelmine August ROGALL
b. 1840 Gumbinnen

Christian August FRASS
b. 1832 Gerdanen

Anna Maria Emma SCHIEMANN
b. 1874 Berlin

Otto Paul FRASS
b. 1869 Königsberg

Werner FRASS
b. 1900 Berlin
d. 1942 Danzig

Herbert FRASS
b. 1902 Berlin
d. 1951 Münster

m. Elisabeth JURKAT

1. Barbara **FRASS** (Varon)
2. Knut FRASS

Barbara's JURKAT Side

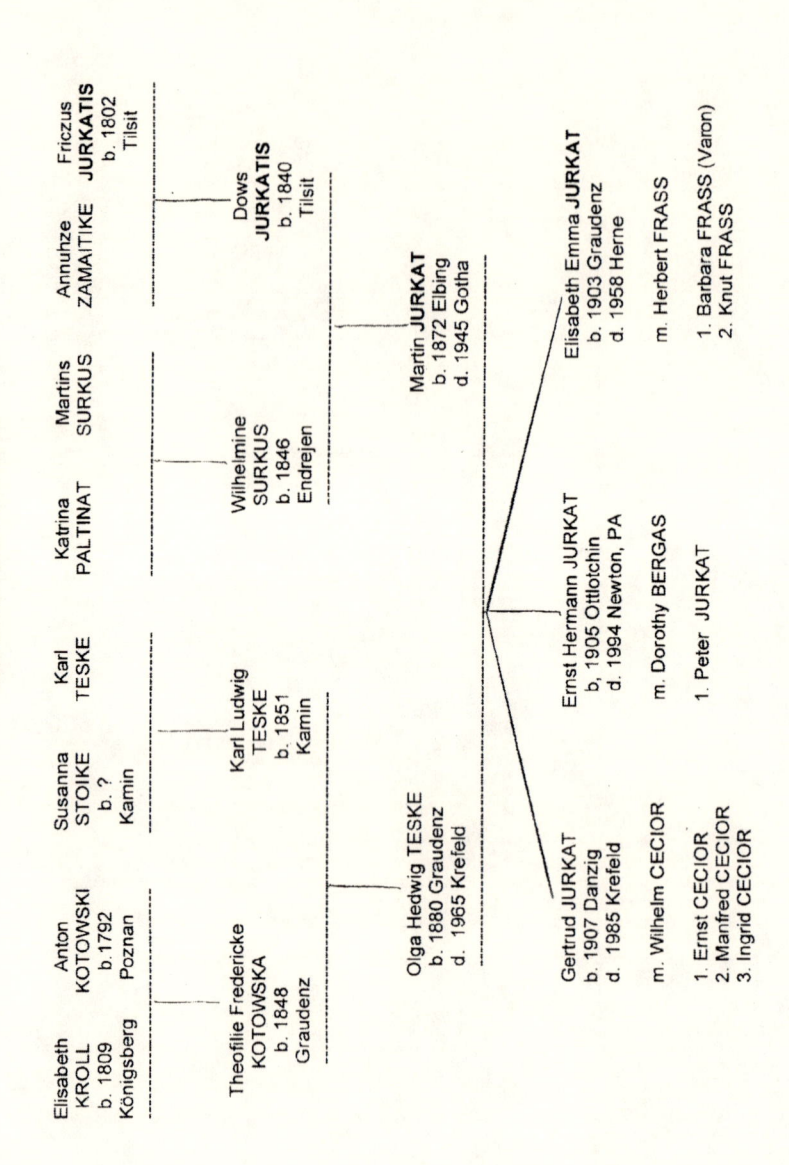

Elisabeth KROLL
b. 1809
Königsberg

Anton KOTOWSKI
b. 1792
Poznan

Susanna STOIKE
b. ?
Kamin

Karl TESKE

Katrina PALTINAT

Martins SURKUS

Annuhze ZAMAITIKE

Friczus JURKATIS
b. 1802
Tilsit

Theofilie Frederickie KOTOWSKA
b. 1848
Graudenz

Karl Ludwig TESKE
b. 1851
Kamin

Wilhelmine SURKUS
b. 1846
Endrejen

Dows JURKATIS
b. 1840
Tilsit

Olga Hedwig TESKE
b. 1880 Graudenz
d. 1965 Krefeld

Martin JURKAT
b. 1872 Elbing
d. 1945 Gotha

Gertrud JURKAT
b. 1907 Danzig
d. 1985 Krefeld

m. Wilhelm CECIOR

1. Ernst CECIOR
2. Manfred CECIOR
3. Ingrid CECIOR

Ernst Hermann JURKAT
b. 1905 Ottlotchin
d. 1994 Newton, PA

m. Dorothy BERGAS

1. Peter JURKAT

Elisabeth Emma JURKAT
b. 1903 Graudenz
d. 1958 Herne

m. Herbert FRASS

1. Barbara FRASS (Varon)
2. Knut FRASS

Engagement Photograph of Maternal Grandparents
Olga Teske and Martin Jurkat

Ernst Jurkat, 12, in Prussian Hussar Uniform.

Top: Elisabeth Jurkat and Herbert Frass, engagement photograph. Elbing, 1940. *Bottom*: Downtown Elbing circa 1940.

With stuffed black bear sent by her father serving in France.

With father on leave in Elbing, East Prussia

Barbara's father Herbert Frass (left) and his older brother, and Barbara's godfather, Werner Frass.

Samstag den 7. November 1931
5. Vorstellung in der Ring-Platzmiete (Deutscher Theaterring)

Neuheit

Marguerite durch Drei

Lustspiel in drei Akten von **Fritz Schwiefert**
Inszenierung: Erich Pabst
Bühnenbild: Werner Fraß

Personen:

Ludwig	Gert Benofsky
Karl	Walter Oehmichen
Lorenz	Wilh. Hoenselaars
Die Dame	Marga Reuter
Jean	Günther Ballier

Der zweite Akt spielt einen Tag nach dem ersten,
der dritte einen Tag nach dem zweiten

Pause nach dem 2. Akt (15 Minuten)

Die Toiletten und Hüte von Frau Reuter stellt die Fa. Landauer zur Verfügung

Anfang 8 Uhr   Ende 10¼ Uhr

Top: Announcement of play (Marguerite Divided by Three)
co-directed by Werner Frass. *Bottom*: Frass, on the right,
in rehearsal probably in Augsburg during the years 1932-1934.

Werner Frass and unknown leading lady probably in rehearsal for a production of Fritz Scherker's opera *Die Gezeichneten* (The Branded) during October 20-26, 1930 in Augsburg

Elisabeth Jurkat (not yet Frass) working
as a bacteriologist in Elbing in the 1930s

Between two Russian soldiers in Gotha,
Soviet-occupied Thuringia, East Germany

Two Frasses: Mother Elisabeth and Daughter Barbara.

Public library membership booklet of
Herbert Frass, Herne, 1950

With high school graduating class in Berlin

Barbara, Herne 1958.
Last picture in Germany

Dorothy and Ernst Jurkat.

In Germantown, Philadelphia, soon after becoming mother.

With former Fairfax County Registrar, friend and mentor Lilyan Spero.

With United States Congressman Gerry Connolly
(then Fairfax County Providence District Supervisor)

Taking the Oath of Office as a member of
the Fairfax Country Electoral Board.

Speaking at Convention of Virginia State Electoral Boards.

The Barbara Varon Volunteer Award

*Presented by the
Fairfax County
Board of Supervisors*

"The best way to find yourself is to lose yourself in the service of others."
Mahatma Gandhi

Part Two

My Journey of Recovery

Chapter Six

The Polish Mystery Man[47]

Barbara had a Polish ancestor named Antoni Kotowski (1792-1875). He was her great great grandfather on her mother's side (see family tree). His memory has survived over six generations largely because he is said to have fought on Napoleon's side against the Russians, to have been imprisoned by the Prussians, and to have written a "history of Poland" while in prison. None of this has ever been verified; sadly, there is no trace of such a history. A few things about him are, nevertheless, better known. They derive from some biographical information scribbled by Barbara's mother on the backside of six 4x6 discarded work-related vouchers from the city agency in Elbing (East Prussia) where she worked as a bacteriologist from 1928 to 1940. The vouchers date from April 1929. Given the German obsession with records and recording, it is unlikely that the vouchers would have been discarded after less than 3-5 years. It is therefore likely that the notations on Kotowski date from the early 1930s at the earliest.

The notes were almost entirely in Polish, which Barbara's mother knew, having been born, grown and lived in a nearly bilingual part of Prussia. Some of them were in the first person, as with

---

[47] I am grateful to Ronald F. Kornell and Elehie N. Skoczylas for their invaluable comments and suggestions and for their reality check of my reality check.

the opening where Kotowski says "I joined the Polish artillery . . ." Others were in the anonymous third person, as with the statement, "Antoni Kotowski died in . . ." And the closing notes were clearly by Barbara's mother, in German. The notes were a mixture of statements copied out verbatim, statements transcribed selectively, and addenda by Barbara's mother. We do not know what sort of document was the basis of these notes. The original source could have been a diary, a Bible, where it was customary to make such entries or notations, something like a memoir, or oral history dictated to Barbara's grandmother. What is certain is that Barbara's mother must have been fully aware of both the importance of the document, and that she might not be able to ever see it again. She took a few things down from it in a hurry on whatever pieces of paper she could find at the moment; she put the six 4x6 pieces neatly in an envelop, which she labeled carefully (all of this before she had any descendants herself), and she managed to preserve the vouchers until they found their way to Barbara's hands and traveled with her to the United States.

A priori, we are fortunate to have two sources of information on Barbara's Polish ancestor: the family lore and the notes I briefly described. However, it is difficult to reconcile the information in the two sources. Moreover, there are serious inconsistencies within each. What I shall do below is lay out what the notes say, provide some necessary historical background, and apply a reality check to the information. I shall not be able to provide definitive answers, especially on the existence of Kotowski's "history of Poland," at this stage. What I shall do is distill the reliable facts about Kotowski the person in order to facilitate the absorption and interpretation of any new information that may become available in the future.

The Notes

The notes start by stating that Antoni Kotowski was born in Bibkowie, Poznan on June 12, 1792. The place with the closest name to "Bibkowie" today is Binkowo, a village in the Sremski district of Poznan province in west-central Poland. Kotowski then says in the first person, "I joined the Polish artillery, Second Group,

The Promise of the Present and the Shadow of the Past

on November 15, 1819, and I ordered my unit to battle at . . . ," listing the following thirteen places:

1. *Liw*
2. *Okuniew*
3. *Wawer*
4. *Grochow*
5. *Deblin*
6. *Ostroleka*
7. Dlugosiad
8. *Rutki*
9. *Tykocyn*
10. Rarygrod
11. *Wilno*
12. *Swaty*
13. Powodymia

Kotowski stressed the *sequence* of the places he took his unit to, numbering them as shown. The nine places in italics are those identifiable on a map of Poland today, with the exception of Wilno, which refers to the capital of today's Lithuania. The other eight are spread over a large part of Poland. Kotowski says that he and his unit went to three more locations but that their names are unknown because they had "crossed the border into Prussia in the dark of night." This seems to have taken place near Dostow on *July 14, 1831*. The text, which is not legible, suggests that the Polish troops were under the command of Generals Guta Chlopowski and Roland Szymanowski, and that those in charge on the Prussian side—those who "accepted us"—were Sztypnagel Krawt, Szmyk J. Vber, and President [*sic*] Szegn Gustem. He continues, "Our troops returned from the border to the village of Pakamory, past Telz, after which we became idle [saw no action] until September [1831], and then we camped in Krolewca." I was not able to locate Dostow where the crossing into Prussia is said to have occurred, nor to identify any of the commanders cited on either side. Telz, or Telsia, the place the troops went by on their return to Polish territory, is located in the north-western part of Lithuania. And

Krolewca, where they camped, seems to refer to Krolewiec, the old name of Könisberg in East Prussia.

Kotowski's account then picks up on April 23, 1832 when he says he arrived in Matawy, a town next to Grudziadz (Graudenz in German) where Barbara's mother as well as her grandmother were born. Kotowski spent the next five years in various places as follows:

> Matawy—April 23, 1832 to June 14, 1832
> Fortyc (?)—June 15, 1832 to October 25, 1836
> Slaska (Upper Silesia in south Poland), Glogow (Lower Silesia in south-western Poland), and Polkowice (Lower Silesia)—October 26, 1836 to February 22, 1837
> Grudziadz—February 23, 1837 to July 10, 1837

He spent the longest time—over four years—during this period in "Fortyc," a place which I could not identify. Nor do we know where Kotowski went after 1837. The rest of the notes are devoted mostly to his offspring.

Kotowski wrote that he had six children between the years 1835 and 1851. He gave the birth place of only one of them—a place, Ogrodzin, I could not locate. But he noted the precise hour of birth of all six, suggesting that he was present at their birth. Only three of the children survived: Fryderyk Wilhelm (1835), Fryderyka Teofila (1848), Barbara's great grandmother, and Maryanna (1851). The Polish text closes by noting that Antoni Kotowski died on May 18, 1875, and that he spent his last days fighting to death "Wielkopoloski" in Poznan. I shall return to this shortly.

At the very end, Barbara's mother writes in German identifying Kotowski's children's mother as Elisabeth Susanna Kroll who was born on June 13, 1809 in Königsberg and died on March 1, 1887. She also refers obliquely to a Konrad Kotowski who married Maria Musulewska. Her switching to her own language suggests that the above information may have come from a different source or from her own knowledge, but that she deemed appropriate to include it where she did.

The Promise of the Present and the Shadow of the Past

Historical Background

Antoni Kotowski's life coincided with a turbulent period in the history of Poland, indeed, of most of Europe. I shall paint the picture in the broadest terms. Kotowski was born three years after the French Revolution (1789), which redrew the map of Europe, and a few months before King Louis XVI and Marie Antoinette were put to death. When he was barely a year old, Poland underwent the second of three partitions among its powerful and competing neighbors: the Kingdom of Prussia, the Russian Empire and Habsburg Austria. The partitions can be viewed as a partition in three stages. The first took place in 1772, the second in 1793, and the third and last one in 1795. As a result, and roughly speaking, Prussia acquired western Poland, including the Poznan province where Kotowski was born, all the way north to Danzig; Austria gained parts of Silesia and Galicia in the south; and eastern Poland, the lion's share amounting to two-thirds of Polish lands, went to Russia. In 1795, the year of the third partition, Poland ceased to exist as an independent, unified state—a status she was not to re-acquire until 1918. Thus, when one talks about the Polish army in the intervening 125 years, one is talking about the army of Poles, not the army of Poland. Understandably, the partitions accentuated the nationalistic feelings of the Polish population and set in motion what has come to be known as the Great Emigration of Polish poets, artists, politicians, noblemen and others to the rest of Europe and the New World.

The Napoleonic Wars (1795-1815) that soon followed and through which Napoleon sought to establish and consolidate his supremacy of Europe made a mess of the partitions. The many battles were fought on, for or through formerly Polish territories. By 1807, Napoleon defeated decisively the armies of the partition partners. He could therefore dictate the terms of the two Treaties of Tilsit with Russia and Prussia that followed days apart that year. The treaty with Prussia resulted in the creation, out of the "Polish territories" which Prussia was forced to give up, of a Duchy of Warsaw—a semi-independent, hybrid state to be ruled by King

Frederick Augustus I of Saxony.[48] The duchy was an anomaly; it was landlocked although not insignificant, as it amounted to one-third of all Prussian territory and it included both Warsaw and Poznan. It was nevertheless on only part of historically Polish lands; the word "Poland" was therefore carefully avoided in its name. The duchy was fundamentally designed to serve French interests, especially, act as a buffer against Russia, and help raise recruits and money for Napoleon. Whether he and his family had left Poznan province by then or not, Kotowski spent his early and mid-teens in the Duchy of Warsaw just described.

Napoleon with his *Grande Armée* crossed through much of partitioned Poland on his way to Russia in 1812 and on his way back in 1813. The Poles in the *Grande Armée* numbered 100,000 of whom just 20,000 survived. The Russian army followed the retreating French army and entered Warsaw in February 1813. For the next two years, the Duchy of Warsaw was ruled as a Tsarist protectorate.[49]

Polish lands were re-allocated again in 1815 by the *Congress of Vienna* which convened after the defeat of Napoleon. The task of the Congress was to redraw Europe's borders, redefine spheres of influence, and reconstruct the balance of power, especially restoring the power of the old dynastic rulers. In the trading of territory that took place, Russia acquired two-thirds of the Duchy of Warsaw, which ceased to exist, and the remainder one-third went to Prussia. Simultaneously, another nominally independent, hybrid state was created, namely, the Congress Kingdom of Poland, to be ruled "in personal union" with Tsar Alexander I of Russia—a constitutional monarchy without its own king but with an absentee king of another nation, in fact, a puppet of Russia. The new Kingdom was smaller than the Duchy of Warsaw, which led to its being referred to by the Polish population "in the

---

[48] This arrangement, whereby a state is ruled by the king of another, is sometimes referred to as two countries being linked by "personal union" and was repeated later.

[49] Norman Davies, *God's Playground: A History of Poland,* Columbia University Press, 2005, Vol. II, pp. 223-224.

affectionate diminutive, *Kongresowca:* the poor little creation of the Congress."[50]

In the beginning, the rule of Tsar Alexander was benevolent and approximated genuine self-rule. The Congress Kingdom had its own parliament (*Sejm*) and army. When Kotowski wrote that he joined the Polish artillery in 1819, he must have meant the Congress army. In addition, Polish was the official language, the Napoleonic Code was applied, and the population enjoyed more freedoms than at any time in the recent past. But things soon began to change. Freedom of the press was abandoned in 1819, the year Kotowski joined the army, and censorship was introduced.[51] The deterioration accelerated after Tsar Alexander I died and was replaced by his more despotic younger brother Tsar Nicolas I in 1825. By 1830, reaction to the increasingly repressive rule, combined with patriotic fervor, led to an uprising by young military cadets, who were soon joined by the general population. By 1831, the uprising and the reaction to it evolved into a full-fledged Polish-Russian war that lasted for ten months. At first, at the battle of Grochow near Warsaw, the Polish forces imposed heavy losses on the unprepared Russian forces. However, the Russians regrouped and defeated the Polish forces decisively at Ostroleka, marking the end of the uprising and, in effect of the Congress Kingdom. The Kingdom was incorporated into Russia and effectively abolished. The event that caused this outcome has entered history books as the *November Uprising.*

The uprising had predictable and painful effects. It accelerated emigration abroad, especially to France which became the center of Polish resistance. Internally, it brought about severe retribution by the Russians, including punishment not just of the uprising leaders, by death, but of the entire population by punitive taxation, confiscation of property, forced military service, closing of university, etc. Worst or most extensive of all were the deportations. As many

---

[50] *Ibid.,* p. 226.
[51] The target of the censors was not merely the Polish population. This was taking place about the time when the Russian poet Pushkin was banished to Russia's southern provinces.

as 80,000 people were condemned to deportation.[52] Many of them perished in Siberia and other remote places, as general amnesty was not declared until 1855, twenty-four years later

The 1830s and 1840s were relatively quiet years partly because of the lasting traumatic effects of the severe repressions. Elisabeth and Antoni Kotowski were busy building a family during this period. Patriotic fervor, never dead, soon reemerged, however. What followed was shaped to a large extent by the activities of Count Alexander Wielopolski (1803-1877). Wielopolski was a Polish aristocrat who, in 1862, was appointed as Head of the Polish Civil Administration by Tsar Alexander II who, in the meantime, had replaced Tsar Nicolas I on his death. He was a defender of Polish culture and interests, including the restoration of greater liberties for the population. He did a great deal for Poland through education, banking and agrarian reform. However, he believed that the best way to achieve more in these and other areas was to seek expanded autonomy, rather than independence, from Russia, and he was confident that this was possible. He went as far as condemning the November 1831 uprising. Russia made limited concessions, while young activists grew increasingly impatient. Fearing the consequences (a new uprising) Wielopolski promoted the conscription of young activists into the Russian Army for twenty years of service. This provoked, rather than prevented, an uprising in January 1863. The youth engaged in urban guerilla activities for a while without marking an important victory. Having antagonized both his Polish countrymen and his masters, Wielopolski went into exile in Germany six months after the uprising, and the uprising was brutally crushed in 1864.

As with the November 1831 uprising, strong reprisals followed. These were more severe, however, because they targeted the soul of Poland, not just its body. In addition to public executions and deportations to remote regions, there were unprecedented attempts at Russification of the education system, abandonment of Polish as an official language, prohibition of printing of Polish books, etc. Polish resistance was crushed. No amnesty followed, even after twenty-five years. For forty years, including the last several

---

[52] *Ibid.*, p. 244.

years of Antoni Kotowsi's life, the Poles of the Congress Kingdom were "submerged into the general stream of life in the Russian Empire. . . . Poland descended once more into the abyss."[53]

Reality Check

Let me start with the information that has come down through the family, which is simple—namely, that Antoni Kotowski fought with Napoleon against Russia, that he was imprisoned by the Prussians, and that he wrote a history of Poland while in captivity. In reality, however, by the time, according to the notes, that Kotowski joined the Polish artillery in 1819, the Napoleonic wars were over, Napoleon and his army had been to Russia and back in defeat, the Congress of Vienna had redrawn the map of Europe, and Napoleon was perishing in the island of Saint Helena. Kotowski, twenty-seven years of age, was serving in the army of the recently created Congress Kingdom of Poland which was ruled by Tsar Alexander I of Russia. Although the plight of the new kingdom's Polish population had begun to deteriorate, there was no armed conflict with Russia until the November Uprising of 1830. Two questions arise:

First, could a young Kotowski have fought alongside Napoleon *before or during* the Russian campaign? He would have been around twenty then. Possible, although had he done so, he would have likely mentioned it in his biographical notes, and with pride. Still, he may have enlisted as an ordinary infantryman, served without participating in the Russian campaign, and been demobilized after 1815. He may have continued studying or returned to farm management afterwards, since the Kotowskis belonged to the landowners class. The experience gained during his earlier army service and in farm management would have contributed to his joining the Polish artillery as an "officer" in 1819. The artillery branch is one where logistics—coordination of procurement, transport and maintenance of big guns and gunpowder—is of prime importance and key to success.

---

[53] *Ibid.*, p. 271.

But who did Kotowski fight between 1819 and 1830 in the thirteen places he so carefully enumerated in his notes? This is more difficult to answer. There may have been skirmishes with the neighboring Prussia, but the localities cited range from literally the suburbs of Warsaw to Wilno in Lithuania and Königsburg in East Prussia. Nor does their sequencing make sense, that is, point to a sensible route; they show instead a zigzag pattern difficult to follow for an artillery unit like Kotowski's. One possibility is that Kotowski was referring to places where his unit was stationed rather than or necessarily to those where they saw combat. More puzzling is the fact that two of the places he mentions first, that is, closer in time to 1819 (namely, Grochow and Ostroleka) are places where major battles occurred—but in 1831 in the aftermath of the November Uprising.

Let me now return to Kotowski's imprisonment and his history of Poland, and start with an assumption and more questions. To write the history of a country—even a simple one, let alone one as complex as Poland's—without access to the necessary documentation, one would need to be in jail for at least 3-4 years *and* be of a certain age. The task can hardly be contemplated from memory and in one's twenties! Where and when could Kotowski have been imprisoned? The Polish army is not likely to have been engaged in hostilities against either Prussia or Russia in the two decades after the November Uprising which, as seen, were a rather peaceful period during which Kotowski and his wife raised a family. Besides, it would have made more sense for Kotowski to have been imprisoned by the more hostile Russians rather than the Prussians, unless the Prussians imprisoned him for or on behalf of the Russians, their allies and former partition partners. This possibility is suggested by the notes copied and left by Barbara's mother, as explained below.

The notes conclude with the statement in the third person that Kotowski, toward the end of his life, *fought "Wielkopowski" to death* or (the translation is not clear) fought "Wielkopoloski" up to his death. The quotes are on the original. Wilekopoloski is the name of neither a place nor a person or family in Poland. There is a place called Wielkopolska (ending with the letter "a"), which is also called Greater Poland and refers to an area of the country corresponding roughly to Poznan province, but no place called Wielkopolski. The quotation marks may have been added by the original writer or Barbara's mother who could not recognize the name. It seems quite logical that the word was mis-spelled and may have been Wielopolski, referring to Count Alexander Wielopolski, the pro-Russian civil administrator of the Congress Kingdom who favored accommodation and autonomy over independence, condemned the November Uprising and caused in part the uprising of January 1863. This would make sense; opposing Wielopolski, as most Polish nationalists did, may have caused Kotowski to be jailed even though he may not have been an instigator of the uprising.

None of the above is certain. The story about Kotowski that has survived is that he fought with (on the side of) Napoleon, was imprisoned in the process and wrote a history of Poland, all back to back, compressed in time. What I believe is more likely is that he may have fought with Napoleon in his youth but was imprisoned by the Prussians and wrote his history later in life. Had he been jailed and written the history earlier in life, there would have been a better chance that it would surface, that he would search for it, that he would rewrite parts of it, leave traces of it or referred specifically to it himself later in life, none of which occurred. What is even more likely is that that the so-called "history of Poland" was, rather, a memoir—an account of Kotowski's experience, which is easier to draft in the isolation of a jail.

In 1960, Barbara wrote, "upon his release from jail, Kotowski derived his sole income from the Catholic Church, having lost his entire estate," without indicating why or what, if anything, he did for the Church. She added, "If my family background is not one of wealth, it is at least, I daresay, a colorful one."[54]

I remember vaguely that, in the 1990s or before the collapse of the Soviet Union, Barbara heard—I don't know how—that Russia had returned Kotowski's history of Poland to the Polish government in a special ceremony. If the history or memoir indeed exists, it must be in the National Archives of Poland, but this remains to be determined.

---

[54] From a school assignment on her family background which she prepared during her junior year at the University of Pennsylvania.

Chapter Seven

The Ambiguous Exit of Werner Frass, Theater Director

Werner Frass was Barbara's uncle as well as her godfather. He was born in 1900 in Berlin and worked for most of his adult life as a technical director of both theater and opera. According to official records, he died in 1942 in Danzig, then part of Germany. Within his close family at least, a question has surrounded the circumstances of Werner's death. The suspicion has persisted that he might not have died of natural causes, given the strong anti-Nazi views of Barbara's family on both of her parents' sides. The suspicion was prompted and sustained in part by the Third Reich's well-documented exploitation of the theater—indeed, of all arts—to spread and impose the Nazi ideology.[55] This chapter highlights what we know and do not know about Werner Frass—the person, the professional, and his death.

---

[55] See Gerwin Stobl, *The Swastika and the Stage: German Theater and Society, 1933-45*, 2007; Amselm Heinrich, *Entertainment, Propaganda, Education: Regional Theater in Germany and Britain, 1918 and 1945*, 2008; and Alan E. Steinweis, *Arts, Ideology and Economics in Nazi Germany: The Reich Chambers of Music, Theater, and the Visual Arts*, 1993.

Werner, the Person

Werner Frass was born on June 18, 1900 in Berlin to Maria Anna Emma Schiemann and Otto Paul Frass. He was the first of two sons and two years older than his brother Herbert, Barbara's father. As an adult, he was strong built, taller than his brother, and lighter skinned. He was devoted to his profession of theater directing, which he seemed to enjoy greatly. In fact, he built his personal life around it. He moved largely in theater circles, enjoying the company of the theater in-crowd, especially actresses. The fact that more photographs survive of him than of his brother—most of them showing him at work—testifies to his pride in his occupation. He did not have to interrupt his work with the advent of the war, since he was never inducted into the military. This was not unusual, given the Regime's desire to convey a sense of normalcy and the opportunity that theater offered for propaganda and indoctrination.

Werner never married. He was nevertheless surrounded by beautiful women who seemed to adore him. He had a sunny disposition, a *joie de vivre*, and lived as a *bon vivant*. He and his brother were quite different in many respects. But one thing they had in common was their individualism and character of free spirit. It is difficult to guess how they developed or from whom they inherited this trait. Apparently, they lost their father at a young age.

Little is known of Werner's family bonds, except that he embraced enthusiastically being Barbara's godfather, sending her a silver baby-feeding set as a gift. He also seems to have established a bond with Barbara's mother, who had a strong individualistic, progressive side herself and was probably responsible for collecting the photographs of Werner at work which have come down to us.

Werner died on October 6, 1942, reportedly, after suffering a heart attack in Danzig, where he had been working since 1939. His death and the cause of death are recorded in the *Deutsches Bühnenjahrbuch* (Theater Yearbook) for 1943, the year immediately following his death.

This is practically all that is known about Werner Frass' personal life. The paucity of it can be explained by the limited nature of the information that has come down directly (through the family) to us. Werner's life overlapped with his brother's, his sister-in-law's and Barbara's only for a very short time. Barbara had no recollection of him, as she was barely two years old when he died. Her mother must have met Werner about the time she married his brother, a little over two years before he died. Contacts in the following years were limited because of the war and the fact that they lived in different cities. So, for the most part, information or news about Werner dried up even before his death. It is, nevertheless, possible to piece together a picture of his professional life that is more complete than one on his personal life.

Researching His Professional Life

The account of Werner Frass' professional life that follows draws heavily on the work carried out by Becke Buffalo of New York City, supplemented by further research. Ms. Buffalo's findings are based on an *ad hoc* investigation she undertook at Barbara's and my request during two trips to Germany in 1997 and 1999.[56] Our interest in the subject and our request to Ms. Buffalo were prompted by the family lore concerning the mysterious circumstances of Werner Frass' death. We also felt a sense of responsibility toward him. Behind this was the fact that Werner Frass had no direct descendant, legal or other. The only person who came the closest to that status was Barbara, his goddaughter; she was the eldest of his only brother's two children.

---

[56] This chapter on Werner Frass would not have been possible without Ms. Buffalo's painstaking and insightful groundwork. Ms. Buffalo is married to Lars Hanson, a graduate of the Yale Drama School, who accompanied her on both trips and had some input into her work. I wish to acknowledge also the helpful comments and suggestions of Simone Seym, Ph.D., Karlsruhe University (Germany), in German Studies, Literature and Culture, and the Sorbonne (Paris), in Performing and Cinematic Arts. Dr. Seym is currently affiliated with the Goethe Institute in Washington, D.C.

The background information we could provide Ms. Buffalo before she undertook the task was limited to a dozen or so photographs of Werner Frass, at leisure and at work. The survival and preservation of these photographs attest to Werner Frass' public persona, the family's pride in his career, and the apparent bond between him and Barbara's mother.

Ms. Buffalo focused her investigation on Berlin (1997 trip) and the cities of Osnabrück, Augsburg and Leipzig (1999), where Werner Frass served as stage or production manager during, roughly, the years 1930-1935. Her research activities encompassed:

- contacting or visiting a range of institutions dealing with theater and the performing arts in general, such as training academies, libraries, museums, and the theaters themselves;
- consulting theater yearbooks, address books, theater staff directories, performance programs, schedules and reviews, theater magazines, and state and local archives;
- and interacting with selected theater personalities in the time available.

Ms. Buffalo presented her findings to us in two stages (November 1997 and December 2001) and in the form of photocopies of the pages of publications (yearbooks, magazines) where Werner Frass is cited; photographs of the theaters which have survived; press announcements and programs (playbills) of the plays shown; and addresses as well as city maps marking the locations of the theaters and the residences of Werner Frass in the various cities, where available. In addition to rich annotations, she supplied some analysis to contextualize her findings to great benefit. The rest of this chapter weaves the story emerging from these documents, other family sources and further research, and expands on Ms. Buffalo's findings and conclusions, in particular.

Werner's Professional Activities: Brief Chronology

The first written reference to Werner Frass as a theater professional dates from 1927 and comes from the German

Theater Yearbook.[57] Beginning in that year and until the middle of 1930, Werner served as production manager (*Theatermeister*) of a touring (itinerant) theater group from Berlin[58] which produced plays in various provinces and cities. Where Werner obtained his professional education and training is not known. The question arises because he was rather young for the post he held.

In 1930/31, Werner Frass worked in the same capacity of production manager at the Stadttheater in Osnabrück, a mid-size city in northwest Germany (noteworthy as the birthplace of the writer Erich Maria Remarque). Frass collaborated there with the *Intendant* (artistic director) Erich Pabst (1890-1955), not to be confused with the Czech-born, Austrian film director G. W. Pabst (1885-1967)—director of the classic Weimar film *Pandora's Box*, among others. The Eric Pabst-Werner Frass collaboration marked the beginning of a long association between the two. As Ms. Buffalo pointed out, it is quite common in the theater world for artistic teams that work well together to continue their collaboration.

From 1932 to 1934, Frass served as production manager *and* stage manager (*Bühnenmeiste*r) at the Stadttheater in Augsburg, working again with Erich Pabst. Augsburg, located in the southwest of Bavaria, has the distinction of being the second oldest city of Germany after Trier. It is also the city where the Frass coat of arms originated in 1284 with ancestor Hugo Frass. The Marxist poet and playwright Bertolt Brecht (1898-1956), a contemporary of Frass, was a native of Augsburg.

The year 1935 found Frass working at two theaters in Leipzig—the Stadttheater and the Neues Theater—the latter being devoted to opera. And in 1936 Frass was listed in Germany's Theater Yearbook as being associated with the Staatlisches Schauspielhaus in Hamburg. This is reportedly a large, 1848-seat theater, which is as well regarded today, as it was then.

The following year, 1937, Frass returned to Berlin to work at the Neues Künstler-Theater, collaborating once again with Erich Pabst. The latter was initially guest director and then formal director of that theater, which was also known as Lustspielhaus. For most of the

---

[57] *Deutsches Bühnenjahrbuch*, 1928.
[58] *Wanderbühnen des Verbandes der deutschen Volksbühnenvereine.*

next 3-4 years, 1938/39 to 1942, when he died, Werner was under contract as operations/production manager with the Staatstheater in Danzig, which was a Free City between the two world wars but a German city throughout the Second World War.

The Work Itself

Information on the substance or focus of Werner Frass' work is available beginning with his period in Osnabrück when he worked closely with Erich Pabst at the Stadttheater there. Pabst was already well known then, thanks to his success as a movie actor and playwright; he was also to become a film director, although not of the caliber or reputation of G. W. Pabst. Frass and (Erich) Pabst may have met earlier in Berlin, but beginning in 1930 their names appear professionally as a pair in both Osnabrück and Augsburg. It seems that almost the entire Osnabrück ensemble moved with Pabst, Frass and company to Augsburg. Understandably, there were also many overlaps in terms of shows; several productions that played in Osnabrück seem to have been remounted in Augsburg. Incidentally, the year 1930 was a pivotal one for the Stadttheater in Osnabrück, since it was in danger of closing because of cuts in government support. Erich Pabst led an aggressive and innovative campaign to increase the subscriber base and was able to keep the theater open. I shall return to this later.

The artistic or political leanings of Werner Frass can be deduced to some extent from the productions (plays, operettas, operas) he worked on or which were being shown in the same theaters. Following is a sample of them, grouped by category. The list does not include those productions which he worked on in the last few years of his life, in Danzig, as Ms. Buffalo's research did not cover this period.

Plays

Alkestis (Alcestis), a drama/tragedy by Euripides
Wilhelm Tell (William Tell), by Friedrich von Schiller
Der Heiratsantrag (The Proposal), a play by Anton Chekhov
Die Weber (The Weaver), a drama by Gerhart Hauptmann

Elga, by Gerhart Hauptmann
Die andere Seite (Journey's End), a drama by R. C. Sherritt
Marguerite durch Drei (Marguerite Divided by Three), comedy by Fritz Schwiefert
Elisabeth von England, by Ferdinand Bruckner
*Der Hauptmann (*The Captain*) von Köpenick,* by Carl Zuckmayer
Reims, by Friedrich Bethge

Operettas

Der lustige Krieg (The Merry War), by Johann Strauss II
Das Land des Lächelns (The Land of Smiles), Franz Lehar
Viktoria und ihr Husar (Victoria and Her Husar), by Paul Abraham

Operas

Aida, by Giuseppe Verdi
Die Zauberflöte (The Magic Flute), by Wolfgang Amadeus Mozart
Boris Godunow, by Modest Mussorgsky
Die Gezeichneten (The Branded), by Franz Schreker
Tristan und Isolde, by Richard Wagner

The productions listed are quite diverse or inclusive in several respects. They cover both classic and contemporary works, both comedy and drama, light operetta as well as serious opera, and works by both German and foreign writers/composers. They display a progressive, anti-Nazi tendency, though one which is not strong, consistent or clear-cut. Hints of such a tendency can be found in the attention given to writers of Werner's and Pabst's generation or of generations overlapping with theirs, such as Abraham (1892-1960), Hauptmann (1862-1946), Sherritt (1896-1975), Bruckner (1891-1958), Zuckmayer (1888-1977), and Shreker (1878-1934).

The list is marked by contrasts, not just diversity. The choice of plays in Osnabrück ranged from the light operetta and comedy of Lehar's *Land of Smiles* to the naturalism of Hauptmann depicting the poverty and hard lives of weavers. His work of that name, *Die Weber,* had been a revolutionary play for the socialist Left when it premiered at the end of the 19th century and was banned for some time. Hauptmann had won the Nobel Prize for literature in 1912 and was a national institution, despite his being Jewish. He was, however, associated with dramas of poverty, exploitation and misery, and blamed by the Nazis for sapping the nation's strength for that reason.[59] Although staunchly anti-Hitler at heart, he stayed in Germany and continued to write after 1933, trying to project some outside conformity. When, in 1938, a Hungarian writer asked him privately why he had not left the country, Hauptmann, who was 76 then, replied shouting angrily, "Because I am a coward, do you understand?"[60]

Another bold choice among the plays Frass was associated with was the war play *Die Andere Seite* (Journey's End). War plays and novels had been in vogue since about 1928, but *Journey's End* was not a typical such play. It was written by a British playwright, R. C. Sherritt, who served in World War I, and it depicted the author's experience at the front in a naturalistic manner. The play's German title, *Die andere Seite*, the exact translation of which would be "The Other Side," seemed to encourage a sympathetic look at the "enemy."

Also an intriguing choice was the production of the opera *Die Gezeichneten* by Franz Schreker, a progressive composer of half-Jewish descent. The Nazis considered Schreker's apocalyptic opera to be degenerate and banned it in 1933, as they did eventually all of his music. He was immediately relieved of all his prominent teaching responsibilities, including at the Prussian Academy of Arts, at the same time as the modernist composer Schoenberg. Soon after, he suffered a stroke and died, his reputation lying in tatters for decades to come. His opera *Die Gezeichneten* was revived in 2005 as the opening production of the prestigious Salzburg Festival in Austria. In the United States, only in 2010 did Schreker's operas begin getting a second look.[61]

---

[59] Strobl, op. cit., p. 178.
[60] As reported in Richard J. Evans, *The Coming of the Third Reich*, 2003, p. 412.
[61] "After a Century, a Composer's Day in the Sun," *New York Times,* July 25, 2010.

With hindsight, the willingness of Frass and Pabst to take risk is suggested by their association with at least two more people. One was Carl Zuckmayer, who had been appointed dramaturge at the *Deutsches Theater* in Berlin, jointly with Bertold Brecht, in 1924. In 1931, his play *Der Hauptmann von Köpenick*, which was also produced in Augsburg, proved a great success, but when the Nazis came to power in 1933, his works were prohibited. Zuckmayer and his family had to flee to the United States via Switzerland in 1939. Frass and Pabst also produced one of the operettas of Paul Abraham who, similarly, felt compelled to flee to the Unites States after the events of 1933, but returned to Germany in 1956, where he died four years later.

Yet the repertoires of Frass, Pabsts and their theaters also included the works of the openly anti-semitic Wagner and the vicious racist Bethge. Unlike the renowned Wagner, Friedrich Bethge was a mediocre playwright who "joined the (Nazi) party in 1932 and crawled his way up via Hinkle (State Commisar for theater affairs) and the SS to become chief dramaturge and acting Intendant [director] in Frankfurt, [but] had little or no success with critics and public."[62] The Bethge productions, such as the play *Reims* that the Frass-Pabst duo mounted, were not as racist as his brutally anti-Polish and anti-Slav *Prussian Trilogy*. Bethge was, nevertheless, a proud and loyal Nazi, who was known and behaved as the "SS playwright." He was not only able to have his plays produced, but he is also said to have come to the theater at least once in his SS uniform. He was a former a military man who had been awarded two Iron Crosses and was wounded five times. As he put it, war was "the primary experience that had made him a dramatist."[63]

The picture that emerges from the choice of productions mostly in Osnabrück and Augsburg highlighted above suggests a tendency to compromise in order to preserve artistic viability in an era of cultural repression. As Ms. Buffalo pointed out on the basis of the theater programs and related writings of the time, "the context [surrounding Frass' and Pabst's work] is mixed, ranging

---

[62] John Willett, *The Theater of the Weimar Republic*, 1988, p. 184.
[63] As quoted in Stobl, op. cit. p. 98.

from harmless to even slightly anti-Nazi. But other materials are clearly pandering to Nazi authorities." This can be attributed to both political and economic factors or realities. Much has been written about the political pressure exerted by the Regime on all arts, theater in particular.[64] Theater had possessed high political significance in the Weimar republic. It had probably been the most consistently controversial branch of the arts. Inevitably, it was also the first part of German culture to undergo thorough nazification, starting with the placing of all arts under the jurisdiction of a newly created Propaganda Ministry led by the infamous Goebbels. Within a few weeks of Hitler's becoming chancellor, the swastika flag was flying on most theaters. In a 1933 photograph that survives, Werner Frass is shown with a group of associates against the backdrop of the Augsburg Stadttheater draped similarly in the vertical Nazi banners. The message could not have been clearer.

The early 1930s, when Frass became very active in his profession, were economically difficult times in Germany in general and for theaters, in particular, which prompted Pabst's intervention to "save" the Osnabrück theater, as noted earlier. Investment funds were particularly scarce. After long delays, the Augsburg theater could be renovated in 1937/38 with fresh government funds. Hitler himself intervened because the theater produced a good deal of Wagner, which Hitler loved and came to see in Augsburg from time to time.

The Osnabrück and Augsburg theaters were not the only ones facing financial difficulty in the early thirties. The most affected were the so-called provincial theaters. To help them, Pabst solicited declarations of support from some of the country's leading or rising artists, including the likes of the composer Richard Strauss, the expressionist dramatist Georg Keiser, the activist playwright Paul Kornfeld, and the writer Max Epstein. Many of the declarations, which Pabst reproduced in the theater playbills, combined the message of support for regional theaters with an anti-war message, and apparently helped the theaters' cause. Typical of the messages was Keiser's succinct statement: "War planes and tanks are not necessary for life; theater is." Epstein's statement stressed theater's

---

[64] See, for example, the works by Stoble, Heinrich and Steinweis cited earlier.

important role in "decentralization," which ran against the Nazis' philosophy. And Kornfeld argued against producing the same plays again and again, stressing the need for new voices. It is ironic that the revitalization of the theaters with the help of leftist, anti-war artists was to serve the fascist regime.

Werner Frass' political views, including his views on artistic freedom, may have been responsible for his rather short service in Leipzig in 1935. On July 1 of that year, he left the *Neues Theater* with a formal resignation. Apparently, the theater had a great many hard-core Nazis who were working assiduously to purge it of those who were not. In one case, an actress, who also worked as a secretary in the theater, felt that Detlef Sierck, director of the Altes Theater in Leipzig, was not Nazi enough to be directing plays there. She was also apparently quite upset that Sierck had never cast her in large roles. She wrote a postcard to some Nazi official stating her concern and requesting that Sierck be removed, and she intentionally left the postcard face-up in the out-tray so that others could see it. Sierck, who learned of it, tried to defend himself, minimizing the event, but he left Leipzig and Germany soon thereafter. Interestingly, the theater administration kept a list of its personnel, especially actors, identifying those who were members of the Nazi party, which must have been common practice then. Frass was not on the list.

Questions: Answered and Not Answered

Many questions arise in connection with the evolution of Werner's life, both personal and professional. The most important or persisting one concerns whether he was killed by the Regime for political reasons. The fact that his death from a heart attack was noted in black and white in the National Theater Yearbook may be dismissed on the grounds that, as Ms. Buffalo put it, "they could write anything they wished in those days." However, there are several arguments against the "killed for political reasons" theory, circumstantial but strong, nevertheless.

- In a letter he wrote from Danzig to Barbara's mother in Berlin on September 17, 1942, three weeks before his death—a letter which has come to light recently—Werner gave no indication of being in any sort of political trouble.[65] The letter dealt with routine, mundane matters such as: the prior exchange of letters and packages; his intention to write to his brother (who was in the navy) later that day and to send her the "fabric" he had promised; inquiring about Barbara, his goddaughter; and including "a little something" (cash) to buy "the little one" some gifts with. Rather telling in the current context is his reporting how extremely busy he was, a situation that was getting "worse and worse," leading him to wonder, "I don't know how I'll make it to the end of the [theater] season." This adds credence to his death unexpectedly of a heart attack brought on by the extreme stress related to work. Incidentally, the letter—the only one of his which survives—reveals him as a warm person, caring for family ties.

- Werner Frass was a technical rather than artistic director throughout his career. Technical directors do not normally have a say on the selection of plays or lead actors, compared to theater management or the artistic director; that is, their *potential* for or danger of antagonizing the authorities is markedly less than in the case of, say, the artistic director. The suspicion about Werner Frass' death survived in the family, including Barbara and myself, partly because of misunderstanding and exaggeration of his role until Ms. Buffalo clarified it.
- Nor is it certain that Werner Frass had the *incentive* to take the risk of revealing his political/artistic beliefs. Although he displayed progressive leanings, there is no evidence that he engaged in strong anti-Nazi behavior which made him a threat or dangerous. He was anti-Nazi and a non-party member but cautious. He did manage, after all, to work professionally for nine years, 1933-42, under Nazi rule. During this period, Erich Pabst, the artistic director he was associated with most closely and longest, managed to remain quite active in theater, mostly in Münster.

---

[65] The letter was among the various family papers stored by Doris, Barbara's sister-in-law, in her basement.

"On the one hand, he [Pabst] seems to have been a loyal democrat during the Weimar Republic, on the other, he appeared almost a devoted admirer of Hitler in the latter half of the 1930s."[66] This is not to imply, for Werner, guilt by association; he and Pabst do not seem to have worked together, in any case, after 1939. It is merely to illustrate the spirit of the time, when many artists were willing to change according to the dominant political atmosphere.

- Frass may have had strong self-preservation instincts, driven partly by his love of the good life, and the fact that the Nazis made sure to shower senior theater professionals with benefits, luxuries, honors, and other rewards. While there is no suggestion that Werner Frass, swayed by these, over-compromised, let alone collaborated, his continuing to work in theater from 1933 to 1942 remains as intriguing as his early death.
- There is no doubt that a large number of theater professionals committed suicide, were murdered or vanished under the Nazis. But the Nazis' control over the arts and the artists was not uniform; that is, they made exceptions whenever they had to. In theater, experienced, non-Nazi professionals—at least those halfway acceptable ideologically, including part-Jewish ones—were retained or tolerated, sometimes with the knowledge and blessings of Goebbels and Goering, who loved opera. Party pragmatists immersed in the arts sometimes won over ideological zealots.[67]
- Finally, had Werner been assassinated for political reasons, there would have been no reason or incentive for the Nazi Regime to fake it, so-to-speak, given their open record of murder and their disregard of public opinion. On the contrary, they would have publicized it to teach theater folk a lesson.

Yet, more light could have been shed on Werner Frass' death by (a) studying more closely his professional life in Danzig during

---

[66] Heinrich, op. cit., pp. 103-104.
[67] Stobl, op. cit., p. 175.

the three years preceding his death, (b) exploring his personal life, including his health records, given his death at a relatively young age, and (c) focusing on his aesthetics . . . on how he carried out his work, his likes and dislikes, priorities, style, etc. It is important to note that he left no letter, neither on this nor on any other matter—this, in a letter-writing society, despite the advent of the telephone. Could this have been an accident?

In closing, aspects of enigma surround the life of Werner Frass, his death, and its aftermath. His memory has been a victim of circumstances. In 1950, when his brother escaped to West Germany, where inquiring about Werner's last days would have been possible—which he no doubt would have initiated—he (Barbara's father) was dying himself.

Chapter Eight

A Life Lost and Remade: The Story of Ernst Jurkat[68]

Ernst Hermann Jurkat (1905-1994) was the younger brother of Barbara's mother, Elisabeth. I talked about their parents in Chapert I. Ernst was born on June 7, 1905 in Ottlotschin, a small town in the region of Western Prussia, which in 1919 became part of the independent state of Poland. The region became known as the Polish Corridor during the interwar years (1919-39), and its capital, Danzig (now Gdansk), was declared a Free City by the League of Nations. Ottlotschin (now Otlotzyn or Ottloczynck) is situated roughly 50 miles south of Danzig and near the city of Thorn (now Torun), a UNESCO World Heritage Site, on both banks of the Vistula river. Although small, Ottlotschin was an important town then, being located on the Prussian side of the Prussian-Russian border. It was the site of a railroad car interchange between the two countries, which must have caused Ernst's father, a career customs official, to be assigned

---

[68] I would like to thank Arden Alexander (Library of Congress), Dr. Christof Biggeleben (economic historian, Berlin), and Dr. Simone Seym (Goethe-Institut, Washington, D.C.) for pointing me to valuable sources of information and for helping me to interpret and contextualize some of the information.

there. Dorothy Jurkat (1904-1990), Ernst's wife, was born on May 3, 1904 in Berlin. She was the daughter of Therese Feilchenfeld and Albert Bergas. They were both Jewish and quite observant. Her father owned a highly successful manufacturing enterprise that produced silverware.

Dorothy and Ernst were married on September 3, 1932 in Berlin and, in 1935, they had a son, Peter, there. They were forced to flee Germany separately in 1938—he first and then, with agonizing delays, his wife and their son. They were not to be reunited until February 1946 in the United States. This chapter deals with Ernst's life journey and that momentous event.

The Kiel Years (1926-1932)

Kiel is the capital city of the northern German state of Schleswig-Holstein. It is located on the Baltic Sea, 56 miles north of Hamburg. It is the site of the University of Kiel known as Christian-Albrecht University in Germany, after the nobleman who founded it in 1665. Ernst Jurkat started his university education at age nineteen (1924) in Kiel, studying economics, philosophy, sociology, and law. In 1926, after spending three semesters at Ludwig Maximilians Universty in Munich, he returned to the University of Kiel, where he would spend the next six years. Soon after taking a course with Professor Ferdinand Tönnies, he became successively his assistant, protégé, disciple, and friend. Ferdinand Tönnies (1855-1936) was a German sociologist and political scientist who pioneered sociology as an academic discipline and published more than 900 works in his lifetime. He influenced Jurkat deeply and on many levels—intellectual, political and personal. Despite their difference in age, the two men were personally alike in many ways. For many years after they met, Jurkat's association with Tönnies shaped not only how others—friends, colleagues and family—saw him, but how he saw himself. Many of the people who helped Jurkat come to the United States in 1941 were people from Tönnies' entourage whom he had met in Kiel. The entourage was like a Who's Who of social scientists. Any review of Ernst Jurkat's life and career must, therefore, start with some background on Ferdinand Tönnies.

Tönnies: His Life and Work[69]

Ferdinand Tönnies was born to a Lutheran family in 1855 on a farm in an area of Germany (Nordfriesland) which was then under Danish sovereignty. He obtained his Ph.D. at the University of Tübingen, one of Germany's oldest, in 1877, and taught at the University of Kiel for most of his life. He began as a "private lecturer" (roughly equivalent to professor without tenure) there and published *Gemeinschaft und Gesellschaft* (Community and Society), the work he is most known for, in 1887.[70] He was thirty-two years old then.

Tönnies identified with pro-labor social causes starting early on in his long career. His outspoken defense of the Hamburg longshoremen's strike in 1896-97 made him suspect. Chancellor Bismarck (1815-1898) was interested in coping with labor movements by legislation and police action rather than through negotiation. As a result, Tönnies' academic advancement was put on hold. He was not made a full professor at Kiel until 1909. In that year, together with Max Weber and others, he founded the German Sociological Association and, two years later, the Statistical Association. He was finally "called to a professorial chair" (earned tenure) in 1913 and continued to teach at Kiel. He joined the Social Democratic Party (SPD, after its German name) in 1930 and spoke as well as published against the rise of the National Socialists (Nazis). As a result, he was declared "politically unreliable" and ousted from his post in 1933, being deprived of his status as emeritus professor and his pension. He died in 1936 lonely, isolated and poor. His financial difficulties were aggravated and perpetuated by his prohibition from publishing to supplement his income, as he had done before. His publications (books, monographs, articles) fell from 31 in 1932 to a meager 2 in 1936.

---

[69] There are at least half a dozen biographies or biographical essays on Tönnies. The latest and most comprehensive among these, and the one with the most numerous and specific references to Ernst Jurkat, is: Uwe Carstens, *Ferdinand Tönnies—Friese und Weltbürger*, Norderstedt, 2005.

[70] The work was first published in Leipzig. It was not translated into English until 1957, a full fifty years later.

Tönnies showed early interest in the then neglected English political philosopher Thomas Hobbes (1588-1679). He made several trips to England and France, where Hobbes had lived, and discovered several original manuscripts by him. In 1896, he published what became a standard work on Hobbes' life and contributions.[71] He interested his students and friends—among them, the historian of philosophy Cay von Brockdorff (1874-1941)—in studying Hobbes. And in 1929, together with Brockdorff, he established the Hobbes Society in England.

Hobbes was a contemporary of Descartes, Galileo and Cromwell. He admired and taught mathematics, among other subjects. He is known for his theory of the state, which he expounded in his major work, *Leviathan* (1651). He believed in individual rights, but he jumped from individuals' innate fear of violence to the need to grant the sovereign absolute authority so as to provide peace and security for all. He advocated that individuals enter into a social contract, a *covenant*, with each other, ceding their natural rights for the sake of protection by a strong sovereign. He was a royalist who believed in the evils of democracy and that despotism is better than anarchy—views that, during the English Civil War (1641-1651), led him into self-imposed exile in Paris.

Hobbes contributed to diverse fields, including history, philosophy, theology, ethics, and political science; he is therefore difficult to classify. While what Ferdinand Tönnies did for Hobbes in terms of reviving interest in him is clear, what Hobbes did for Tönnies—his contribution to Tönnies' own views—is subject to speculation.

Tönnies laid the foundation for scientific, systematic sociology beginning with his seminal work, the aforementioned *Gemeinschaft und Gesellschaft*, in 1887. In it he distinguished between two types of social grouping. The first, *Gemeinschaft,* is akin to a pre-modern rural community which is formed by itself, out of its members' interest in and bonds with each other, and reflects the shared desire to preserve those bonds. The second, *Gesellschaft,* resembles instead a modern, urban community where *self-interest,* rather than care for others, predominates, and the

---

[71] *Hobbes: Leben und Lehre* (His Life and Teachings), Stuttgart, 1896.

objective is serving individual aims and goals. Broadly speaking, the work contrasted a traditional society and a modern-day capitalistic one. While Tönnies did not defend either type of society, his distinction between the two was at the cornerstone of his theory of dynamic social change, which contrasted with the static, romantic view that preceded him.

Tönnies' work was not received well by academic/governing circles under Kaiser Wilhelm II (1859-1941). The distinction between *Gemeinschaft* and *Gesellschaft* was criticized for over-generalizing differences between societies. It was also seen by the authorities as favoring the demands of the increasingly vocal labor movement in an era of rapid industrialization. Yet the book went through several printings during the Weimar Republic and spawned follow-up research, which continues to this day.

Tönnies did not stop there. He distinguished between three types of sociology: *pure or theoretical* sociology, which dealt with abstract constructions, as *Gemeinschaft und Gesellschaft* did; *applied* sociology, which took account of the impact of economic, political and cultural forces on society; and *empirical or inductive* sociology, *based* on observations on the ground through field studies. He focused increasingly on empirical research as a tool for formulating social policy and guiding social work in order to bring about social change. However, he did so without abandoning his interest in pure and applied sociology. He believed, in fact, that sociology should combine all three approaches. His interest in social reform through empirical research involved him in the study of numerous fields such as history, economics, ethnography, demography, and the sociology of crime, in all of which he made significant contributions and involved Ernst Jurkat, his last known assistant. Tönnies was especially drawn to *sociography*, the proper use of statistical data to describe social phenomena.

Jurkat and Tönnies

Ernst Jurkat must have impressed Tönnies soon after he came to Kiel University. In 1927, even before becoming his assistant formally, together with Eduard Georg Jacoby, who preceded him in that role, he helped Tönnies complete a major work titled *Suicides in Schleswig-Holstein: A Sociological-Statistical Study.*[72] Tönnies had several assistants, but he considered Jurkat the "most gifted" among them, even among a group that included Rudolf Heberle, his own son-in-law.[73] He relied on Jurkat for a variety of tasks on a variety of subjects: drafting presentations, papers and books dealing with pure and applied sociology. He took him to professional meetings and retreats, as well as on professional trips, both within Germany and abroad. And he made him part of his inner circle, as well as his family.[74] The person who came closest to playing this role was the aforementioned Jacoby, although he left Kiel before Jurkat did.[75]

I should add parenthetically that since Tönnies was, for years, identified with *Gemeinschaft und Gesellschaft* (GuG) and Jurkat was identified with Tönnies, within his family at least, Jurkat became identified with this work specifically. GuG was, however, completed forty years *before* Ernest Jurkat began working with and for Tönnies, although neither man ever strayed far from GuG's theses intellectually.

Following are illustrations of the range of activities which Jurkat carried out with or on behalf of Tönnies in 1928-29:

- In 1928, together with Lauritz Lauritzen, Jurkat helped Tönnies to prepare a lecture on *Wirtschaft—Politik—Geist*. Lauritzen (1910-1980) was a native of Kiel. He studied law and political science at Kiel University, where he met Tönnies. A social democrat, he served as head of various ministries in the West German government after the war.

---

[72] *Der Selbstmord in Schleswig-Holstein. Eine statistisch-soziologische Studie.*

[73] Carstens, op, cit, p. 254.

[74] Tönnies had five children: Gerrit, Franziska, Jan Friedrich, Carola, and Kuno. Ernest Jurkat got to know all of them.

[75] Eduard Georg Jocoby (1904-1978) studied law at Kiel but was a great admirer of Tönnies and did some field work for him. Being the son of a Jewish father, he had difficulty in finding and holding a job after he left Kiel. He was, therefore, forced to emigrate first to England and then to New Zealand where he had a successful career and made a mark in education planning. He maintained an interest in sociology and Tönnies' teachings throughout his life.

- The same year (1928), Jurkat accompanied Tönnies to a professional retreat, possibly a meeting of the German Sociological Association, in Assenheim, also attended by: his son, Kuno Tönnies; the historian of philosophy, Cay von Brockdorff; and Else Brenke, a devoted follower. Assenheim was the locus of a "researchers' home" established in 1924 by Max Graf zu Solms, a sociologist of aristocratic background, with his inheritance. It was a permanent meeting place for social scientists—a place for work, debate, rest and recreation. The home was closed in 1932, a victim, in part, of the Great Depression.
- Also in 1928, Jurkat helped Tönnies to prepare a presentation on "the population question" for a conference in Berlin—a foray into the field of demography which would help him professionally later.
- In 1929, he co-authored with Tönnies a book on *Crimes in Schleswig-Holstein in the Years 1899-1914.*[76] Jurkat was 24 years old then and had not yet earned his Ph.D. degree.
- The same year (1929) he accompanied Tönnies to Oxford, England—Herford College specifically—for a commemoration of the 250th anniversary of Hobbes' death and the launching of the Hobbes Society in the same year.

In 1931, Ernst Jurkat received his Ph.D. from the University of Kiel. Although he was associated with the University's Institut für Weltwirtschaft (Institute for World Economics), his degree was in philosophy and his doctoral dissertation on sociology. It was titled *Die soziologische Fragestellung in der Werttheorie und die Theorie der sozialen Werte* (The Sociological Question in the Theory of Values and the Theory of Values). It was completed in 1930 and published in 1931.[77] The dissertation adviser was Tönnies himself. In it, Jurkat took issue with some of Tönnies' views. This did not hurt him; rather, it may have gained him Tönnies' respect. The dissertation, which was just 47-pages long, was well received both in Germany

---

[76] *Die schwere Kriminalität von Männern in Schleswig-Holstein in den Jahren 1899-1914.*

[77] The publisher was Schmidt & Klaunig, Kiel.

and abroad. Rudolf Heberle, an eminent German-American sociologist, wrote, "Through his Ph.D. dissertation, Dr. J [sic] has made a real contribution to theoretical sociology."[78] An indication of this is the fact that today, the dissertation can be found at the libraries of the Universities of Chicago, Columbia, Harvard, Yale, and Pennsylvania, among others.

Dr. Jurkat stayed in Kiel for nearly a year after receiving his doctorate. He married Dorothy Bergas of Berlin in 1932 and moved there that year. It is not clear which event came first: did he move because he got married or did he get married after he moved?

The Berlin Years (1933-1938)

Dr. Jurkat's activities in Berlin fall into in three groups: what he did to make a living; his continued involvement with Tönnies and his work; and his political activities, which led to the fleeing of the Jurkats from Germany for life.

Making a Living

It was not easy for German intellectuals of any political persuasion to find a job in 1932/33, partly because of the lingering effects of the Great Depression. This applied to Dr. Jurkat, too, and for additional reasons. While he no doubt had strong socialist leanings, Jurkat, unlike his mentor Tönnies, had not joined the SPD. Yet Jurkat was closely associated with him, and he had a Jewish wife—a fact which was widely known. Jurkat appears to have been unemployed for a while. After April 1933, when the *Law for the Restoration of the Civil Service*, aimed at Jews, was passed, jobs started opening up, as Jews began to be released in droves. It was not easy, however, to be "approved" for one of those jobs. It helped to be a member of the *Bund Nationalsozialistischer Deutscher Juristen* (Association of Nationalsocialist Lawyers). This was a sub-organization of the NSDP (the Nazi Party), one not as influential as others but one which, in the Spring of 1933,

---

[78] Letter by Dr. Heberle to the Emergency Rescue Committee (ERC) in New York City, dated April 10, 1941, in the ERC files.

played a key role in replacing all Jewish experts in nearly every trade association and chamber of commerce in Germany. Jurkat joined this association and, in June 1933, was able to get a job with *Verein Berliner Kaufleute und Industrieller* (Association of Berlin Merchants and Industrialists), known as VBKI.

VBKI, established in 1879, was one of the oldest and most prestigious business clubs in Germany. It is as powerful and influential today as it was then. It is strongly market-oriented and known for, among other things, its elitist and sumptuous business and social gatherings. A question that poses itself is why Dr. Jurkat joined VBKI at the very time when it was replacing its entire Jewish staff—and why, before then, he had become a member of the *National Socialist Lawyers' Association*. Perhaps he needed the job, any job. Perhaps he thought that the VBKI job would provide him cover to continue his relationship with Tönnies and engage in anti-Nazi activities. The humiliation of Tönnies by his ousting in 1933 without pension must have devastated Jurkat.

Dr. Christof Biggeleben is a contemporary German economist/historian who wrote his doctoral dissertation at Humboldt University (Berlin) on VBKI's history from 1879 to 1961, and published several papers on the subject. He provided me valuable information on Dr. Jurkat's work there. Jurkat joined VBKI as secretary of the association and editor of its trade publication. His predecessor there was August Koppel, a Jew, who was dismissed after 27 years of service. Until Dr. Jurkat's arrival, VBKI's trade publication consisted of a sort of newsletter edited by Koppel. Jurkat transformed the publication into a substantive monthly magazine, called *VBKI Spiegel* (Monitor), which continues to be published under that name. Jurkat worked at VBKI until 1938.

According to Biggeleben, as editor of the VBKI magazine, Jurkat was "quite moderate." He published neither openly anti-semitic articles nor anti-Nazi pieces critical of the regime's autarchic economic policy. The management of VBKI itself was moderate in the mid-thirties, but this era ended when Heinrich Hunke, a leading Berlin Nazi and prominent economic thinker and supporter of the regime, became VBKI president. There is little doubt that had Jurkat not fled the country for political reasons in 1938, as we shall see, he would have either resigned or been fired once Hunke took VBKI's helm. Incidentally, Biggeleben believes that Jurkat may have been replaced in his job by Dr. Paul Reinitz, an NSDP member, like Hunke.[79]

Homage to Tönnies

VBKI must not have been Ernst Jurkat's priority while he worked there. His mind was elsewhere and his heart belonged to Tönnies, as the cliché goes. He maintained contact with him, met him on several occasions, and showed his admiration for him with action before his death in 1936, as illustrated below.

In February 1933, Tönnies came to Berlin to make a presentation on Free Speech at a conference on the same subject endorsed by Albert Einstein and Thomas Mann, who could not attend. Ernst, who was married by then, attended with his wife. The occasion was notable because, as Tönnies himself reported later, the authorities stopped his presentation before he could finish it and cancelled the conference at the same time.[80] This was, after all, 1933.

In 1935, Jurkat and Jacoby, Tönnies' other favorite ex-assistant, who was also in Berlin, prevailed on Tönnies to pick up the work on *Geist der Neuzeit* (The Spirit of Modern Times) which he had started many years ago. This was to be a study in applied sociology analyzing the transformation of Europe from the Middle Ages to modern times. It had been conceived as a companion to *Gemeinschaft und Gesellschaft* and planned in two volumes. Tönnies reacted favorably and completed volume one in pieces, which he would send to Jacoby and Jurkat (they were known as the two J's) for their review and suggestions. They, in turn, would send it to Else Brenke, a Tönnies protégé who lived with his family and who would put the pieces together. Although volume one did see the light of day, a mystery has surrounded volume two. Was it ever written? For years, the rumor was that any draft, if there was one, must have ended up in the hands of Ernst Jurkat. Jurkat, who died in 1994, left no such draft. Carstens, the eminent biographer of Tönnies, has reported

---

[79] Based on my correspondence with Biggeleben in November/December 2009.
[80] Carstens, op. cit., p. 288.

the existence of a file marked "Ernst Jurkat Soziologie" in a Moscow archive and wondered whether the missing draft might be there. Tönnies expressed his gratitude to Jacoby and Jurkat for the risk they took by assisting him with volume one. But this was nothing compared to the risk that Jurkat would take shortly thereafter.[81]

In 1935, Tönnies was hospitalized for a few days in Kiel. Some time later, Ernst Jurkat visited him at his home. This was probably the last time the two men—master and pupil, leader and follower, virtual father and son—met.

Tönnies died in 1936 at eighty-one years of age. As his eightieth birthday was approaching, Ernest Jurkat began conceptualizing and then actively preparing a collection of memorial essays by his admirers and followers to celebrate that occasion. Jurkat's efforts as planner, coordinator and editor culminated in the publication of *Eine Festgabe für Ferdinand Tönnies zu seinem achtzigsten Geburtstage* (Essays in Honor of Fredinand Tönnies Eightieth Birthday),[82] unfortunately a few months after Tönnies' death. The 404-pages long collection contained 28 papers by scholars from 19 different universities spanning four continents. The academic homes of the various contributing scholars included the universities of Amsterdam, Athens, Basel, Berlin, Bogota, Giessen, Halle, Innsbruck, Kiel, Köln, Kyoto, Marburg, New York, and Rome; Cambridge, Columbia and Harvard Universities; the Technische Hochschule in Dresden; and the New School for Social Research in New York City. The list testifies to both the richness and diversity of Tönnies' admirers and the ambition of Jurkat's undertaking.

This, moreover, was no ordinary memorial volume praising the honoree. It consisted of original, scientifically important contributions. Jurkat himself contributed one: *Die Soziographie des moralischen Lebens* (The Sociography of Moral Life). Furthermore, the focus was not on the past but on the outlook for the then young science of sociology and the most important problems it needed to address. As one reviewer put it, this memorial collection had an "orienting value."[83] The papers were grouped under five

---

[81] Ibid. pp. 300-301.
[82] Published by Hans Buske Verlag, Leipzig, 1936.
[83] Review by Ernst Harms, *The Philosophical Review*, Vol XLVII, 1938, p. 84.

headings: the history of sociology; theoretical sociology; empirical sociology; the philosophy of history; and Tönnies, the man and his contribution.

The risk that Ernest Jurkat was taking with the above initiative cannot be overstated. He was honoring a man who had been ousted from academia by the regime (apparently with Kiel University's collaboration) as soon as the regime came into power. The contributors of the memorial essays included people who had fallen out of favor themselves, including some who, like the famous anthropologist Dr. Franz Boas, had been blacklisted. One wonders if Jurkat might not have had a protector (at VBKI or elsewhere) or if the regime might not have noticed the hidden anti-regime messages of some of the essays. The answer to both is probably not.

Tönnies commanded a lot of respect and loyalty from his colleagues and former students long after his death. A good example is Jacoby, his favorite assistant other than Jurkat, mentioned earlier. Trained as a lawyer, Jacoby worked in trade, banking, government, and education planning—fields removed from pure sociology—throughout his career. Yet roughly thirty-five years after Tönnies' death, and while living in New Zealand where he was forced to emigrate because of his Jewish heritage, he wrote two major works setting out and defending Tönnies' legacy.[84] Jacoby, however, was not taking the risk that Jurkat took in 1936.

Leaving Berlin—and Germany

During his first 2-3 years in Berlin, Ernest Jurkat's time was taken up by adjusting to a new city, a new job, married life, and becoming a father (1935). He was also putting together the collection of memorial essays in honor of Tönnies. He published, moreover, two additional papers during that period, both of them

---

[84] Eduard Georg Jacoby, *Philosophie und Soziologie: Ferdinand Tönnies' wissenschaflischer,* Kiel, 1970, and *Die moderne Gesellschaft im sozialwissenschaftlichen Denken von Ferdinand Tönnies. Eine biographische Einführung,* Stuttgart, 1971.

in Germany's Yearbook of National Economy and Statistics.[85] This must have left him very little time to engage in political activism, although opposition to National Socialism was embedded in his family. Hans Bergas, his brother in law, had been a staunch supporter of the Weimar Republic and had aggressively opposed the rise of National Socialism. He had to flee Germany for that reason in mid-1933. He worked actively against the Nazi regime from France and paid dearly for it. (See Chapter 9.)

Jurkat's active, if clandestine, opposition to the regime would start with the creation of the *Deutsche Volksfront* (German Popular Front or German People's Front) in late 1936. The *Deutsche Volksfront* was a political alliance of leftist parties established in resistance to National Socialism. It was founded by a group led by Hermann Brill (1895-1959), an ex-SPD politician, as a reaction to the SPD leaders' passive attitude towards Hitler. Brill and his co-founders drew up a manifesto of ten points intended as a platform for all the liberal, democratic, socialist and communist groups in the country. The founders vied for a democratic Germany—politically, socially and economically—with a foreign policy oriented towards peace and reconciliation, and a less autarchic economic policy calling for, among other things, an end to the nationalization of major industries.

Ernst Jurkat joined the *Deutsche Volksfront* early on and worked closely with Brill. His membership as an active participant in the Front is substantiated in a major study on Germany's political refugees in the period leading to and during the Second World War.[86]

The *Deutsche Volksfront* was inspired by and modeled on the "popular fronts" of France and Spain. The French *Front Populaire* had succeeded in bringing to power the socialist government of Leon Blum in 1936. The *Volksfront* was allied with these, as well

---

[85] Ernst Jurkat, "Demodynamik: Bemerkungen zu dem gleichnamigen Buche von Mächler," and "Die soziale Verbundenheit und ihre Gestaltungen," in *Jarbücher für Nationalökonomie und Statistik,* 1934.

[86] Heinz Boberach and others, *Quellen zur deutchen politischen Emigration, 1933-1945* (Sources About German Political Refugees, 1933-1945), Munich, 1994, p. 152.

as the Soviet counterpart, namely, the Soviet Communist Party. The common objective was to create a joint front or *international alliance* against Hitler. The intellectual center of the alliance was in Paris and the political center in Moscow, which pushed for the joint front the most. This is why, according to Carstens (Tönnies' biographer), many of the files of the international alliance members are found in Moscow, including apparently one on Ernst Jurkat. (I have found no corroborating evidence of the existence of such a file on Jurkat.)

The efforts, neither of the *Deutsche Volksfront* nor of the alliance of national fronts, succeeded in their objective, due to dissensions within and among the individual fronts, which had to deal with the long-standing socialist-communist animosity, a co-existing Socialist International (centered in Brussels), German communist party (KPD) exiles in Moscow, SPD exiles in Prague and elsewhere, etc. Affiliation with the *Volksfront*, nevertheless, caused Jurkat to flee Germany under dire conditions, leaving his wife and child behind.

Thanks to Christopher Isherwood (1904-1986), the British-American author, there is a written record of the circumstances under which Ernst Jurkat left Berlin. To jump temporarily ahead, shortly after he arrived in the United States in mid-1941, Jurkat spent a few months at a "hostel" for political refugees run by the American Friends Service Committee. The purpose of the hostel, which was located in Haverford, Pennsylvania, near Philadelphia, was to impart to the refugees the English language and other skills they needed in order to adjust to and work in the United States in their respective fields. This was a very unusual undertaking which merits attention on its own and to which I shall, therefore, return later. Isherwood, who had recently emigrated to the United States himself, was a language teacher at the hostel, and he apparently valued his experience there. In his 1000-page long diaries, which were published posthumously, he devoted nearly fifty pages to his Haverford years and, in October 1941, included this passage about Jurkat:

"Ernst Jurkat was another non-Jewish refugee. . . . He was an expert on statistics, and had worked in Berlin at a government institute which dealt with trade and economics. When the Nazis took over, Ernst stayed at his job. But at night he went home and printed pamphlets, inciting the nation to revolt against Hitler. The penalty for this kind of illegal work was to be beheaded, facing up toward the axe. Ernst lasted quite a long time—until shortly before the outbreak of the war. One day, while he was at his office, his wife called him on the phone and gave him the prearranged signal. The Gestapo were watching his home.[87] Ernst always carried his passport in his pocket, so there was nothing to take with him but his hat. He got out of Berlin by train, found his way to the Swiss frontier and dodged over the line in the twilight, when the guards can't see so well to shoot and the searchlights don't help much. The Nazi consulate in Bern hadn't been advised of his escape, and he was able to walk boldly in and get money and permits to go to France. In Paris, he offered his services to the Second Bureau [France's external military intelligence agency then, which later became the country's Intelligence Service], on condition that they smuggle his wife out of Germany to join him. This the French did. During the war, he had fought in the French army. He was now badly worried about his wife and child, who were still interned in France. The wife was Jewish."[88]

The above account is believable because Isherwood must have heard it directly from Jurkat and recorded it in his diary before time could cloud the memory. Other participants in the hostel who have written about their experiences there support the essence of it. Furthermore, the account is broadly consistent with the version of the event that has survived in Jurkat's family—of which I was a member through marriage—with the following two exceptions.

---

[87] They were living at Wartburgerstrasse 27 in the Schönberg area of Berlin.
[88] Christopher Isherwood, *Diaries*, Volume one: 1939-1960, Harper Collins, 1997, pp. 190-191.

Ernst must have been viewed by the Nazi authorities with suspicion for some time, being an openly loyal follower of the disgraced, Social Democrat Tönnies, and the brother-in-law of Hans Bergas who, like Dorothy Jurkat, was Jewish. What had tipped the scales against him? The family always believed that Ernst was pursued by the Gestapo in 1938 because of some specific action he took against the regime and that he was singled out because of it. There is no evidence of such an action; it is far more likely that he was pursued as part of a round-up of *Volksfront* members. Such a round-up did occur. As recorded in the *Encyclopedia of German Resistance to the Nazi Movement*, in September 1938, "the Gestapo broke up the group despite its camouflage."[89] (Camouflage referred to the secrecy in which the group operated by necessity.) Indeed, Brill, the *Volksfront* founder himself, was arrested as part of the round-up on September 21, 1938, very likely on the same day the Gestapo came after Jurkat, too. This, incidentally, was a few weeks before the infamous anti-Jewish pogrom known as *Kristallnacht* (The Night of the Broken Glass) of November 9-10, 1938. It seems that few of the *Volksfront* cadre escaped. Brill and some of his and Ernst's collaborators were sentenced to 12 years in jail.

The other discrepancy, though minor, between Isherwood's account and the story the family heard concerns the escape of Ernst's wife and son. Isherwood wrote that this was achieved through the intervention of France's Second Bureau, whereas the family attributed it to the efforts of Ernst's loyal friends. Both may be true; that is, the Second Bureau may have been able to carry out the task with the help of Ernst's friends. It is also possible, indeed likely, that Hans Bergas played a role in it. While living in Paris, he was already engaged in resistance activities as a double spy and was well connected in Berlin. He must have played a role at least in the escape of his widowed mother, Therese Bergas, who accompanied Mrs. Jurkat into exile abroad.[90]

---

[89] Wolfgang Benz and Walter H. Pehle, Eds., *Encyclopedia of German Resistance to the Nazi Movement, 1997*, p. 170.

[90] Therese Bergas was listed as living alone in the address book of Greater-Berlin Jews for 1931. (*Jüdisches Adreßbuch für Groß-Berlin,*

Two coincidences, both of them involving Brill, are worth noting. After being imprisoned in two different jails, Brill was sent to Buchenwald in 1943, where Hans Bergas was to arrive a few months later. Bergas mentioned him in his unpublished memoir. The two men must have met without knowing of each other's relation to Ernst Jurkat. Following the end of the war, and after surviving Buchenwald, Brill moved to Thuringia, attracted by the fact that this region was occupied by the Americans. After Thuringia became part of the Soviet zone, however, Brill escaped to the American zone.

Understandably, after leaving Germany through Switzerland, Ernst Jurkat came directly to Paris—understandably, because, as noted, this was the intellectual capital of European opposition to Hitler, and because Hans Bergas, his brother-in-law, had been there since 1933. France—particularly Paris—became the most important center of German emigration until 1938-39. Approximately 3,000 Social Democrats and around 5,500 Communists settled there, as did representatives of other leftist parties and organizations from Germany. A considerable number of exiled German or German-speaking writers found haven in France. Exiled publishing houses relocated there, as did German-language daily newspapers and other periodicals. And clubs, circles, cafés, and other establishments, run almost exclusively by Germans, abounded. Prague in Czechoslovakia also became a center of German political refugees but not to the same extent as Paris.[91] In Paris, Ernst worked for a while at the *Deutsches Archiv für Dokumente der Zeitgeschichte* (The German Archive for Documents of Contemporary History), one of several such centers in Europe. He probably also wrote economic columns for local newspapers.

In 1939, the inflow of political refugees from Germany and other countries turned into an avalanche. As the war was approaching and in anticipation of a German victory, Hans Bergas moved to southern France where the nucleus of an organized resistance was forming. The Gestapo continued to pursue Ernst in

---

Ausgabe 1931.) This indicates that she lost her husband before Dorothy and Ernst Jurkat were married (1931).

[91] Encyclopedia of German Resistance, op. cit., p. 92.

Germany by putting pressure on his wife, Dorothy, who was still there and surviving with the help of Ernst's friends. Ernst joined the French army. Many political refugees did the same. The army provided cover from his pursuers and a chance to fight the Nazis. Dorothy Jurkat and her son were able to escape to France. The war broke out in September 1939 with disastrous consequences from the beginning for France. Barely nine months later, the Allied forces, which were cut off by the German army, had to be evacuated from the beaches and harbor of Dunkirk in northern France. According to the Jurkats' son, Peter, who was barely seven years old then, he and his mother went to Dunkirk in the hope of being evacuated with the troops but they did not succeed in this goal. France surrendered days later. Ernst was released from the army as the war ended for France, without seeing action, and sought refuge in Vichy France.[92]

The precise dates of some of these events—in particular, the enlistment of Ernst in the army and the arrival of Dorothy and their son in France—are not certain. But the *sequence* was roughly as I indicated it. What needs to be stressed is that Ernst and Dorothy could not and did not meet in France. The reunion was still many years away.

The Slow Road to the United States

Several private groups and individuals helped the Jurkats to come to the United States. The process, not simple in normal times, was complicated by the need to secure emigration permission, entry visa, sponsorship, affidavits, identity papers, a place on a ship, and the means to pay for it, all under the watchful eyes of the Vichy authorities or the Gestapo itself. Furthermore, the situation faced by the political refugees like the Jurkats was utterly chaotic, with literally hundreds clamoring for attention and competing for the limited permits, places, and funds under the pressure of time. The dominating reality was uncertainty—uncertainty about the

---

[92] The unoccupied southern "free zone" of France administered from 1940 to 1944 by a wartime government subservient to Germany, named after the place where its administrative center was located.

rules, the regulations, the people in charge, the ship departures, etc. Uncertainty characterized also the work of the rescue or relief agencies themselves, some of which were new and still improvising. Three things were at a premium: *information* that was reliable, *communication* about or with one's relatives stranded somewhere in Europe; and *coordination*—for what needed to be done went beyond the authority or means of a single agency or individual.

Among the agencies that benefited the Jurkats the most and the longest were the Emergency Rescue Committee (ERC) and its successor, the International Relief and Rescue Committee (IRRC).[93] The Committee fulfilled the three roles noted above—information, communication and coordination; it did so for the duration of the war; and it did it with a human touch. The ERC was a grassroots organization founded in 1940 in New York City by activists concerned about the fate of European political and intellectual refugees—Jews and non-Jews—trapped in Vichy France. Among the ERC's founders was Varian Fry, a journalist/humanist, whose activities have been the subject of books, including a book for young adults, and a movie.[94] The ERC enjoyed the political, moral and financial support of many influential people, including Eleanor Roosevelt.

The refugees who were the object of the ERC were concentrated in France's southern port of Marseille, far from German-occupied Paris, where the United States had a consulate. Varian Fry took it upon himself to rescue as many of them as he could, and he went there in August 1940 with a list of 200 endangered refugees to be helped. (Ernst Jurkat was not on that list.) He worked hard and under harrowing conditions to that end, overachieving his

---

[93] In 1942, the ERC merged with the International Relief Association (IRA), created in the early 1930s to help the Germans suffering under Hitler, to form the International Relief and Rescue Committee, shortened to International Rescue Committee.

[94] See Fry's own account of his activities, *Surrender on Demand*, 1945, as well as Sheila Isenberg, *A Hero of Our Own: The Story of Varian Fry*, 2001, Andy Marino, *A Quiet American: The Secret War of Varian Fry*, 1999, and the made-for-television movie, *Varian's War*, with William Hurt playing Varian Fry.

objective, until the Vichy government deported him in September 1941. In its thirteen months of operation through Fry, the ERC helped more than 2000 political, cultural, labor, and academic leaders. It owed its success to the sense of mission, flexibility, dedication, and imagination of its supporters and staff at all levels. Its staff also displayed a sense of history by preserving the records of ERC's activities meticulously for future generations, which has greatly benefited this research.[95]

Prior to Departure

Ernest Jurkat came to the attention of the ERC central office in New York first in April 1941 through the *Centre Americain de Secours* (hereafter referred to as the *Centre*)—a sister relief organization of the ERC, established by Varian Fry under the auspices of the French government and used to evacuate endangered refugees through illegal means, as necessary. By that time Jurkat, who was in Marseille, had obtained an immigration visa from the United States consulate, most probably with the help of the *Centre*. He had also applied for visas for his wife, child and mother-in-law, who were in Paris, without knowing, though, when they might be able to join him in Marseille. He was at the time penniless and under severe time pressure. His family was being detained in Paris and harassed about his whereabouts. He could have been arrested and extradited any day under the "surrender on demand" clause of Article XIX of the Franco-German Armistice. The clause stated, "The French Government is obliged to surrender all Germans named by the German Government in France, as well as in French possessions, Colonies, Protectorate Territories, and Mandates." Years later, Varian Fry got the title for his memoir of that period, *Surrender on Demand*, from that same clause.

In those days, securing a booking on a boat and raising the money for it were bigger challenges than obtaining a United States visa. Even if a visa was "approved," it was not actually issued unless

---

[95] The ERC files are kept under the individuals' names in the M. E. Grenander Department of Special Collections and Archives, University Libraries / University at Albany / State University of New York, Albany, New York.

and until the applicant could produce proof of a paid reservation for a definite departure. The financial question, therefore, dominated everyone's concerns in the spring of 1941.

To address the financing challenge, the *Centre* asked Jurkat to draw up a list of the people who might help him raise the necessary funding for the passage, although the initiative for contacting them was left to him. Dr. Jurkat identified eight people in the following order but without the brief background information on them which I am providing. All of them were people whom he had met in Germany and who, he thought, were residing in the United States at the time. The list is important because it throws light on the people whom Dr. Jurkat identified with both personally and intellectually at the time.

Dr. Gerhard Colm (1897-1968). Fiscal economist. He had been professor and director of research at the Institute for World Economics in Kiel during 1927-1933, where Dr. Jurkat met him and probably worked with him. He was also a contributor to the collection of essays in honor of Ferdinand Tönnies' eightieth birthday edited by Jurkat, mentioned earlier.[96] Colm immigrated to the United States in 1933 where he had a brilliant and long career. He was professor of economics at the New School of Social Research in New York (1933-1939), assistant chief at the Bureau of the Budget (1940-1946), principal fiscal analyst and member of the Council of Economic Advisers (1946-1952), and chief economist at the National Panning Association (1952 until his death in 1968).

Dr. Fritz Levy (1887-1957). Pathologist and Ernst Jurkat's brother-in-law through marriage. Dr. Levy, a Berliner, was first married to a sister of Dr. Jurkat's wife, after whose death he remarried and, in 1936, moved to Elkins, West Virginia. Dr. Levy proved quite attached to his first wife's family, providing assistance, including financial assistance, to Ernst and both his ex-mother-in-law and his ex-sister-in-law while they were refugees in Europe through the end of the war. (See Chapter 10.)

---

[96] Gerhard Colm, "Probleme der Finanzsoziologie" (Problems of the Sociology of Finance), in *Eine Festgabe für Ferdinand Tönnies*, op. cit. The paper was contributed while Colm was already at the New School in New York.

Prof. Rudolf Heberle (1896-1991). Eminent sociologist. After a Rockefeller Foundation fellowship (1926-29), Heberle taught at Kiel University for nearly a decade (1929-1938), during which period he married Ferdinand Tönnies' daughter Franziska, a social worker, and was, by his own account, in almost daily contact with Ernst Jurkat. He was among the contributors to the collection of papers in honor of Tönnies' eightieth birthday, planned and edited by Jurkat.[97] Dr. Heberle and his small family moved to the United States in 1938. He served as professor of sociology at the Louisiana State University in Baton Rouge throughout his life and career in this country, while writing more than ten books and presiding over several academic and professional associations.

Dr. Paul Hertz (1888-1961). Son of a Jewish merchant, and lifelong SPD politician. He obtained his Ph.D. in "national economy" from the University of Tübingen (same as Prof. Tönnies) in 1914. He joined the SPD in 1917 and rose quickly to a leadership position in the party. He served in the Reichstag (German Parliament) as an SPD representative for twelve years and joined the German *Volksfront* against Hitler, which is probably how he met Ernst Jurkat. When the SPD was outlawed in 1933, he went into exile, first to Prague, and he emigrated to the United States with his family in 1939. He became a labor leader in New York City. Dr. Hertz returned permanently to Germany, West Berlin specifically, in 1949. He distinguished himself as administrator of the Marshall Plan activities and in other posts he held there. And he served as Economic Minister in the West Berlin government, under Mayor Wili Brandt, from 1955 until his death in 1961.

Mrs. Wachenheim (?). I have not been able to find out who she was, as Dr. Jurkat gave neither her first name nor her address.

Dr. Gerrit Tönnies (1898—?). Ph.D. chemist. Eldest of Ferdinand Tönnies' five children, living, according to Dr. Jurkat, in Philadelphia at the time.

Jan Friedrich Tönnies (1902—?). Certified engineer (*Diplomingenieur*). One of three sons of Ferdinand Tönnies, who,

---

[97] Rudolf Heberle, "Die Bedeutung der Wanderungen im sozialen Leben der Völker" (The Importance of Migration in the Social Life of Tribes), in *Eine Festgabe für Ferdinand Tönnies,* op. cit.

according to Dr. Jurkat, may have been living in New York at the time, but who, Prof. Heberle (above) emphatically stated, had left the U.S. in the interim.

Prof. Paul Hermberg (1888-1969). Economic statistician. He taught at numerous universities—Kiel, Leipzig, Jena, and Bogota (Colombia)—before moving to the U. S. in 1940, where he lectured at the New School for Social Research (New York) and played a key role in the development of the Marshall Plan. While not being on the list of seven people drawn up by Dr. Jurkat as candidates for raising the funds he needed, Hermberg was very helpful in this regard. The Hermbergs, husband and wife, and Ernst Jurkat must have known each other well from their days in Germany. Prof. Hermberg contributed a paper to the collection of essays in honor of Tönnies.[98]

Dr. Jurkat wrote to some of the above people from southern France asking for their financial help and for them to contact the others for the same on his behalf. Some did and, among these, the actions of three stand out. On April 10, 1941, Prof. Heberle wrote a strong letter to the ERC in New York, giving Jurkat's background, explaining his dire predicament, and pleading for the Committee's assistance. A few days later, Prof. Heberle's wife Franziska, the daughter of Tönnies, as previously mentioned, took the remarkable initiative of writing to *Dr. Franz Boas*, the eminent anthropologist then teaching at Columbia University, setting forth Jurkat's case.

Boas (1858-1942) had been a contemporary of Tönnies, a member of the initial intellectual crowd from Kiel, and a strong anti-fascist like the rest of the group. His seminal work, *Mind of a Primitive Man*, and others advanced an idea that was anathema to Nazi ideology, namely, that various races have equal capacity for cultural development—that differences among races are generally the result of particular historical events rather than physiological destiny. His book was burned by the Nazis and his Ph.D. degree rescinded when they came to power. Boas, in the meantime, had emigrated to the United States, where he came to be regarded as the

---

[98] Paul Hermberg, "Über das Rechnen mit Erscheinungen: Eine Vorarbeit zum Problem der Schätzung und Mittelnung," in *Eine Festgabe für Ferdinand Tönnies,* op. cit.

founder of American anthropology and ethnology. He was, by all counts, the intellectual dean of the people on the list submitted by Jurkat and known well to him, having been one of the contributors to the commemorative essays honoring Tönnies.[99] Franziska Heberle, who had met Boas and knew his background, pressed all the right buttons in her passionate letter to him and made two important points. She stressed that Jurkat was in imminent danger of arrest for handing over to the Gestapo. And she remarked that the assistance that many of Jurkat's friends in the United States could provide was limited because most of them had been very recent immigrants (unlike Boas, who had been in the country since 1886) and had, therefore, limited financial means.

The third notable initiative to help Jurkat came from Dr. Paul Hermberg, who was residing in Washington, D.C., as mentioned earlier. He volunteered to centralize the collection of financial contributions and involved his wife in the effort.

Although contributions did come in (we are not sure of the exact amount), apparently they fell short of the amount needed to cover the cost of the passage. Many of the people approached, including Dr. Boas, passed on Jurkat's request to the ERC. (Boas was 83 at the time and died a few months later.) The ERC could not help directly, but it enlisted other agencies, notably the Jewish Labor Committee (JLC), in the effort. The JLC, which continues to exist, was an American secular Jewish organization dedicated to promoting Jewish interests in labor unions and labor union interests in Jewish communities. In the late 1930s and early 1940s, its activities focused on supporting anti-Nazi labor forces in Europe, sending relief to Jewish labor institutions there, as well as, more generally, assisting the anti-Hitler underground movement and aiding the victims of Nazism, both Jewish and non-Jewish. Jurkat was brought to JLC's attention initially by the Women's International League for Peace and Freedom (WILPF)—a non-profit, non-governmental women's peace organization, founded in 1915, with headquarters in Geneva. The JLC embraced Jurkat's case without hesitation and assumed responsibility for him

---

[99] Franz Boas, "Die Individualität primitiver Kulturen" (The Individuality of Primitive Cultures), in *Eine Festgabe Ferdinand Tönnies*, op. cit.

from departure through arrival. Although Jurkat had acquired an immigration visa, to minimize problems at entry, the JLC obtained a "special visa" for him—the kind introduced at Eleanor Roosevelt's initiative to help threatened scientists and artists. And it succeeded in booking him passage, making up most probably the shortfall in the funds collected privately.

The Voyage from Hell

While the process of obtaining a visa, a booking and a paid ticket was messy and uncharted, the time lapse for Dr. Jurkat and others like him was not long, averaging six weeks. All the parties concerned were aware of the time factor—the ERC, the WILPF, Varian Fry and his *Centre American de Secours*, and most of all, the refugees themselves, many of whom were, like Dr. Jurkat, traumatized and under the threat of arrest. Earlier, Dr. Jurkat had applied for visas for his wife, young son and mother-in-law, as well as secured JLC's commitment to finance their passage. It was his intention to wait for them to arrive in Marseille from Paris, where they had been detained and harassed by the Gestapo. But as waiting further became too risky, Dr. Jurkat had to leave at the first opportunity that presented itself—the earliest booking that the JLC could make, namely, on the steamship *Winnipeg* leaving Marseille on May 6, 1941 for the French colony of Martinique. As it turned out, Dr. Jurkat's wife and son arrived in Marseille three weeks after he left. After coming so close to a reunion, they were not to see each other for another five years!

Ships had been leaving Marseille for Martinique carrying refugees regularly. Jurkat's was not a routine voyage, however. I refer to the sailing part only, for there was nothing routine about how one got to the point of boarding the ship either. This particular voyage from hell was to take 39 days.

The atmosphere at the pier on the day of departure was tense. Varian Fry, who had been coming to the pier regularly to see his protégés off, was there and witnessed first-hand how several people were forcibly taken off the ship for different reasons just before it sailed. Jurkat and some of the other refugees must have observed this, too, and been horrified by it. Fry himself was under intense suspicion at the time. His own government had been refusing to validate his passport unless he returned to the U. S. He was eventually arrested and deported by the Vichy authorities with the prior consent of the United States government.

On May 6, the *Winnipeg* sailed with 750 passengers, of whom 300 were German and Austrian refugees.[100] Also on board, in addition to the crew, were some 70 French military personnel allied with or sympathetic to the German bosses of the Vichy regime. The refugees included some eighty so-called political refugees, or "clients" of Fry. Among these, other than Jurkat, were: Lothar Popp, an anti-Nazi peace activist and champion of workers' causes; Erhardt Konopka, a militant leader of the anti-Nazi labor and youth movements, with connections to the French underground;[101] Wilhelm Herzog, a German historian of literature and culture, playwright, encyclopedist, and pacifist; and Eduard Fendler, well-known music conductor.[102]

The political refugees on board also included the wives of Rudolf Breitscheid and Rudolf Hilferding, two long-time enemies of Hitler. Breitscheid (1874-1944) was a left-wing German politician who had been the leader of the Social Democratic bloc in the Reichstag. Rudolf Hilferding (1877-1941), a former Minister of Finance, was an Austrian Marxist economist of the hard left and a social theoretician. They knew and had collaborated closely with each other. They had gone into exile in 1933, fearing persecution for their views, and ended up in Marseille after living in various countries. Arrested in 1941, Breitscheid was sent to Buchenwald and Hinferding to a prison in Paris, where, Fry believed, they were both murdered. Others, however, suspect that Hilferding committed suicide.[103]

To set the *Winnipeg*'s journey of May 6, 1941 in perspective, six days before her departure, the painter/sculptor Max Ernst and the American art collector Peggy Guggenheim had left similarly by

---

[100] Isenberg, op. cit, p. 189.

[101] Konopka, like Jurkat, owed his rescue largely to the ERC. and his file is, therefore, in the same ERC archives as Jurkat's.

[102] See Marino, *A Quiet American*, op. cit., p. 285.

[103] Eric D. Weitz, *Weimar Germany: Promises and Tragedy*, 207, p. 366.

boat. A day after the *Winnipeg* sailed, the painter Chagall left for Lisbon to catch a boat bound for New York. And a few days after, the sculptor Jacques Lipchitz followed Chagall's route. These were some of the hundreds of the scientists/writers/artists rescued by Fry. The list included also Hanna Arendt, Jean Arp, André Breton, Marcel Duchamp, Wanda Landowska, Alma Mahler, Max Ophüls, and Franz Werfel, and earned Fry the reputation of being "the American Schindler."

The event experienced by Jurkat is described vividly in Sheila Eisenberg's 2001 biography of Varian Fry and is based largely on a report by Konopka, one of Jurkat's fellow-passengers . . .[104] The account below draws heavily on Eisenberg's text. The *Winnipeg* was no first-class liner. It was one of a handful of ships, like the *Mont Viso* and the *Wyoming*, making the Marseille-Casablanca-Martinique run. They were adapted to accommodate as many passengers as possible by putting bunks in the hold. The *Winnipeg* was particularly crowded on this crossing. "Food was inadequate and the passengers slept jammed together in poorly ventilated barracks."[105]

On May 26, twenty days after leaving Marseille and just before she reached Martinique, the *Winnipeg* was stopped on the high seas by a British ship. According to one eyewitness, armed Dutch soldiers (free-Dutch, presumably) from the British vessel boarded the ship, arrested the crew and ordered the ship to sail southward to Trinidad in the British West Indies. This took place in the dark of night, with "the earsplitting noise of planes roaring overhead and alarms ringing," and the terrified passengers looking on. Upon arrival at port, the passengers were interned behind barbed wire, but those who had a U.S. visa, mainly the protégés of Fry, were trucked to a special camp. "Food was brought in huge amounts. For the first time there was butter and soap . . . a shower room . . ."[106]

Once their status was cleared up, the political refugees were allowed to continue their journey. Shortly thereafter, news broke that the *S.S. Evangeline* was in port and due to leave for New York

---

[104] Isenberg, *A Hero of Our Own*, op. cit., p. 189.
[105] *Ibid.*
[106] *Ibid.*

on June 5. This created euphoria among the refugees, mixed with panic, given the need to raise funds to pay for the passage. A traffic of cables between passengers and relatives/friends ensued. Jurkat was virtually penniless.[107] The ERC fortunately agreed to cover his fare. And the *Evangeline* sailed as scheduled, with him on board.

According to the ship's manifest, Jurkat identified himself as a writer, of Polish citizenship, born in Warsaw (which was not correct) and giving his residence before boarding in Marseille as Paris. Jurkat hid his German citizenship and city of birth clearly out of concern of being arrested and deported under the *Surrender on Demand* clause. Although Jurkat was in possession of a U.S. visa, he was nevertheless anxious, and on June 9 he cabled the ERC from the *Evangeline* asking to be met on arrival, *before* disembarking, aboard the ship. Two representatives of the Jewish Labor Committee's New York office did, and Ernst Jurkat entered the United States on June 13, 1941. He was a free man for the first time since he left Germany nearly three years earlier, but still haunted by worries over his wife and son.

Ernst Jurkat in America

The Haverford Hostel

Shortly after he arrived in the United States in mid-1941, Ernst Jurkat came to a hostel run by the American Friends Service Committee (AFSC) in Haverford, Pennsylvania, near Philadelphia. Who recommended or sent him there is not certain. It may have been the International Relief and Rescue Committee or the Jewish Labor Committee, which had paid for part of his journey and received him in New York harbor. Ernst was at the hostel between September 1941 and July 1942, when the hostel stopped operating. His experience there proved far more important than the nine-month duration of his stay would indicate, for several reasons.

---

[107] One recollection that has come down through the family is that when Jurkat was unable to give even a tip to a porter that had helped him with his meager luggage, he apologized and promised to send him the tip from the United States . . . which he did, as soon as he earned some money.

This was his first sustained exposure to the United States The contacts he made there eventually led him to choose a career path, settle in Philadelphia, and become affiliated with Pennsylvania for the rest of his life. (He died and was laid to rest in that state.) Also, he became acquainted with Quakerism at the hostel, as a result of which a few years later he (born Lutheran), his wife (born Jewish) and their son would join the Society of Friends. His fellow-refugees in the hostel were a group of people of diverse scientific background with a special group dynamic. Furthermore, this was a critical time for all—the organizers as well as the participants—as the war was still going on in Europe and the United States was about to become a participant in it. For these reasons, and since very little has been written about the hostel to date, I shall describe the hostel first, before turning to Ernst Jurkat's own experience there.

The hostel, called *Collective College Workshop*, was conceived and came into being in 1940.[108] The intended beneficiaries were the growing number of political refugees, mostly from German-speaking countries, nearly all of whom had an academic background, and many of whom were Jewish. The number of people attending the hostel at a given time was in the 25-30 range. The objective was to help them adjust professionally, psychologically, socially, and spiritually, and—most important of all—to find them employment. Since many of them had been teachers, the priority was to teach them English, including phonetics, introduce them to American pedagogy, and expose them to the "American way of life." This was not an easy task. The participants had widely different backgrounds. They included, while Ernst Jurkat was there, several lawyers, a judge, a poet, a botanist, several teachers, a writer, a translator, an accountant, a philosopher, a biologist, an art historian, an economist, a psychoanalyst, a physicist, and a couple of professional Marxists/Communists. Furthermore, while some were there with their spouses, many had left their wives and children behind. They were worried about them, in addition to

---

[108] This was one of several such hostels run by the AFSC. Two others were in Scattergood, in West Branch, Iowa, and Quaker Hill, in Richmond, Indiana. There were also "recreation hostels" in Skyland, Nyack and Aberdeen, New York.

their future. Most had broken spirits. This manifested itself either in self-isolation or in a desire to speak, to let off steam, to share.

The hostel was organized and run in typical Quaker fashion: with a low budget, limited staff, and the help of volunteers. Christopher Isherwood was the only full-time English teacher on the staff, which consisted of a mere six people. Volunteer teachers from Haverford and Bryn Mawr Colleges and the Baldwin School complemented him in this task. The hostel was run communally, with the participants sharing the various daily chores, from dishwashing to housekeeping. The physical, manual work was therapeutic in a way for the many broken spirits, generally welcome, and even enjoyed. A few years later, one of the participants gave an illustration of the communal work as follows:

> "It was almost a foregone conclusion that the translator of Romain Rolland, himself the author of a well-known book, would converse with the story-teller, who was the head dishwasher, about epical problems, while drying glasses. No one was astonished when the Russian-Jewish philosopher, holding silver forks in his hand, defended certain sociological phenomena in Europe against the already Americanized viewpoint of a former (non-Jewish) assistant of one of the best German sociologists, who had to flee, in 1938, because over there he had belonged to a secret anti-Nazi group and been very active [the reference is unmistakably to Ernst Jurkat]; or that a student of the philosopher Heidegger, carefully drying a frying pan, should deliver a quick lecture about an essay on Hölderlin by his teacher. Meanwhile, the once-famous theater critic from Vienna recited an old folk song, very appropriate when peeling potatoes, and the former judicial counselor from Berlin talked about Indian philosophy and religion with an English poet."[109]

---

[109] Jacob Picard, "Meeting the Quakers," in *Jewish Frontier*, Vol. 2, No. 15, May 1945, p. 22.

Communal living kept costs down. The fees charged for room, board and instruction were $30-40 per participant per month. They were paid on behalf of the participants by several refugee service committees or from a grant by the Treasury Department. The AFSC encouraged the donors to provide also some pocket money to the participants. Costs were also minimized by obtaining free access for the participants to lectures at Haverford and Bryn Mawr Colleges. It is of some interest that the British philosopher, social critic and writer Bertrand Russell, was living near Haverford at the time. Under an arrangement with the pharmaceutical millionaire and art collector, Dr. Alfred Barnes, he was giving lectures at the Barnes Foundation. The hostel made no attempt to draw the famed philosopher into its program, although Isherwood, who knew him, visited him on a couple of occasions. Meanwhile, as Isherwood put it, "He [Russell] had to waste his lectures on a small and pretty stupid group of Barnes' friends."[110] Russell broke his relations with Barnes and went back to England soon thereafter.

The atmosphere at the hostel was liberal and informal. The only obligatory activity was attending the English language class. Participants were also expected to attend the Sunday morning "meeting" at the Haverford Meeting house. There was thus plenty non-programmed time and ample opportunities to socialize. This allowed Isherwood, who already had the novelist's eye for detail, to get to know most of the participants well. The modest size of the group helped in this regard. For years to come, he modeled some of the characters in his writings on people he had met at the hostel.

But why had Isherwood been attracted to the hostel to begin with? Why had he come? Why had he stayed? The answer lies in the phase of life he was in. After coming to the United States for good with his friend and co-writer W. H. Auden in 1939, Isherwood went to Hollywood, where he did some writing and lived a wild life for a while. Having gotten a taste of Hollywood's competitive environment, the quiet life offered by the hostel appealed to him. He had been, moreover, anti-war since the death of his father, a British officer, in combat during the First World War. The pacifist and other views and beliefs of the Quakers thus no doubt attracted

---

[110] Isherwood, op. cit., p. 202.

him. He also yearned privacy. For the first time in a long while, he concealed his homosexuality, although he offered no reason for it in his diaries. Finally, he seems to have genuinely enjoyed himself at the hostel, owing to his prior favorable experience in Germany. Because of the homophobia they had encountered in their youth in England, he and Auden had lived and worked in Germany between 1929 and 1933. As the editor of Isherwood's diaries put it, at the hostel, Isherwood must have enjoyed ". . . the time spent living among the diaspora of the culture by which he had been familiar during the early 1930s in Germany."[111]

Ernst Jurkat at Haverford

Isherwood described Ernst at the hostel as follows: "A pale, fair-haired, bespectacled little shrimp of a man with a big adam's apple, quite young. When you looked at him more closely, you saw that he was muscular and tough. He had bad teeth, no chin, a long nose and immense boyish charm. His grey eyes behind his glasses were courageous and serene."[112] Jurkat had no money. His stay at the hostel was financed by the Church of the Brethren, which, like the Mennonite Church, joined the AFSC in many of its service activities.[113] It is very likely that the Church of the Brethren did not select Jurkat specifically; rather, it probably indicated to the AFSC that it wished to help one or more individuals and that the AFSC recommended Jurkat.

In his diaries, Isherwood mentioned Jurkat among his favorite people—a claim that is supported by his nearly dozen references to him. Jurkat must have been one of the participants who took *private* rather than group language lessons from Isherwood and worked closely with him. The detailed account that Isherwood gave of Jurkat's escape from Germany is not the sort of thing that

---

[111] Diaries, op. cit., p. xvi.
[112] *Ibid*, p. 190.
[113] The Church of the Brethren was started in Germany roughly three centuries ago. Like the Quakers and the Mennonites, the members of the Church are service oriented; they practice peaceful living and were traditionally recognizable because of their plain dress and reserved ways.

emerges from a group lesson. Furthermore, the letters that Jurkat wrote to the Emergency Rescue Committee during 1942-46 reveal a high level of proficiency in English that he may have attained thanks to Isherwood's personal help and attention.

Jurkat does not emerge from Isherwood's diaries as a person with a broken spirit. Rather, he was active, almost energetic, talkative, involved, and sociable. He also had two back-to-back amorous/flirtatious relations with female participants at the hostel—one with an art historian, the other with a young economist. These have to be seen in context. Such relationships within the hostel fraternity and sorority were not rare, given the emotional and other needs of the participants. A case in point is that of a married female participant who died in the hostel. Her widowed husband fell in love with another person from the hostel and married her at the hostel less than two months after his wife's death. Neither of Jurkat's amorous mini-adventures had any lasting consequences. Yet Isherwood wrote dutifully and somewhat gleefully about them, falling himself prey to the gossip mill that churned away in the hostel.

It is interesting that on arrival and throughout his stay at the hostel, Ernst Jurkat assumed exclusively the identity of an academic—an ex assistant professor of sociology at Kiel University. He rarely referred to his five years at the VBKI, the businessmen's club, in Berlin. He must have made one exception, however, with long term benefit to him. It involved Wroe Alderson (1898-1965). Alderson and his family lived a few blocks from the hostel. He was a rising marketing expert with a bright future ahead of him. After spending six years at the U.S. Commerce Department in Washington, he was now working at the Curtis Publishing Company in Philadelphia. He was a recent but committed Quaker. On Sunday mornings, he conducted a Bible class for adults at the Haverford Meeting, which the hostel students and staff attended. As the hostel was preparing to close down in July 1942, he hired Jurkat to carry out research for a book on marketing, which he was revising—a task for which Jurkat was quite qualified. Alderson could not have known that and offered him the job without being familiar with Jurkat's experience in marketing which he had acquired at VBKI in Berlin. Alderson offered to house Jurkat in his home while he worked for him. Their association would develop into a longer-term relationship. After a two-year interlude at Princeton University, Jurkat would return to work with Alderson and make marketing his chosen career focus for a number of years.

Ernst Jurkat at Princeton

Ernst Jurkat's priorities after leaving Haverford and the hostel were to get a permanent paying job, to resume efforts to be reunited with his wife and son, and to help them survive wherever they might have been stranded until then. He succeeded in all three in different degrees. A few months after his Haverford period, he joined Princeton University's Office of Population Research as a Research Associate, a position he held for the next two years.[114] The Office was founded and headed by the eminent American demographer Dr. Frank W. Notestein (1902-1983), who later became the first director of the Population Division of the United Nations.

How did Jurkat, not a demographer specifically, get the job so quickly or smoothly? His Ph.D. from Kiel University was not focused on a single field; it was, as doctor of philosophy degrees in Germany were then, broadly speaking, in the social sciences. At various stages in his career, Dr. Jurkat worked as an economist, a marketing consultant and an urban planner, but he was a sociologist in essence and at heart, as his work for and close association with Tönnies indicates. He had, nevertheless, worked on demographic issues in Kiel, preparing, for example, a critique of a book on the subject.[115] This may have come to the attention of Princeton's Office of Population Research and of Dr. Notestein specifically. Besides, Dr. Jurkat had been well connected abroad. Authors from outside Germany supplied nearly half of the papers he had solicited for the book on Tönnies which he edited. But the person who helped him get the Princeton job the most was in all likelihood

---

[114] Through most of his stay at Princeton University, Dr. Jurkat lived at 21 Hawthorn Avenue, Princeton, New Jersey.

[115] The book was *Demodynamik*, by the architect Martin Mähler. Jurkat's review appeared in *Jahrbücher für Nationalökonomie und Statistik*, 1934.

The Promise of the Present and the Shadow of the Past

Dr. Rudolf Heberle, the son-in-law of Tönnies, who knew Jurkat well, and had been one of the people who helped him come to the United States. Heberle had come to the this country first and was already well-established as a sociologist.

During his work at Princeton, Jurkat authored or co-authored a number of significant studies, including the following three:

- Frank W. Notestein and Ernst Jurkat, "Population Problems of Palestine," in *The Milbank Memorial Fund Quarterly*, October 1945.
- Ernst Jurkat, "Prospects for Population Growth in the Near East," in *The Milbank Memorial Fund Quarterly*, July 1944.
- Ernst Jurkat and Louise K. Kiser, "The Peoples of the Mohammedan World," in *The Annals of The American Academy of Political and Social Science*, January 1945.

The above studies formed part of the program of Princeton's Office of Population Research on long-term global population projections, in which the Office specialized.

Incidentally, Dr. Jurkat's past affiliation with Princeton's Office of Population Research had, years later, a significant impact on my life. In 1961, when I was working part-time at the Population Studies Center in Philadelphia, I recommended Barbara, my future wife, whom I hardly knew then, for a research assistant position that had just opened up there. She would have probably gotten the job on her own, but her relation to Dr. Jurkat, her uncle, accelerated and assured the decision. The Center's director, Prof. Dorothy S. Thomas, who interviewed Barbara, knew Dr. Notestein of Princeton's Office of Population Research personally. Once she heard of Barbara's relation to Jurkat, the interview was cut short and a hiring decision made without interviewing any other candidate.

In October 1944, Dr. Jurkat left Princeton to join the consulting firm Wroe Alderson & Company, with responsibility for marketing research—a position he held for several years, past reunification with his wife and child, and beyond. A question that arises is why he left Princeton when he did. The question is relevant because, with hindsight, the decision may not have been optimal.

Although, intellectually, he was supremely suited to everything he did professionally, personally, he was suited best to the life of a thinker, a researcher, and a writer, like Tönnies was. He may have left Princeton because he had to. He may have been at the Office of Population Research for a fixed term or on a rolling annual contract. He was not a member of the faculty with teaching responsibilities, let alone tenure. He may also have needed to increase his income, given the financial assistance that he was providing his wife and child stranded in Europe, which was not insignificant. This is suggested by his often being late with or skipping one of his monthly transfers to them. Besides, almost coincidentally with his change of jobs, his wife had asked for an increase in the monthly transfers.

To recapitulate, by war's end, Ernst Jurkat of Berlin at the start of the war, was working at Wroe Alderson & Co. on the 25th floor of Lewis Tower in Philadelphia and living, by himself, at 4 Dreycott Lane, in Haverford, Pennsylvania.

Family Reunification

In the United States, Dr. Jurkat lost no time to resume his efforts to be reunited with his wife Dora, as she was known, and their then six-year old son, Peter. He reestablished and maintained contact with them through the ERC central office in New York and its branch in Marseille, where his wife and son arrived three months after he (Ernst) left. Contact was key for both sides. When contact was lost for 2-3 months at a time, which was unavoidable in a wartime environment, the ERC staff helped in an understanding way and with the human touch I referred to earlier. Dr. Jurkat also reapplied for U.S. visas for his wife, son and mother-in-law, since the visa regulations had been changed on July 1, 1941, necessitating restarting the process, submitting new forms and affidavits, etc. And as soon as he got a job, he began sending them subsistence money, roughly $60 a month, mostly through the AFSC. Although visas for them were approved by December 1941, the visas would not be issued until November 1945, when the war was over.

Not long after he arrived in the United States, Dr. Jurkat must have gotten in touch with at least some of the people who had helped him get a visa earlier and raise the money for his passage. We know that he visited Dr. Fritz Levy, his wife's ex-brother-in-law, in Elkins, West Virginia. And he contacted Dr. Gerhardt Colm, who submitted one of the affidavits needed for his wife's new visa application.

There is a break in the information available about Dr. Jurkat's close family from about mid-1942 to March 1944, at least in the ERC files. While Ernest Jurkat kept sending subsistence aid for them through the ERC and the funds were delivered, we do not know where they were living. Dora and her son surface in the ERC correspondence next in July 1944, after being "liberated" (released) from an internment camp in Criens (Krienz), near Lucerne (Luzern), Switzerland. We do not know when and how they had arrived there. Also, apparently, Dora and Peter were separated from her mother, Therese, at one point and, consequently, Therese reached Switzerland after they did. She was interned at the Hotel Tivoli with hundreds of refugees, like they themselves had been before. About this time, the financial demands on Dr. Jurkat to assure the subsistence of his close family increased significantly. Release from internment could be secured only by an outside commitment of a monthly subsistence payment. Dr. Fritz Levy was very helpful by assuming responsibility for his ex mother-in-law, and the IRRC (the metamorphosed ERC) also helped by making up the difference between what Dr. Jurkat could provide and the amount needed for decent survival. I describe the substantive role that Dr. Levy's assistance played in Chapter 10.

Dr. Jurkat's financial assistance during this critical period generated a great deal of correspondence with the ERC in particular. His letters reveal a strong and unflinching commitment to helping his wife and child, his readiness to make any sacrifice necessary, and, throughout, the pain of a worried husband and father—all expressed with elegance, sensitivity, and gratitude toward the ERC/IRRC. On July 25, 1944, he wrote the IRRC:

> "I certainly am very grateful to your organization for paying the necessary difference for the maintenance of my family, thus making possible that my wife can live in liberty and together with our son. The separation of

mother and son was a constant worry for me, knowing how much it means for both of them to have each other. For a boy the age of my son, the education by his mother very likely is of importance for his whole development."

As the war was winding down, two unexpected events concerning the Jurkat family occurred. Dr. Jurkat's mother-in-law became seriously ill in November 1944 and died seven months later (June 1945) in Lucerne, Switzerland. And at about that time, news came that Dora Jurkat's brother, Hans Bergas, who had worked for the French underground, survived Buchenwald, where he had been held since January 1944, but in very poor physical condition. (See Chapter 9.) Neither event had an impact on the next and ultimate challenge—Dora and Peter's emigration to the United States.

The challenge for Dr. Jurkat was again threefold: to get visas, bookings and financing, and in a concerted way. Even before obtaining the visas, which had been pending for two years, Dr. Jurkat focused his attention on the tickets. The JLC had bought tickets for his wife and son two years earlier but had had to dispose of them when Dora and Peter were unable to leave. Dr. Jurkat and the IRRC hoped that the JLC could do the same this time, too, but the JLC declined. The IRRC first offered the JLC the option of sharing the cost with it. When that did not work either, the IRRC agreed to advance the full amount against an oral pledge by Dr. Jurkat to reimburse it after his wife's arrival in the U. S. "in whatever way is suitable to you."

Dorothy and Peter finally got their visas in November 1945. The next challenge was obtaining a booking. Dora herself took the initiative in this regard in consultation with her husband by mail, and weighing the various cost alternatives. The most attractive was travel by a "liberty ship"—one of the cargo vessels made famous by World War II, which were quick and cheap to build and usually took along a few civilians. As Dr. Jurkat expressed it, "this would represent the cheapest kind of transportation" and with the advantage of "good food and medical care." Passengers interested in a voyage would be normally informed not more than five days in advance.

The Promise of the Present and the Shadow of the Past

Mother and son left Lucerne on January 23, 1946, hoping to get on a liberty ship bound for the United States on January 25. While their voyage did not approximate Dr. Jurkat's hellish one five years earlier, it was not without unforeseen difficulties and it took longer than anticipated, adding to the tension coming from the now seven years of separation. Dora and son, on arrival in Antwerp, could not get passage on a liberty ship; they were stranded there until February 4 when they boarded the steamer *Edward Steppard* for Boston. The steamer was due to arrive at its destination on February 21, but on that day a heavy storm drove her back in the eastern direction, and only when the storm subsided on February 24, 1946 was she able to dock at the Boston port. Dr. Jurkat was there, of course. The following day, he wrote the IRRC:

> "My wife and son arrived in good condition, healthy and happy. I suppose my wife will write you herself as soon as she gets to letter writing. She is full of praise and thankfulness as to the splendid job your people abroad did in her case."

The Jurkats settled on arrival at 501 Oakley Road in Haverford, Pennsylvania. It took only five weeks for Dora Jurkat to write to the IRRC herself, enclosing the first payment ($10) of reimbursement for the tickets, adding, "You can be sure that we take care to pay so regularly as possible." The statement is typical of her, a proud, assertive woman who, even when she said hello or thank you, did it with an air of being in command. She signed the letter Dorothy, the name she would be known by, by her choice, for the rest of her life.

On January 23, 1947, the Jurkats formally joined the Religious Society of Friends at Haverford, thus becoming Quakers for life. Their son Peter (12) became a "birthright member" of the Society on the same day. Might their experience before and during the war have had anything to do with it?

For the next fifteen years (1947-62), the Jurkats made Philadelphia their home. During this period, Dr. Jurkat worked as a marketing consultant, first for Wroe Alderson, mentioned earlier,[116] and then as head of his own firm. In the late 1940s, he also served briefly on the faculty of the Graduate School of Business Administration of New York University, commuting from Philadelphia. Over time, Dr. Jurkat's work extended to the fields of urban planning and regional development. In the early 1960s he worked closely for entrepreneur Milton J. Shapp with whom he prepared an economic revitalization plan for the state of Pennsylvania.[117] Three years later, Shapp ran for governor of the state partly on the strength of that plan. Although he lost the election narrowly, his collaboration with Jurkat on the plan was the beginning of a close and enduring association and friendship.

In 1963 Ernst Jurkat was recruited by the United Nations Development Program (UNDP)—the development assistance arm of the world organization—as an urban planning adviser for Turkey, and the couple moved there. On the way to their destination, Istanbul, they stopped over in Germany to visit Ernst's surviving relatives. This was the Jurkat couple's first visit to Germany in twenty-five years. After Turkey, Ernst served for the UNDP in the same advisory capacity in Ethiopia and Tanzania until 1971. This was a most rewarding period for him, for his wife, as well as for the people they worked with. They served longest in Turkey—first in Istanbul, then in Ankara, the capital. Ernst was quite knowledgeable about and sympathetic to Turkey and the rest of the Middle East, having done significant research on the region at Princeton University in the early 1940s. His quiet, fatherly and professorial demeanor, in addition to his expertise, endeared him to his counterparts and assistants, especially in Turkey. He developed a group of young enthusiastic devotees and followers not only in Turkey but in Ethiopia and Tanzania, too. Dorothy Jurkat did the same and gained wide admiration, both by assisting her husband and on her own. While in Ethiopia, for example, she assisted the daughter of Emperor Haile Selassie in managing the numerous charities she supported and oversaw. This was not the first occasion on which Dorothy assisted—complemented is a

---

[116] He was officially director of research for Alderson & Sessions, Inc.

[117] *New Growth, New Jobs for Pennsylvania*, A Shapp Foundation Report, 1962.

better term—her husband. She had some background in sociology and had co-authored some research with him in the late 1940s.[118]

Dr. Jurkat could have worked longer for the UNDP, but in 1971 he responded to a new challenge: Milton Shapp was elected Governor of Pennsylvania in 1970, and he did not waste time to ask him to join his administration. Shapp was as devoted to him as his young disciples had been. The Jurkats relocated to Harrisburg, the state capital, soon thereafter. And for the next eight years—Shapp was re-elected in 1974—Ernst worked as personal adviser to the governor and Chairman of the Governor's Council of Economic Advisers.

Ernst retired soon after the end of Governor Shapp's term in office in 1979. In 1980, the Jurkats moved to Pennswood Village, a Quaker retirement community in the town of Newton, located in Bucks County, Pennsylvania. Dorothy passed away there in 1990, and Ernst followed in 1994. They are buried side by side at the Newton Friends Meeting House grounds.

To step back, in closing, on August 21, 1979, Ernst Jurkat wrote Barbara, by hand, a warm personal letter asking her to translate some of the papers he had published decades earlier in Germany. Clearly, he was thinking of publishing a collection of his writings. His wish did not materialize; neither he nor Barbara followed up on his request. I do not know the reasons, since Barbara never discussed the letter with me; I discovered it among her papers after her death in 2003. It would have been extremely unlikely for her to refuse his request, and not simply because of her respect for him, but because she was eminently, almost uniquely qualified to carry out his wish. She had been working as a part-time, freelance technical translator for some time; she had studied sociology in graduate school; and she had a highly analytical mind, like he did. The letter is nevertheless intriguing for at least the following reasons.

Dr. Jurkat's request came very shortly after the conclusion of Governor Shapp's term of office, when he retired. This suggests that

---

[118] See, for example, Ernst H. Jurkat and Dorothy B. Jurkat, *Economic Function of Strikes*, Industrial and Labor Relations Review, July 1949.

he may have started thinking about it—about his legacy—before his retirement.

Over his long career spanning half a century and two continents, Dr. Jurkat authored a multitude of papers and reports on a variety of subjects. His particular interest in the work he had carried out mostly during his Kiel years in Germany suggests to me that he remained a sociologist and an academic at heart.

Could his interest in publishing a collection of his writings have been a step toward writing his memoirs, breaking the long silence about his leaving Germany, the war and its aftermath? We will never know. What we are sure about is that had he proceeded with his memoirs, the world would have been better for it, and my task would have been easier, to say the least. Besides, it would have been so much better if HE, rather than I, wrote about Tönnies, if HE described Christopher Isherwood rather than the other way around, to give two examples. I have written about what Ernst Jurkat did. HE could have told us what he saw—and thought.

Chapter Nine

The Buchenwald Memoirist

Hans Bergas (1898-1969) was the elder brother of Dorothy Jurkat, Barbara's aunt through marriage. I was not aware of his existence until I came across a letter by Dr. Jurkat, dated June 11, 1945, in his wife's Emergency Rescue Committee file welcoming the news of "the release of Hans Bergas from Buchenwald." He added, "To know this meant much comfort to Mrs. Bergas [Hans' mother] in her hour of death." Mrs. Bergas had died in Luzerne, Switzerland, two days earlier. Almost immediately, I went to the United States Holocaust Memorial Museum in search of a trace of Hans Bergas among the Holocaust survivors. I found not only a trace but also his entire Buchenwald file. The American soldiers who liberated Buchenwald on April 4, 1945 had the good sense of photographing all of the files. The Bergas file quickly revealed that he had been held in Buchenwald as a French political prisoner, not as a Jew, although he had been a Jew by birth. I also learned at the museum that after the war Hans Bergas had written an unpublished memoir of his Buchenwald experience, which had found its way through a circuitous route to the Friends Historical Library of Swarthmore College in Swarthmore, Pennsylvania. I visited the library soon thereafter and acquired a copy of the memoir.

This account of Hans Bergas' life is based largely though not exclusively on his unpublished memoir.[119] Understandably, his case has attracted considerable attention in recent decades and has been the subject of discussion or references in numerous articles which, though not in all cases reliable, have proven useful in my research. My account also draws on an unpublished interview which Bergas' only surviving daughter, Suzanne Bergas-Legé, gave a French reporter in February 2009 near Paris.

In the Beginning

Hans Bergas was born on July 23, 1898 in Berlin. His birth certificate lists both his mother and father, Therese and Albert Bergas, as *mosaisch* (Jewish). At the beginning of the First World War, at age sixteen, he enlisted in the army "like all good German youth."[120] He served with the Imperial Marines. He was seriously wounded during combat, but he survived. Like many others, he soon began to question the justification for the war, and he participated in the mutiny of 1917 in an attempt to stop it. The mutiny did not succeed; its participants were condemned as traitors; the fighting continued; and Germany lost the war. The birth of the Weimar Republic in late 1918 was, for Hans Bergas, a dream come true. He joined the Social Democratic Party at that time. Years later, he wrote, "I have been loyal to it [the Party] and shall continue to be loyal to it. Socialism on a democratic foundation is and will remain my ideal."

Internal resistance to the Weimar Republic started almost immediately. Those opposed to it included the reactionaries who thought only of revenge for the lost war, and the communists. The resistance became increasingly generalized and violent. Defamation and murder were common. During the Weimar period, 1919-1933,

---

[119] I wish to express my gratitude to Christopher Densmore, Curator of the Friends Historical Library of Swarthmore College, for giving me access to and guiding me through Hans Bergas' memoir and correspondence.

[120] To allow young people to volunteer for the army, the last year of the *Gymnasium* (high school), was practically canceled, and the final examinations were substituted by the requirement to write an essay.

Bergas held a variety of posts and took part in various activities to fight the enemies of the republic. He worked for a while as a reporter for *Die Welt am Abend* (The World in the Evening), a communist daily tabloid published in Berlin, but he resigned from it in 1927. By his own account, he held "high political offices" during part of the Weimar period, although we do not know what or where they may have been.[121] He also notes in his memoir that, during this period, he was for a while in prison, because "I was bold enough to write articles disclosing the secret rearmament of Germany," which he claimed started as early as 1921.[122]

The environment for Weimar supporters deteriorated rapidly. When the Nazis came to power in 1933, Bergas and like-minded activists were designated as "November criminals," November referring to the month in which the Weimar Republic was founded in 1918. Bergas was immediately relieved of all his positions, his possessions were confiscated, a warrant was issued for his arrest, and his close family began being harassed. A few years earlier, Hans had married Anna Wieczorek, born in 1900 in Schmarse, now Poland. She was a pious, Catholic woman very supportive of his politics. They had a son, Horst Albert, born in 1930 in Berlin, who later adopted the name Henri. In July 1933, Hans escaped by train to Switzerland. His wife and child fled a few months later to Paris, where Hans joined them. This was the first of several occasions on which Hans would escape in advance of his family, only to be joined by them later. Such a pattern was not uncommon among dissident German men.

The Bergases lived in Paris until 1939/40 and began their resistance activities as soon as they arrived there. I said "their"

---

[121] His Buchenwald file lists his prior occupation or post as *Ministerialdirektör* without further specification.

[122] We do not know where the articles were published. More importantly, this claim conflicts with a similar claim about disclosing Germany's secret rearmament attributed to Dr. Jurkat by some surviving family members in explanation of his forced escape from Germany in 1938. Bergas' claim is more believable because we have it in his own words and in writing. Besides, Germany's rearmament would hardly have been news and constitute the disclosure of a secret in 1938.

because Hans' wife took part in such activities then as well as later, as did members of her family. She had a brother who was tortured and went mad in the process. The Bergases lived in a two-room apartment in Vincennes, a suburb of Paris. Their activities were not yet classical resistance activities, as the war had not started at the time. What had started was the influx of political refugees from Germany and neighboring countries threatened by it. Most prominent among the Bergases' activities was forging identity papers, providing sponsorship or cover for illegal refugees, and helping young people especially to emigrate legally or clandestinely to Africa, Britain and its colonies, and elsewhere. An overarching objective was to fight fascism by exposing its ills through every means available, including the distribution of leaflets among German troops as well as to the civilian populations of France and Britain. Another activity as the war approached was to prepare, organize and train the nascent resistance. To support the family—they had a second child, a daughter, shortly after arriving in Paris—Anna Bergas did house work for "rich Jewish families." And Hans engaged in counter-espionage before the war by working as a bellboy-messenger at the plush Ambassador Hotel, frequented by Germans, and passing on the intelligence he gathered to the forming French resistance.[123] As the German armies were occupying Paris, Hans fled to Montauban in southwestern France and his family joined him there later.

Montauban

Montauban, which is almost synonymous with the Hans Bergas saga and French resistance at a broad level, is a town of about 50,000 people (40,000 before the war) in the Tarn-et-Garonne *Département* of which it is the capital. It is in a largely agricultural area and located 31 miles north of the city of Toulouse. Throughout the war, southwestern France, of which Montauban is a part, was an important center of resistance both by accident and by design. The

---

[123] Apparently, the Ambassador Hotel functioned as a hub of espionage and counter-espionage like the Park Hotel did in Istanbul before and during the war. See my *Cultures in Counterpoint*, op. cit. p. 70.

area had a large concentration of German political refugees, as those who fled Germany before the war were soon joined, once the war began, by those fleeing arrest and persecution by the Vichy Regime. Moreover, early on in the war, the German Communist Party, the Social Democratic Party and the labor unions had instructed their ex-members and sympathizers in France to assemble in designated places in this region of the country. The Germans who were rounded up first by the pre-war government and later by the Vichy government were sent to camps located in the South-West, to keep them far from Paris.[124] The camps consisted of both internment centers and labor camps (*camps de préstation*) where the detainees were organized into so-called "foreign workers brigades." Although the camps were periodically inspected by the Gestapo to spot dangerous people and activities, camp security and inspection were not thorough. As a result, literally hundreds fled the camps but remained in the region and joined the resistance.[125]

Two remarkable individuals played an important role in forming the resistance base. Adolf Ludwig, born in 1892 in Germany and a Social Democrat, had been living with his immediate family in France since 1935. He served in a labor camp but was released after a year (perhaps thanks to a French parent), and was considered a legal citizen of the country. In 1941, he managed to lease a large farm with some private Swiss capital, and he established in rather short order a large, successful collective agricultural colony employing the numerous unemployed German refugees. The farm's success can be gauged from the meticulously-kept records of its diverse and large agricultural output produced year after year. The farm soon became a source of manpower and womanpower for the resistance.

At about the same time, another German, Siegbert Simenauer, born in 1890 in Berlin, was laying the ground for a similar resistance

---

[124] The camps included also political refugees from other countries such as Poland, Czechoslovakia, Belgium, Italy, and Spain.

[125] Mauntoban has a happier association than the one it acquired during the Second World War. It is the birthplace of the French neoclassical painter Ingres (1780-1867) and boasts the world's only museum devoted entirely to his work.

capability in Montauban. Like Ludwig above, Simenauer had been in France before the war (since 1928) and even served in the French army. A former industrialist, he had connections with labor leaders in both Germany and France, including Vichy France, through whom he managed to identify both those who needed help, for example, false papers, and those who could provide it (artists, forgers, etc.).[126]

When Hans Bergas arrived in Montauban he found a resistance network, not simply a cell, in the making, although much work lay ahead in terms of both preparation and action. While at Montauban, he was employed by the local office of the American Friends Service Committee (AFSC) and received, in addition to a salary, food and board for himself and his family. What Hans did for the AFSC is not clear, although it could not have conflicted with his resistance work; in fact, there may have been synergy between the two. Nor is it clear why the Quakers would have an office in Montauban or employ Hans. While Hans' cause was in tune with Quaker ideals, one could hardly say the same of his tactics.

Concerning the logistical preparation of the resistance, Hans Bergas wrote:

> "In the underground we had many different kinds of jobs and divisions which specialized in specific tasks. There were couriers, radio senders, radio receivers, mailboxes, photographers for passport photos, printers, specialists in forging official seals, drivers, butchers, bakers, nurses, doctors, fliers, social workers, priests, hotel managers, frontier guides and many, many others. In short, we had to set up an organization to direct an

---

[126] For a more detailed account of the establishment of French resistance in southwestern France and the key players, see Annette Röser, "Les réfugiés Allemands dans le Sud-ouest Pendant la Seconde Guerre Mondiale," in *Arkheia* Nos. 11, 12, 13, 2004. *Arkheia* is, as it defines itself, a Review of History and Remembrance of the Twentieth Century in the South-West of France. It aims to revisit the history of that century through the "prism of regional history," that is, from the parts to the whole, with the participation and help of academics, students, historians, journalists, and testimonials.

army of workers, and had to do it secretly, and we had to care for the dependents and relatives of an army."

The resistance activities encompassed all classical resistance actions such as sabotaging supply trains and troop transport, informing the Allies "hourly" of German troop movements, distributing anti-Nazi leaflets, forging ration cards and identity documents, smuggling people, etc.

Hans was not a resistance *leader* and, in fairness, he never claimed to be. He was nevertheless an important player and a reliable, trusted team member. He had most of the time the job of overseeing "the work of the foreigners"—Poles, Yugoslavs, Russians, Austrians, Belgians, "Jews," etc. in the resistance. To provide the refugees some income, he and others helped establish a toy factory or workshop and a farm on a more modest scale than the one mentioned earlier. And when she was not participating in the resistance activities herself, his wife (called Anneliese instead of Anna in France) did some housework for others to make ends meet.

Regarding Hans Bergas' personal contribution, the testimonials he received after the war singled out, among others, his help to the Jews fleeing the police, his warning them of imminent deportation to allow them to escape, his assistance to needy families, and his serving as liaison between the Resistance and foreign powers. While all of these were important contributions, the honors he received after the war—Legion of Honor and *Croix de Guerre* medal (more on them later)—appear to have been just as much for his work *at* Buchenwald to help the other French prisoners. But how did he get there?

Bergas was arrested on September 14, 1943 in Montauban when the wife of an elderly Jewish couple whom he and the Resistance had been hiding in a hospital was discovered and, under the threat of death, revealed his whereabouts—an act for which he never blamed her. The arrest took place as part of *Aktion Meerschaum* (Operation Seafoam) designed to round up and punish the members of the Resistance in occupied countries. Bergas was immediately taken to Prison Saint Michel in Toulouse where he spent the next five months, three of them in solitary confinement, deprived of food, clothing, blankets, etc., and being beaten, flogged and tortured. The torture he received in Toulouse was the worst of his life and resulted in the mutilation of his internal organs. His wife was being threatened and maltreated concurrently. The object of the torture he was subjected to was to force him to reveal the identities of the leaders of the Underground, which he never did. He was then taken to Compiègne in northern France for trial, but the trial never took place. And on January 29, 1944 he was delivered to the Gestapo in Paris for transport to Buchenwald, with his mutilated internal organs still exposed.

Buchenwald

Since, as stated earlier, the bulk of Hans Bergas' memoirs are about Buchenwald, this is a good place to introduce them and to dwell on them. But the subject consists of two equally interesting stories: how the drafting and preservation of the memoirs came about, and what the memoirs actually say.

Drafting of the Memoirs

We need to jump ahead, and then back, before turning to the post-Buchenwald period. Hans Bergas was liberated from camp seriously ill, with tuberculosis lodged in both lungs. After a period in hospital (probably a sanatorium), he returned to his family in Montauban but was confined to bed for 21 hours a day. He could not work and had no income, except for what his wife could bring in through housework. There was not much to buy anyway, even among the bare necessities, due to the horrendous economic situation which followed the horrendous war. He and his family had the good luck, however, of being adopted almost literally by a teacher of German and her class thousands of miles away.

The teacher was Gertrude Weaver, a Quaker, who had studied the German language and German history at Swarthmore College in Pennsylvania and spent her junior year, 1936/37, in Munich, Germany. The class was the German language class she taught, after graduating from Swarthmore and attending Columbia University, at Chester High School in Chester, Pennsylvania. She learned about the postwar plight of German refugees, developed a keen interest in helping them, and identified a few, including Hans Bergas, presumably through her Quaker connection. And she enlisted her class in the endeavor. Miss Weaver and her students engaged in a regular correspondence with the Bergases—husband, wife and sometimes their children—to inquire about their needs; they collected money by soliciting contributions from family, friends and neighbors; they purchased and packed the goods as a team; and they shipped them. This was repeated many times and generated quite a bit of correspondence, which was, in a way, the payoff for teacher and students. The incoming letters from the Bergases (all in German) were translated by the students, as part of their homework, under Miss Weaver's supervision.

The goods requested by the Bergases and shipped to them reveal both the dire postwar situation of scarcities and the loving attention that it must have taken to procure, pack and send them. They included: coffee, sugar, meat, soap, clothes (ranging from gloves to underwear and sleepwear), razor blades, sewing materials and tools, colored pencils for the children, and paper, for the correspondence itself. The Bergasses also requested shoes, by sending with their letters outlines of the feet, plus leather and nails, "so we can have our shoes soled,"

In return, Hans Bergas offered to write his memoirs for the class. The idea may have been suggested by Miss Weaver—she had the personality and imagination required to take the initiative—although it must have appeared attractive and doable to Bergas, who was confined to bed and undoubtedly eager to return the kindness he and his family had been receiving. He wrote the memoirs over time by hand, and mailed them in installments, as he completed each one. And the students translated them as they arrived. The completed whole, referred to hereafter as "the memoir," is a document of 77 pages, titled *Buchenwald Experiences of Hans Bergas Written for Chester High School Students: 1914-1946*. It was written and mailed in sixteen segments between April and July 1946.

Before turning to the memoir, it is important to note that the Buchenwald topic was not an easy one for adults, let alone for young people like the Chester students, in 1946. Moreover, digesting the memoir required more than a beginner's knowledge of German. It necessitated literally dissecting what Hans Bergas was writing and knowledge of the context—political, historical, economic—which Miss Weaver was no doubt providing. In the end, a group of high school students in a small town called Chester acquired inside knowledge of what took place in Buchenwald when half the world was ignorant of it. The students certainly knew more about it than their parents. Whether they discussed their homework with their parents is one of the many questions posed by this remarkable story.

After or in addition to teaching at Chester High School, Weaver worked in the Newark (Delaware) School District, at Penn State College, as well as at a college in China. She also continued her education at the University of Maryland and the University of Pennsylvania. Ms. Weaver was killed in a car accident in 1998. But the Bergas memoir survived. It was passed on first to Anna Janney DeAmand, a Swarthmore graduate and lifelong friend of Weaver, and was subsequently transferred to the Swarthmore College archives.

The Memoir Itself

The first few pages of the memoir describe briefly Bergas' political awakening at age 16, his departure from Germany, his arrest in Montauban, and his torture in Toulouse, which I have covered above. Bergas also describes graphically his horrendous rail journey to Buchenwald under the bestial conditions in such journeys to hell that have been depicted in several motion pictures since. According to his Buchenwald file, which I obtained from the United States Holocaust Museum, upon arrival, Bergas was registered as a Roman Catholic and a French "political prisoner," not as a Jew. The description of his physical condition and traits noted a permanent scar on the left side of his skull, which was probably due to an injury suffered during the previous world war. There was no reference to his more recent bodily wounds, which were still bleeding. The shape of his nose—clearly a stipulation designed to identify Jews—was given as "straight."

The Promise of the Present and the Shadow of the Past

The Buchenwald concentration camp (Buchenwald for short) had been established in 1937 and was the first and one of the largest camps on German soil. Its location and name had ironic links. The camp was located near Weimar, which gave the social democratic republic preceding the Third Reich its name. And the camp's name, German for *beech forest,* was obliquely related to Goethe. The eminent German writer used to visit a favorite oak tree in the area, which was later named after him and incorporated into the camp. Inmates, or internees, included Jews but also a large number of political prisoners (communists, anarchists), criminals of all kind, religious prisoners (Jehovah's Witnesses), and prisoners of war from many countries. Among the prisoners were writers, doctors, lawyers, and artists. Most of the political prisoners from occupied countries were members of the resistance. The camp was not an extermination camp like Auschwitz—one whose main purpose was mass extermination—although prisoners were starved or worked to death in the camp quarry or adjacent arms factories. Many were put to death through transfer to other camps.

Hans Bergas' description of Buchenwald is comprehensive. It covers the camp layout, its inmate composition, its management and internal organization, the living (or survival) conditions and camp life, the nature of the compulsory work, and the internal power structure; and it closes with the liberation of the camp. Before embarking on the task of writing, Bergas recognized that what he had experienced and was about to describe would be shocking to young people. He therefore asked Miss Weaver for guidance about how open he should be in that regard. Her reply was not among the Swarthmore College files, but we can guess what it was, for Bergas did exercise some restraint. Although he mentioned all the horrors of the camp—the crematoria, the brothels, the medical experiments on human beings, and the maltreatment of children—he did not describe his own torture and the suffering of others graphically. His restraint notwithstanding, he left no doubt whatsoever about the end objective. "It was murder," he wrote, "murder, murder. Murder for sadistic reasons; murder for expediency and murder for security. Murder practiced by the S.S. for further murder."

Much of what Bergas revealed is common to other accounts of concentration camps. One thing that distinguished his account is that he seemed more concerned with the behavior of the inmates, the group he belonged to, than with the behavior of the Gestapo or the S. S.—at least he oscillated between the two in his account. He stated emphatically, "The worst crimes of the S.S. were only possible at all because of the complicity of the prisoners themselves." He cited cases of denouncement, cheating, stealing and false accusations—even inmate killing inmate—that resulted out of the instinct for self-preservation. And he did not exclude himself from this. He noted that even when he had rescued someone from death, he had been aware that someone else was would be killed instead. He cast this behavior in the context of what he labeled the Buchenwald Code, which he claimed operated at the camp.

The Buchenwald *Code* (I am not sure that this is the correct translation of the word he used) seems to me to be almost a term of Bergas' creation to explain the inexplicable: namely, the immoral, irrational behavior of the inmate population, which was governed by terror and the instinct for self-preservation. The Code did not refer to a set of dictated or imposed principles of conduct—there weren't any. It referred, rather, to the reality on the ground, that is, to behavior governed by the law of the jungle, where anything was possible. Bergas believed that, ". . . the amorality of the Buchenwald Code was the assistant helper of the S.S."

To convey what this meant in practice, Bergas took pains to describe the composition of the inmate population and the governance and power structure. The inmate population consisted of seven groups, as determined by the S.S: political prisoners, criminals, hardened criminals, labor deserters, Jews, sex criminals, and religious fanatics. The camp governed itself internally, under orders and supervision by the S.S. Cleverly, the S.S. delegated and spread the governing responsibilities among the above prisoner groups in a way that created rivalries and enmities. The result was internecine war since the various jobs to be performed carried vastly differing hardships and prospects of death.

> "The functionaries of the camp management were put in their jobs by the S.S., at the recommendation of the prisoners. Sometimes the criminals were bosses of the camp, other times the political prisoners. If the

criminals were in charge, they sent the political prisoners on the death commandos [tasks] and vice versa. If the political prisoners were in charge, they sent the criminals to their death."

Because of his language skills and possibly prior contacts with some the German inmates, which included old political friends, Hans Bergas played the role of go-between in the life-and-death situations that arose almost daily.

The most powerful prisoner group in the camp were the German Communists, partly because they had been there the longest and knew the ropes, so-to-speak. They enjoyed the most privileges and had the biggest say on assignments, which worked to the detriments of others, including the French prisoners. At one point, toward the end of the war, the two groups entered into negotiations to develop common position on issues like "Work or Sabotage, National Justice or Collective Justice in the Camp, Proportional Representation in the Secret Camp Command," and others. Hans was charged both with bringing the two sides face to face—not an easy job—and with providing translation and other assistance during the discussions. The French were representing the other prisoners as well, and the recalcitrant German communists, who wanted to hold on to their privileges, dominated the German side. The negotiations failed to produce results and Hans returned to assisting inmates on an individual basis.

The Allies were advancing and the end of the war was approaching. Bergas' account of the last days displays literary flair. It describes grippingly and in a crescendo-like way the joy, hope, chaos, and terror—that the S.S. may carry out the orders to kill all remaining Jews, as rumored—the actual loss of 3,000 Jews 48 hours before liberation, and the camp's takeover by the inmates minutes before the American forces arrived. The last words of the memoir state that once a radio was connected with the loudspeaker system, the first news that came was the announcement of the death of Roosevelt, "our liberator."

The Memoir in Perspective

The memoir, its translation and preservation are the product of two remarkable people and call for some comments and questions.

The German language instruction which Gertrude Weaver offered was at a much higher level than was typical for a high school. How come? Chester did not have an ethnic German population; in fact, the city was founded by Swedish immigrants and was known originally as "Finlandia." The quality of the English text is also of a higher quality than one can reasonably expect from high school students. The text is quite sophisticated in places and flows like non-professional translations rarely do. Did Weaver translate, write or edit any of it? My guess is probably yes. Also, every memoir segment that arrived must have led the students to ask and Weaver to answer a multitude of questions about the events, not just the language.[127]

The memoir combined elements of reportage, testimonial, confession, and reflection in a *stream of consciousness* way. Bergas went out of his way to stress that he was not an inmate leader, a block captain, a *capo*. He was an important player, but not a lead player. He talked in detail about his role and some of his actions, but he avoided placing himself at the center of the memoir. He wrote, rather, as a witness, which makes the memoir valuable to historians.

What is relevant and noteworthy—and this observation has been made by others—is that Bergas wrote his memoir barely a year after he left Buchenwald and over a period of just three months, that is, while the events he recounted were still fresh, his anger raw, his emotional wounds open, with little time to reflect on his experience, check facts, etc. How did this affect what he wrote? Would the memoir have been different in any way had he written it, say, 8-10 years after the facts, like Elie Wiesel?

---

[127] One wishes that the exchanges between Weaver and her students had been taped. Since they were not and Weaver is not alive, it would be interesting to locate some of those students and ask them to share their recollection of this rather unique experience.

And there is something which he left out. In addition to the Buchenwald Code, the camp had produced the Buchenwald *Manifesto*. As the war was ending, the representatives of the various political groups in the camp started devoting attention to Germany's post-war governance, especially to reconciling the significant differences between the communists and the Social Democrats, which had caused destructive hostility. This led to intense discussions within each group and between the two. The Social Democrats were led by Hermann Brill (1895-1959) who advocated the unification of the two parties. To rally the Social Democrats around common goals, their representatives at camp, headed by Brill, drafted the Buchenwald Manifesto, which was signed immediately after the liberation of the camp.[128] Bergas did not mention any of this; his memoir contained a single, casual reference to Brill in the "one day I bumped into him" way. This suggests that Bergas may not have been a party to the substantive discussions, which would be hard to believe, given his strong political views and strong identification with Social Democrats. He probably omitted the subject in his memoir on purpose, considering it of lesser interest to the Chester High School student.

The picture of Bergas that emerges from his memoir is one of a man led, obsessed and consumed by ideology, anti-fascist ideology, just as much as his opponents were by theirs, and who lived his life by it, regardless of the pain or the circumstances.

The Aftermath

Hans Bergas was declared invalid for life at the end of the war. His dual priorities were, therefore, physical and financial survival. He survived his acute tuberculosis, which had severely damaged his two lungs, thanks to the nowadays much maligned French health system. Thanks to the many testimonials on his wartime contributions both outside and inside Buchenwald, he was granted a military pension with free housing for life. He also received

---

[128] Brill went on to become, sequentially, a senior state government official of the Federal Republic, a member of the Bundestag for the SPD and, later, a university professor, before his death in 1959.

damages for the personal property he lost in Paris, as well as, years later, compensation from the German government. At the same time, he was awarded a Legion of Honor and the military medal known as *Croix de Guerre*. Thus, he enjoyed financial tranquility for the balance of his life, with his health and honor restored. He sided with Algeria in the French-Algerian war and helped Algerian refugees. He spent most of his remaining years assisting needy women and children, including those seeking compensation from Germany. He died 1969 in Livry-Gargan outside Paris, and his wife died in the same place in 1982. Of their two children, only the youngest, their daughter Suzanne Bergas-Legé, a psychiatric nurse, survives. Their son Henri died in 1977. Of their six grand-children, one, Jean-Luc Bergas, lives in Montauban where much of the drama evolved.

Relevance—Direct and Indirect

I did not set out to research Hans Bergas for himself, that is, as a resistance hero, although his story is gripping. I did it because of his connection to Barbara, my wife, through the Jurkats—Hans' sister and brother-in-law. I ended up with many questions and maybes, rather than answers, in this regard—intriguing questions, nevertheless.

Ernst Jurkat had been the assistant and protégé of the staunchly anti-Nazi, Social Democratic Prof. Ferdinand Tonnies in Kiel. Therefore, his political views could not have been too different from Hans' views, although Hans was militant, while Ernst was not. The two no doubt knew each other and each other's thinking. Yet while Hans was fleeing Berlin in 1933, Ernst was starting a new career as editor of a magazine of the Berlin business establishment.[129]

When Ernst Jurkat himself fled Berlin in 1938 and joined the French army soon thereafter, his first stop must have been Paris where Hans Bergas and his small family had been living and engaging in clandestine political activity for nearly five years. Hans may have suggested or facilitated Ernst's joining the army.

---

[129] I discuss Dr. Jurkat's association with the business group, *Verbein Berliner Kaufleute und Industriellier*, in Chapter 8.

One of Jurkat's early letters in his Emergency Rescue Committee file is one which he wrote on March 16, 1941 from *Montauban* to an acquaintance in the United States requesting assistance in raising the funds for his passage to this country. The letter leaves no doubt that Ernst Jurkat visited Bergas there and suggests that the two may have maintained contact while they were in Paris and Montauban. Also, on the ship's manifest upon coming to the United States, Jurkat declared his citizenship as Polish and his place of birth as Warsaw, neither of which is true. This indicates that he traveled with false papers—papers which he may have obtained through Bergas or his associates in the resistance.

Bergas' memoir, indeed his entire Swarthmore College file, contains just a single reference to his mother and sister, but one which shows that he cared about them. It reads, "I stayed in Germany until July 1933 but when they began to annoy, to beat and to arrest my mother, sister, wife and child because they could not find me, I left the country." We do not know if he stayed in touch with them; in all likelihood he did. After Dr. Jurkat's hasty escape, his wife (Hans' sister) may have left with the help of her husband's connections and friends. However, Hans may have had a role in arranging for his mother's escape.

No written communication between the Jurkats and the Bergases before, during or after the war, has come down to us. But some independently taken photographs have. They show, in my view, a strong resemblance between brother and sister, each with a round face and a small distance between the eyes. They may even have had similar personalities. When Hans' daughter was asked by an interviewer in 2009 what her father was like, she replied "Emmerdant. Pas facile," which mean annoying, difficult to deal with or, with some translator's liberty, stubborn and willful. These adjectives describe Hans' sister as well, especially later in life. They were both apparently easy to admire but difficult to love.

Chapter Ten

From Berlin to Elkins, West Virgnia[130]

Dr. Fritz Levy, a medical doctor, was born in 1887 in Berlin. He was the brother-in-law of Dorothy Jurkat, wife of Barbara's uncle Ernst Jurkat. He is of interest not only because of the financial help he provided Dorothy and her mother when they were refugees during World War II in Europe, but also on his own merit. Like many German Jews of his generation, he had an unlikely life journey.

It will be recalled that Dorothy Jurkat, born in 1904 in Berlin, was the daughter of Therese and Albert Bergas, both of them Jewish. She had an older sister named Suzanne, born in 1891, and an older brother, Hans, born in 1898.[131] Suzanne, who married Dr. Levy, was a surgeon—quite unusual for a woman then even in an advanced country like Germany. They had a son, Albert Gunther David Levy, born in 1920. Suzanne died prematurely in 1925,

---

[130] I acknowledge the valuable assistance of William H. Rice, a historian and resident of Elkins, West Virginia, especially on the town of Elkins itself and on the footprints of Dr. Fritz Levy and his family there. Much of the information on Dr. Levy's life and descendants outside Elkins comes from his loving grandson, David Levy, of St. Louis, Missouri.

[131] See Chapter 9 on Hans Bergas, who joined the French resistance during World War II, was sent to Buchenwald, and wrote an unpublished memoir of his experience there.

after which her husband married Elsa Anna Weyl, born in 1887 in Berlin. Dr. Levy came to the United States in April 1936. His second wife and son joined him there a year later. They settled as a family in Elkins, West Virginia.

Elkins, the Town

Elkins is a small, quiet town in north-central West Virginia at the heart of the state's Mountain Highlands. It is located about 70 miles south of Morgantown, home of West Virginia University, and at an elevation of about 2,000 feet. It is the seat of Randolph County, West Virginia's largest. Elkins' population of nearly 8,000 is mostly white, with African Americans and Latin Americans each accounting for less than one percent of the total. The largest proportion, one-fifth, are of German ancestry, followed closely by those of Irish descent. The town, like the county, is mostly rural. The most important economic activities are lumbering, coal mining, mostly in the west, and tourism, due to the recreational opportunities such as skiing offered by the many state parks.

In the late 1930s, when the Levys arrived, Elkins would have been of about the same size and composition demographically as it is today, still a quiet town, but more active and diversified economically. Rail transport—both commercial and passenger—played a particularly important role then, as it connected the remote town to the wider world. Most of the rail tracks have been pulled up since. Some of the manufacturing activities such as textiles have disappeared, too, giving way to service activities like a large Western Union "call center." Elkins functioned like a real town then, more so than it does today, enjoying public transportation, taxi service, and a busy downtown. The town experienced a major surge in population during 1944-1945, when it became a training center for the military. A mountain corps and other units were moved in for training purposes to exploit the area's physical similarities to the Alps in Europe. Although this did have a positive impact on the local economy and even generated a sense of pride in the community, the impact was temporary.

The Levys in Elkins

Dr. Fritz was a pathologist. He did early cancer research and published some of his work. He established several contacts overseas and traveled to the United States to meet fellow-researchers. The ascendance of the Nazis and the demand for his skills in the United States led him to seek to emigrate there in 1936. It was not easy to leave Germany with one's family and find a position in the United States in those days. He managed both through his contacts. Elkins, West Virginia had the attraction of being a small, isolated place where he would not be noticed and where medical skills were in high demand because of the frequent injuries in the coal mines. The town had a medical clinic operated by Dr. Benjamin Golden and founded by his father William, also a doctor. The clinic, which was known as the Golden Clinic, was part of Davis-Memorial Hospital in Elkins. Dr. Levy may have known about the clinic and Dr. Benjamin Golden before he left Germany, although neither Golden, Benjamin or William, seem to have had a prior connection to that country.[132]

Upon coming to Elkins, Dr. Levy practiced for a while (shared offices) with Dr. Perthas Chenowith, a surgeon, but he soon moved to the Davis-Memorial hospital and worked there for the rest of his stay in Elkins. His wife Elsa also worked there as a lab technician for some of the time. The Levys lived in rental quarters on 124 Elm Street. In the meantime, their son Albert graduated from Davis-Elkins College, started teaching in local schools, and lived with his parents initially, before moving to 127 Elm Street across the street. Albert must have been very gifted and highly proficient in English, because he earned his B.A. degree in arts in 1938, at age eighteen, less than a year after arriving in the United States. He continued his education at the University of Chicago, where he received a doctoral degree in international law in 1944.

---

[132] Benjamin Golden was born in New York City and his father William in Russia.

Davis-Memorial Hospital and the Golden Clinic split in 1946, after which time the Levys left Elkins.[133] Whether their departure may have been associated with the split of the two medical facilities or not is not known.

The War Years

Dr. Levy was quite attached to his first wife's family. He showed this with his actions toward Ernst and Dorothy Jurkat and his mother-in-law to their great benefit. Ernst relied on him as reference provider, sponsor and supporter when he applied for a U.S. visa from Marseille in 1940, and when he tried to raise funds for his ocean passage. He visited Dr. Levy in Elkins soon after arriving in the United States, and he maintained contact with him through correspondence. Beginning in 1944, the two entered into an arrangement to share the financial support for Dr. Jurkat's wife, his son and his mother-in-law, who was also Dr. Levy's (ex) mother-in-law. The support was needed to obtain their release from the refugee camps were they were interned, allowing them to live modestly, though independently, as private citizens. Under the sharing arrangement, Dr. Levy was to support his ex mother-in-law, and Dr. Jurkat his wife and young son, Peter.

The support payments took the form of money transfers through the American Friends Service Committee or the International Rescue and Refugee Committee (IRRC). They averaged about $50 per month for both Dr. Jurkat and Dr. Levy at the beginning, but a higher amount for Dr. Jurkat with time. Dr. Levy's payments were reliable and punctual—more so than those of Dr. Jurkat who was a newer refugee and less well established economically. Moreover, Dr. Levy was extremely cooperative, adjusting his payments as needed. Three actions he took illustrate this well. When his ex mother-in-law passed away in Luzern, Switzerland in June 1945, Dr. Levy volunteered to pay for the funeral, as well as for the

---

[133] The clinic was absorbed by Memorial-General Hospital, also founded by Dr. William Golden, which was dissolved in 1988. The building is still refered to by local residents as the "Golden Clinic."

pre-death medical expenses. After the mother-in-law's death, rather than discontinuing his payments for her, he redirected them to Dr. Jurkat's wife. And when the latter requested, through the IRRC, an increase in the payments she was receiving, Dr. Levy came through again.

The role which Dr. Levy filled in the financial support of his ex relatives during that critical period was conveyed by Dr. Jurkat himself when he wrote to the IRRC about the need to raise the payments to his wife. He wrote: "As far as the increase of the support for my wife and son are concerned . . . I will get in touch immediately with Dr. Fritz Levy in Elkins, although I do not like very much the idea to ask further help from Dr. Levy who has shown such a wonderful attitude toward the family all these years. Would you write a little note to Dr. Levy telling him whether more than 100$ [*sic*] monthly can be sent to my wife and son?"

According to the itemized records of the IRRC, roughly 30 percent of the support transferred to Mrs. Jurkat and her son through them in 1944 and early 1945 came from Dr. Levy.

Family Dynamics

Dr. Levy's devotion to his first wife's family was highly remarkable. It remained strong twenty years beyond her death when, at war's end, her mother died in Switzerland. His devotion extended to her sister, Dorothy Jurkat, and was shared by Levy's son. When, in late 1945, Dorothy requested, through the intermediary of the IRRC, a significant increase in the support she was receiving, Dr. Jurkat wrote back that this would be possible because both Dr. Fritz *and* his son, Albert Levy, were willing to help. Moreover, there seems to be every reason to believe that Dr. Levy provided this help with his second wife's knowledge. The contribution, after all, was not negligible and lasted for more than a couple of years.

Dr. Levy's first wife must have died less than ten years after they were married. His close and enduring attachment to her family must reflect above all the strong feelings that he must have had for her. Theirs may have been an epic love story. Being both doctors, they had a strong professional bond, in addition to a personal bond. Her untimely death and the common grief it caused must have drawn him closer to her family. A contributing factor may have been that Dr. Levy remarried two years after her death, during which period not just his mother-in-law but his sister-in-law Dorothy as well may have cared for his young son of five years.

The assistance provided by Dr. Levy to Dorothy herself after his ex mother-in-law's death can be seen as a desire to help Ernst Jurkat, who had the primary responsibility for her, out of a special bond of friendship with him. Yet Fritz was eighteen years older than Ernst. An intriguing fact is that apparently Dr. Levy knew Gerritt Tönnies, oldest son of the famed sociologist Dr. Ferdinand Tönnies. Since Ernst had been an assistant to Tönnies in Kiel and was treated almost like a family member by him, he may have known Dr. Levy when he was young, that is, before he met his future wife Dorothy. Could he have met her through Dr. Levy, who married into the family first?

Dr. Levy seems to have been quite open about his lasting attachment to his first wife, Suzanne, née Bergas. While his son Albert and his grandchildren cared deeply for his second wife, Elsa Weyl, interest in their blood relation to Dr. Levy's first wife and her Bergas clan never faded. Albert Levy kept in touch with some of his Bergas relatives, and his son David Levy of St. Louis, Missouri visited one of them—his father's first cousin, Suzanne Bergas-Legé—in Paris in 1973.

The Aftermath

Dr. Levy died in Washington, D. C.'s Maryland suburbs in 1957. He and his wife Elsa must have followed their son Albert there (see below) around 1950. Elsa died in 1983, at the ripe age of ninety-six, in Rockville, Maryland. Albert Levy led an interesting and successful life beginning almost with his arrival in Elkins, West Virginia in 1937 at seventeen years of age. As noted earlier, he graduated from college at age eighteen and earned a Ph.D. degree from the University of Chicago at age twenty-four. He met his future wife, Syvia Cohn of Alabama, at the University. Albert's Ph.D. thesis had been on the prosecution of war criminals. Undoubtedly on the strength of it and of his knowledge of German, he was recruited as an assistant prosecutor at the Nuremberg Trials (1945-1949). His wife went with him to Germany as his assistant. At Nuremberg, he served as lead prosecutor in the civil trial of I. G. Farben, the conglomerate which supplied the poison gas *Zyklon B* used to exterminate millions in the concentration camps and was found guilty of war crimes. Over his long, diverse and distinguished professional life, Albert Levy taught briefly at Hiram College in Ohio, worked for the Tariff Commission, and was associated with several think tanks and consulting firms in Washington, D. C. In the early 1960s, he started his own consulting firm, Albert Levy Associates, Inc. He and hs firm did a great deal of work for the federal government, especially the Defense Department, state and city governments, intelligence agencies, and the private sector. He also served on community organizations and received several civic awards. Dr. Albert Levy retired in 1985 and died, at age 68, in 1988. His wife died in Silver Spring, Maryland, in June 2008.

The Jurkats and the Levys maintained contact in the immediate postwar period. Ernst and Dorothy Jurkat's son Peter, a mathematician, remembers visiting the Levys in Elkins with his parents. The contacts must have stopped or fizzled out after Dr. Levy's death. The descendants of the two couples, Albert and Peter, both born in Berlin, both successful in their fields, and the children of two loving sisters, never met . . . at least, not as adults.

The Levy's story is just as much an American story as it is a German story—a story of a Berlin Jew, a successful professional, who came straight to small-town America, of his Berlin-born son educated in America who returned to Germany to prosecute, in Nuremberg, those who contributed to the events that caused his father to come to America and who, on his return, raised all-American children brought up in freedom. One of those children, David Levy, remembers accompanying his father on Sunday mornings to the Pentagon, for which his father did consulting work, and "sitting outside the Air Force War Room with a big marine, reading the Sunday comics." David's father, Albert, was part of the team that developed the War Room and the system of flying command posts (planes out of the Strategic Air Command in Colorado). He was also involved in developing a national plan for large civilian fallout shelters in major cities in the early 1960s and worked on developing, among other things, the 911 emergency system in the early years. Through Albert and Elkins, West Virginia, a German story was transformed into a classical American one combining love, toil, justice, and a happy ending.

Edwards Brothers, Inc.
Thorofare, NJ USA
July 1, 2011